Songs of the Serbian People

Pitt Series in Russian and East European Studies

Jonathan Harris, Editor

Songs of the
Serbian People

From the Collections of
Vuk Karadžić

Translated and edited by Milne Holton
and Vasa D. Mihailovich

University of Pittsburgh Press

Published by the University of Pittsburgh Press, Pittsburgh, Pa. 15261

Manufactured in the United States of America

Printed on acid-free paper

10 9 8 7 6 5 4 3 2 1

Library of Congress Cataloging-in-Publication Data

Songs of the Serbian people : from the collections of Vuk Karadzic / translated and edited by Milne Holton and Vasa D. Mihailovich.
       p.   cm. — (Pitt series in Russian and East European studies)
    Includes bibliographical references (p.).
    ISBN 0-8229-3952-5 (alk. paper).—ISBN 0-8229-5609-8 (pbk. : alk. paper)
    1. Epic poetry, Serbian—Translations into English.   2. Folk songs, Serbo-Croatian—Texts. I. Karadzic, Vuk Stefanovic, 1787–1864. II. Holton, Milne. III. Mihailovich, Vasa D. IV. Series: Series in Russian and East European studies.
PG1465.S66 1997
891.8´21008—dc21   97-4561

A CIP catalog record for this book is available from the British Library.

Contents

Pronunciation Guide

c	as in ca*ts*
č	as in *church*
ć	as in *t*une
dj	as in en*d*ure (British)
dž	as in *j*ob or *George*
j	as in *y*es
lj	as in mi*lli*on
nj	as in ca*ny*on
š	as in *sh*e
ž	as in plea*s*ure

Other Serbo-Croatian letters are pronounced very much the same as in English. We have followed transliterated Serbo-Croatian spellings except in those instances in which they would cause confusion for readers of English.

Preface

It is our undertaking here to present in English translation and in a form as close to its original as possible a body of songs that constitute a central tradition of the Balkans. For we believe that only by the fullest possible encounter with that form can the reader experience the full impact of these historically important poems. We are aware that examples of the oral poetry of the South Slavs have been translated into English with some frequency over the course of the nineteenth and twentieth centuries: from Walter Scott's version of "The Wife of Hasan Aga" in the late eighteenth century to Anne Pennington and Peter Levi's *Marko the Prince,* a collection of the songs in English translation issued in 1984. But we are also aware that it is rare indeed for translators of the songs to attend to their form—a form peculiar to themselves—and to attempt, metrically, to reproduce the experience of hearing them sung.

In following the tradition of identifying our subject as "Serbian," we have certainly not desired to feed the flames of ethnic divisiveness that have so long ravaged the historical experience of the South Slavs. We are fully aware that the Croats, the Bosnians, the Macedonians, and the Bulgarians lay legitimate claim to their share of this body of poetry and to the history it embodies. We have called the poems "Serbian" in reference to a nation and its language, never to any modern state, yet we have done so in full recognition of the complex nature of the literary identity that existed in the minds of the collector and the singers whose work we present here.

For everyone speaking the "Serbian" language—today the Štokavian dialect of Serbo-Croatian—no matter how nationalist may be his or her politics, that problem of literary nationality is a knotty one. In the first place, any thinking person must immediately recognize that all nationalities are in a sense imposed from without, by historical or geographic circumstance or perhaps more recently by the will of politicians, yet in another sense all are inherited through a developing sense of shared linguistic or historical/ethnic/geographic community. Also, one must be aware that these two sources of identity are really one and the same, that the circumstantial identity of today is the historical and linguistic identity of tomorrow.

It now seems likely that the day will come when the songs of the South Slavs will be fully recognized by all as a broadly shared cultural heritage, a heritage that may well extend beyond the limits of Slavic Europe. For much of what is to be found in poetry is the product of a preconscious that is historically and linguistically shaped. Yet, as Vuk Stefanović Karadžić would have been the first to recognize, that awareness is today still enforced by language, by orthography, by much of the machinery of literary experience. And certainly—especially in the Balkans—language is at once the badge of ethnicity and a primary justification for nationhood.

In a certain sense, the historical lineage inherited by those poets who perceive themselves as Serbian is perhaps as rich, and certainly as full and complete as any of those held among the Slavs of the Balkans. It began to take shape at least as early as the twelfth century. In spite of subsequent conditions most adverse to its continuity, it has remained in the consciousness and has been reified in the poetry of a significant number of poets ever since. In presenting once again the heroic songs, it is this identity as well that we have undertaken to present. The Serbian identity, and the historical experience and poetic canon that has shaped it, is in more than a geographical sense a central one to the Balkans. An understanding of it can, if nothing else, lead the reader of English to a fuller awareness of the rich literary heritage of all the South Slavs.

Of course, a truly representative selection from such a full and diverse tradition is in any real sense an impossible task, and it is made no less so when one is limited to the confines of a single volume. The oral songs may seem to have their origins in the imaginations of ill-lettered and sometimes blind singers—imaginations that one would hardly expect to extend far beyond their own time and place. But the tradition these singers practiced presumed the knowledge of a body of songs that were themselves generated by historical and social circumstance reaching back in time, sometimes perhaps more than a thousand years, and that included primitive animistic beliefs, courtly medieval cultures, and the urbanity of Mediterranean Renaissance merchants, as well as the attitudes and practices of their own time.

To us it appears that these imaginations were thus deeply shaped by history and tradition, perhaps much more so than has been traditionally recognized. This translation of this oral poetry sets a difficult task for the translator in the effort to represent, celebrate, and establish it in another culture. Although we recognize that every act of translation is in itself a critical interpretation, in every poem included here we have attempted to avoid any change of syntax or word meaning as we have understood it. We have attempted, wherever possible, to repeat the recurring epithets and phrasings that mark the poems in Vuk's versions. Throughout we have regarded the lining of poems to be of particular importance, and only in unusual cases have we permitted ourselves the liberty of altering the poet's arrangement of the lexical elements of the original within lines.

For the most part, and unless noted, the oral narratives translated here were composed in the traditional *deseterac,* the ten-syllable poetic line especially reserved for the *junačke pesme,* or "heroes' songs" by the singers, or *guslari,* for they traditionally accompanied themselves in their singing by playing upon a single-stringed, bowed instrument known as the *gusle.* We believe that the connotation or implication of the rhythms of the original oral poem (for in a sense, even Vuk's transcriptions are translations) are better suggested to the Anglophone reader's ear by the original form of transcription. Thus we have rendered the *deseterac* whenever possible in a ten-syllable divided line (in Serbian the term *deseterac* suggests ten units), the first part of which is held rigidly—as it was by the singers—to four syllables in a predominantly trochaic pattern (thus forming an obligatory caesura), the second part also metrically patterned, but variously so, to achieve a relief from monotony. In these translations we have attempted to suggest mnemonic artifice (and traditional convention) by preserving phrasal recurrence of half lines. We hope that the English reader, accustomed to the greater metrical variation of written poetry, will not find these recurrences overly annoying and will accept them as a reminder of the very different poetic and social tradition from which these poems are generated.

Thus we depend on the forbearance of our reader to encourage us to believe that in our efforts we have not entirely failed. For Serbian oral poetry, with its deep engagement to its own myth and history, its special response to the demands for expression of the individual consciousness, often under conditions appallingly adverse, and its persistent development over a thousand years or more of a turbulent history, has earned the attention of the world's readers. If nothing else, we would wish that our undertaking might stand as testimony of our own attention to this body of poetry, and of its riches, from which we have been so amply repaid.

Acknowledgments

Our first thanks go to all those—both students and other friends—who have assisted in the translation process; their names are acknowledged beneath appropriate texts. But we are pleased to remember those who at the inception of our work on this book offered us encouragement and valuable advice. Among them must be included Charles Simic in this country and in Yugoslavia Krinka Vidaković Petrov, Aleksandar Petrov, and Ivan Gadjanski. There have been many other friends and colleagues in Belgrade who deserve our thanks, but foremost among them would be Miodrag Pavlović, whose careful and expert advice guided the very conception of our book. Unfortunately, the late Ivan V. Lalić, a poet and translator whose love of Serbian poetry is sadly no longer a vital center of Yugoslav intellectual life, is no longer with us to receive our thanks.

In the preparation of the manuscript, William S. Peterson has wisely guided us in the intricacies of computers as well as in the aesthetics of book design.

Last but certainly not least, it is only with the patience and encouragement of our wives, Sylvia and Branka, that this work would have been brought to its consummation.

Songs of the Serbian People

Introduction

Vuk Stefanović Karadžić and *Songs of the Serbian People*

HE ORAL POEMS TRANSLATED herein are taken from a single work of collection undertaken by one man, Vuk Stefanović
Karadžić (1787–1864), a scholar and linguist living in the city of
Vienna in the early years of the nineteenth century. He began his work in
1813, around the time of the collapse of the first Serbian insurrection
against the Turks.

Vuk Stefanović Karadžić was born in 1787 in the village of Tršić in
Western Serbia, the son of a Serbian peasant. A sickly child, he was given
the name Vuk (Wolf), supposedly to ward off evil spirits. As a youth he
became involved in the service of the *hajduk*[1] rebels against the Turks and
later in the first insurrection. Later he attended briefly the famous high
school at Sremski Karlovci and then studied for a time at the new *velika
škola* (later university) in Karadjordje's Belgrade. But he soon left Belgrade and, after an illness that left him crippled for life, went to Vienna in
1810. It was here that he met Jernej Kopitar, a Slovene scholar of some distinction who was then living in Vienna, where he occupied the post of
official censor for Slavic literatures.

Kopitar was only three years older than Vuk but much more intellec-
tually sophisticated, and he soon assumed the role of mentor. Both in his
official capacity and as a result of his absorption of Herder's ideas of the
importance of "popular"—as opposed to literary—cultures as the legiti-

---

1. Outlaw brigands living in bands in the highlands of the Balkans, some of whom may have
been politically motivated to rebellion against Turkish rule.

1

mate expression of national character, Kopitar was committed to the support of the language and culture of the Slavic peasants in the Balkan lands. It was his belief, and the policy of his government, that the encouragement of the Slavic populations of the empire in their nationalist aspirations would protect them from Russian influence even as it would commit them to the protection of the Habsburgs. Kopitar, who read an essay written in the vernacular Serbian by Vuk, recognized in the younger man the ideal advocate for that vernacular.[2]

Kopitar proposed a three-part program for the young scholar: the establishment of a vernacular grammar, the writing of a dictionary, and—most important for our purposes—the collection of the oral songs of the people, for he had become aware that Vuk remembered many of them.[3] Certainly Kopitar was right, for with his encouragement and assistance, Vuk would first produce a grammar of the vernacular Serbian language in 1815 and a Serbian dictionary three years later. In these works he reduced the complex Slavo-Serbian alphabet from forty characters to thirty, following the then radical principle of the elimination of all unpronounced letters. These works, both of which were of crucial importance to South Slavic linguistics, letters, and history, and neither of which Vuk could have completed without Kopitar, attracted the hostility of the Orthodox Church fathers, who, although recognizing the importance of a vernacular literary language, saw Vuk's radical reforms as attempts that played into the hands of the Austrians and Catholics by turning Serbian loyalties away from Russia, her religion, and her language.[4]

As the imperial authorities perhaps also recognized, Vuk's commitment to the vernacular was radically subversive. For in a sense what Vuk had undertaken was a redefinition of South Slavic nationalism—or indeed of the Serbian nation itself. No longer was that nation, or people (the two words are one in Serbian, ever since Vuk, in his 1818 dictionary, offered one word, *narod,* to bear both meanings), defined by a shared Or-

2. Much of the biographical information in this section is taken from Duncan Wilson's remarkable biography, *The Life and Times of Vuk Stefanović Karadžić: 1787–1864* (Oxford: Clarendon Press, 1970), and from George Rapall Noyes and Leonard Bacon, eds. and trans., *Heroic Ballads of Servia* (Boston: Sherman, French, 1913). Antun Barac's *A History of Yugoslav Literature* (Belgrade: Committee for Foreign Cultural Relations, 1955, and Ann Arbor: Michigan Slavic Publications, 1973), and, of course, Svetozar Koljević's authoritative work on the epics in English, *The Epic in the Making* (Oxford: Clarendon Press, 1980), subsequently cited as "Koljević," have been of inestimable critical value.

3. Duncan Wilson, *The Life and Times of Vuk Stefanović Karadžić,* 2–3; subsequently cited as "Wilson."

4. See Wilson, 2.

thodox Christian faith and the literary tradition that faith had generated. For the nation Vuk reified in his grammar and dictionary, and later in his collections of songs, was much more broadly based, the great *raja*[5] of the Balkans, oppressed and on the edge of rebellion, a potential for disorder in Ottoman lands, yet attracting only occasional support from Vienna. It was the language spoken by that *raja* that Vuk privileged by establishing its textuality. And it would be the poetry of that language that Vuk would offer to give legitimacy to the language itself.

Thus, in a sense Vuk redefined the South Slav nationality. He provided it with a realistic and viable identity, which would survive the censorship of his collections in Vienna, the early years of Obrenović rule,[6] and Vuk's own exile from Belgrade after 1832. In his years of exile, the 1830s and 1840s, he traveled in Croatia, Dalmatia, and Montenegro, came to know the peoples of those lands, and attempted to minimize their linguistic differences from the Serbs. Then—after the Obrenovićs themselves were exiled to Vienna in 1842—he received the financial support of Miloš's son and successor, Prince Mihailo. Vuk would also be supported by the "Illyrian" movement centered in Zagreb, which would demand more independence for all the empire's Slavs. Thus Vuk was an honored figure at the Pan-Slav Congress in Prague in 1848.

After that year of revolution Vuk's assumptions, and his Serbian language, were taken up by a new generation, the generation of the United Serbian Youth movement, which throughout the second half of the nineteenth century rejected the traditional culture of the Serbs in Austria and south Hungary and turned to that of the people in the Balkan homeland.

Duncan Wilson has pointed out that there are two aspects of Vuk's importance, that of the radical reformer and that of the conservative—the conservator of the heritage of oral singing in the Balkans. He has observed that while Vuk's countrymen often overemphasize the first, it is the second that has received the attention of foreign scholars. Certainly, it is the latter aspect that is the more important for our purposes; Vuk was responsible for the collection of the oral poetry that was to become the foundation of the literary culture of the South Slavs. But it was also that work which, by providing the exotic and romantically heroic flavor fashionable in literary circles of the time, attracted the attention of Europe's

---

5. The *raja* were the Christian peasantry of the Balkans under the Ottoman Empire.

6. The second modern Serbian dynasty, established by the leader of the second insurrection, Miloš Obrenović, who ruled from 1815 to 1839 and from 1858 to 1860. The first dynasty began with Karadjordje.

leading writers, generated translations—and fakery—in English, French, German, Russian, and Polish and, more importantly, helped bring Serbia and the Balkans to the European consciousness.

Even before he had undertaken his grammar, just after the crushing of the first insurrection in 1813 and the flight of yet more refugees into the Srem (the Austrian lands between the Danube and the Sava whose population was then composed mostly of South Slavs), Vuk had also begun to gather from his own memory and from the recitals of relatives and other Serbian exiles a collection of Serbian oral poems, mostly lyrics. He published his first collection, *Mala prostonarodnja slaveno-serbska pjesnarica* (A Simple Little Slaveno-Serbian Songbook) in 1814.

Vuk then moved into the Srem and prepared a second collection, where he met the *guslari* and *guslare* (for there were women singers), who would serve him as sources: Tešan Podrugović, a Bosnian Serb freedom fighter of prodigious size and memory; Filip Višnjić, a blind *guslar;* and "the blind Živana," an old woman who would give him "The Kosovo Maiden" and other songs. The songs Vuk heard from these singers were the basis for a second collection, *Narodna srbska pjesnarica* (A Serbian Book of Folk Songs), published in Vienna in 1815, in which the first of the "heroic" songs, the long narrative histories in *deseterac,* the ten-beat line of the peasant songs, especially songs of the Battle of Kosovo, of Marko Kraljević, and of the insurrection appeared.

In his work of collecting, Vuk received the encouragement of Lukijan Mušicki, then archimandrite of the monastery at Šišatovac in Srem, who had taught at Sremski Karlovci during Vuk's years in the school there. But it was Vuk's friend Kopitar who showed the collection to the renowned German scholar, Jakob Grimm, then attached to the German diplomatic delegation in Vienna. It was through Grimm that Vuk would meet Goethe and that his collections would establish the fame of Serbian poetry throughout Europe.

Vuk also journeyed east into the Banat to collect more songs from other refugee *guslars* and *hajduks*. It was these singers who can be seen as the authors of the songs, for they never sang from texts; their songs were memorial reconstructions set out in *deseterci*. It is not clear what is meant by "knowing" a song—whether to "know" a song was simply to have the ability to correctly set forth a narrative line and the skill to set it forth in one's own lines, or whether to "know" described an act of memorization of prescribed linguistic structures, or whether the true meaning lay somewhere between these extremes. It is clear, however, that to a great or lesser extent, each singing was a compositional and not purely a recitational act, for each singer sang the songs differently (indeed Vuk himself often collected many versions of a single song). So in a certain sense, regardless of the "age" of the songs, what Vuk was collecting were early nineteenth-century folk songs, all of which, after having been passed on from generation to generation, had passed through the minds and memories of their singers and had been reformed according to their tastes or experience and in the vocabulary of their own cultures.

Vuk's two most important singers had been encountered in Šišatovac as early as 1815. The first—the first singer Vuk heard as an adult—was Tešan Podrugović, a huge man of about forty years who as a youth in Bosnia killed a Turk who had raped a girl in his family. He fled to become a *hajduk,* then joined the first insurrection under Karadjordje. He fought bravely, but quarreled with his commanding officer and left the army to cross the Danube into the Austrian Srem after the Turks recaptured Serbia. He made a living there as a gatherer of reeds. Vuk made his acquaintance through Obrad, Lukijan Mušicki's cousin, shortly before Easter of 1815, a week after the beginning of the second insurrection under Miloš Obrenović. Vuk was barely able to restrain him from a return to the fighting, and he soon departed to join the other rebels. However, in the summer he left the army again, killed a bey,[7] and again became an outlaw in Bosnia. There he got into a fight in an inn, where he was beaten by some Turks and died shortly thereafter. Podrugović recited (he did not sing) his songs to Vuk, many of them very funny, with a straight face, never smiling. He knew hundreds; Vuk had a sense that many remained unsung. He collected twenty-two songs from Podrugović, notably comic songs and *hajduk* songs, of the experience that he knew so well. Vuk called Podrugović "the first and the best" of his singers.[8]

Shortly after Podrugović had departed with his unsung songs, Vuk met his second singer, a successful *guslar* (the only professional singer Vuk would encounter) named Filip Višnjić. Višnjić, who had been born in Bosnia in the vicinity of Bijeljina and had been blinded by smallpox at eight, had fled after his father died, members of the family were tortured and killed, and his uncle Marko was hanged for killing a Turk who had

7. A "bey" (beg) is a Turkish district governor.
8. See Wilson, 106–8; Karadžić's introduction to the Leipzig edition, vols. 1 and 4; and Koljević, 311–14 et passim.

raped a member of the family. Višnjić became a professional singer, singing both to Turks and Christians, and traveled as far south as Skadar, then came to Serbia in 1804, found himself in the midst of the battles of the first insurrection, crossed into the Srem in 1810, and settled in the village of Grk. There he was well received and well paid for his singing. Vuk met him when Višnjić was about fifty years old, well-off and successful as a *guslar* who regularly performed in public. He was perhaps Vuk's most popular singer and was remembered by the villagers for years afterward. When Višnjić died in Grk in 1834 he was buried with a *gusle* carved on his cross.[9]

Višnjić was extremely capable as a singer. His songs—notably songs of the first insurrection—were worked with new formulas, perhaps the most accomplished of the songs collected by Vuk. Vuk transcribed from him a total of nearly forty songs—over ten thousand lines all together. It was this transcription that formed the nucleus of what was to be Vuk's extensive and monumental collection, *Narodne srpske pjesme,* published in Leipzig between 1823 and 1833, the so-called Leipzig edition.

There would be other singers. There was "the blind Jeca," a woman singer whom Vuk met in Zemun and who sang "The Death of Duke Prijezda" for him;[10] there was "the blind Stepanija," who gave him both a version of "The Building of Skadar" and "Tsaritsa Milica and Duke Vladeta." There was an unnamed blind woman from the village of Grgurevci from whom Vuk took three of the finest of the Kosovo songs, "The Fall of the Serbian Empire," "The Death of the Mother of the Jugovićes," and "The Kosovo Maiden."[11] Indeed, it is strange to discover how many of the historical songs, and many of them among the finest, were sung by blind and presumably illiterate women singers, whose access to their material must have been either mnemonic or purely imaginative.

There were other great male singers as well: "Old Milija," whose "Banović Strahinja," perhaps the single greatest of the poems, reflected the tragedies of his own life; "Old Raško" (in the patriarchal culture of Vuk's Serbia the attribution of "old" was honorific and not merely descriptive), the singer of several of the medieval songs: Stojan the Outlaw, who, in prison in Serbia for having killed a woman who (he said) "ate" his

9. See Wilson, 110–11, and Koljević, 306–10 et passim; see also Karadžić's introduction to volume 4 of the Leipzig edition.
10. See Koljević, 89–90.
11. See Koljević, 319.

child, in 1820 gave Vuk the magnificent "The Wedding of King Vukašin";[12] and several others. These were the true authors of the heroic songs; in the final analysis Vuk was really only their editor and collector.

The fruits of Vuk's work as a collector of the oral songs came between 1823 and 1833 in the now famous and greatly expanded Leipzig edition. For in spite of his recognition abroad Vuk had difficulties at home. The Office of the Censor in Vienna, probably provoked by the Orthodox clergy in Austria, denied permission for Vuk's *Narodna srbska pjesnarica,* so it was in Leipzig that the book appeared. In this edition were many new songs that Vuk had more recently collected. And with its four volumes Vuk established the arrangement of the poems that was to become the basic pattern of all subsequent editions. Volume 1 (1824) presented the *Ženske pjesme* or "Women's Songs," the lyric poems, usually not in *deseterci,* short, mythic narratives, many of pre-Christian origins, and the round dances. The second volume (1823)[13] was identified by Vuk as the *Pjesme junačke najstarije,* or the "Oldest Heroic Songs," the narrative and historical songs in *deseterac* that—because they made no mention of firearms—Vuk regarded as the oldest. The third volume (1823), *Pjesme junačke srednjijeh vremena* (Heroic Songs of the Middle Period), consisted mainly of *hajduk* narrative songs and other songs set during the years of the Turkish occupation. A decade later there appeared Volume 4, *Pjesme junačke novijih vremena o vojevanju za slobodu* (Heroic Songs of the Recent Times of the War for Freedom), where were collected the songs of the Montenegrin and Serbian insurrections.

After the Leipzig edition Vuk, with the uncertain patronage of Prince Mihailo Obrenović, then exiled to Vienna, traveled south, to Montenegro and its Bay of Kotor, to Dubrovnik and Lika on the Dalmatian coast, places he had not visited before, known for their oral songs. His search there for other *guslari,* for new poems, and for variants of poems he had already heard was in preparation for what would be a definitive "Viennese" edition of the collection—some 1,045 poems—entitled *Srpske narodne pjesme* and published again in four volumes, in 1841, 1845, 1846, and 1862.[14]

---

12. See Koljević, 127

13. The second and third volumes were published in 1823 before the first, in 1824.

14. Koljević, 345. V. Nedić reproduced this edition, correcting only misprints, in *Srpske narodne pjesme,* Belgrade: Prosveta, 1969.

Throughout his life—or at least until he received the support of Prince Mihailo—Vuk suffered from lack of money, so he did not confine his literary activities to his collections but col-

There have been many subsequent editions of the songs—a somewhat bowdlerized edition by Ljubomir Stojanović in 1891–1901 (it was reprinted between the world wars); an annotated edition by Djurić, Matić, Banašević, and Latković in 1953–1954; Nedić's edition of the Viennese edition in 1969; and an edition with the "objectionable" poems separated in a volume not publicly sold, in 1973–1974.[15] For the Serbs, *Srpske narodne pjesme* constitutes the "classic anthology" (in the Confucian sense) of Serbian oral poetry.

Vuk Karadžić was neither the first nor the last to collect or to transcribe the oral songs of the Balkans. As Koljević tells us, there are references to the singing of the South Slavs throughout the seventeenth century. But much earlier, as early as the twelfth century, at least one hagiography and several of the Dukljanin's chronicles may have been based on oral narrative songs. There is a transcription of a fragment of a Slavic oral song, transcribed by Ruggiero Pazienza, a court poet of the Queen of Naples, in the village of Gioia del Colle in southern Italy in 1497; it is extant in the fifth volume of an eight-volume courtly epic, *Lo Balzino,* the manuscript of which is presently located in the City Library in Perugia.[16]

Around 1555 a *bugarštica,* a heroic song conducted in the "long line" of fourteen to sixteen syllables and associated with a courtly tradition of oral performance, entitled "Marko Kraljević and his Brother Andrijaš," was transcribed on the island of Hvar, then the richest Venetian community in Dalmatia. In 1568 Petar Hektorović, a nobleman from the same island, published in Venice a poem written in the long line of the *bugarštica,* a fisherman's eclogue (then popular in Italy), which contained transcriptions of several of the oral songs sung by his fishermen companions on a fishing expedition. And many other *bugarštice*—recounting the collapse of the Serbian Empire at the end of the fourteenth century and the events

laborated with Leopold von Ranke on a history of contemporary Serbia (which contained accounts of the insurrections) in 1828 and a first description of Serbia's now famous monasteries in 1821. Moreover, also on Kopitar's advice, he undertook a translation of the New Testament into vernacular Serbian.

15. Ljubomir Stojanović, ed., *Srpske narodne pjesme,* by Vuk St. Karadžić, 9 vols. (Belgrade, 1891–1901); Vojislav Djurić, Svetozar Matić, Nikola Banašević, Vido Latković, eds., *Srpske narodne pjesme,* by Vuk St. Karadžić, 4 vols. (Belgrade, 1953–1954); Vladan Nedić, ed., *Srpske narodne pjesme* 4 vols. (Belgrade: Prosveta, 1969), and *Srpske narodne pjesme iz neobjavljenih rukopisa Vuka Stef. Karadžića* (Serbian Folk Poems from the Unpublished Manuscripts of Vuk Stefanović Karadžić) 4 vols. (Belgrade, 1973–1974).

16. See Koljević, 11–28. We are much indebted to Koljević for the following discussion.

of the subsequent Turkish occupation—were transmitted and published in the towns along the Adriatic Sea and elsewhere in the seventeenth and eighteenth centuries—by Nikola Ohmučević, a merchant, later by the poet Ivan Gundulić, by Djuro Matijašević, a cleric (all citizens of Dubrovnik), and by others living in or around Kotor in the Bay of Kotor, another major Venetian colony and a city long important to Serbs, and elsewhere.

These *bugarštice* were poems that exemplified the degeneration of an older poetic form prevalent in feudal court poetry and then surviving as a form of popular entertainment in various cities and towns along the Adriatic coast. No longer feudal poetry, the *bugarštice* had become urban poems, essentially bourgeois in their assumptions. They described banquets and toasts, concerned themselves with the appropriateness of manners and clothing, showed familiarity with money, and demonstrated an awareness of a greater world and its political realities. But the *bugarštice* still contained elements—motifs, stylistic devices, even stock phrases and formulaic patterns, which belonged to their courtly predecessors and may originally have been mnemonic in function.

However, it was not the *bugarštice* but the *deseteračke pesme* (*deseterci*), the songs conducted in ten-syllable lines, being sung at the time in the patriarchal peasant villages of the Serbian, Bosnian, and Montenegrin uplands, even in Croatia, that were Vuk's concern. The *deseterci* were products of a different culture, not urban but peasant, not bourgeois but patriarchal, and as such they told their stories in a different vernacular— less sophisticated, perhaps, more metaphorical and less accurately realistic in representations of things like money and banquets and fine clothes. But their shorter line gave for a certain economy of epithet, and the narrative moved more cleanly. The motifs and patterns and phrasings surviving in the *bugarštice* were tightened and simplified in the *deseterci.* Also, the heroes of the *deseterci* seemed to live in a less ordered world, a world of violence and uncertainty, of pragmatic values and compromise, the world of the uplands, not in the more ordered world of the songs sung on the civilized coast.[17]

The *deseterac* line is dominantly trochaic, end-stopped, and unrhymed (occasionally internal rhyme is employed). Most important, each line is

---

17. Koljević discusses the *bugarštice* in his chapter entitled "The Grand Stammer"; see Koljević, 31–68. The *bugarštice* are presented in English translation in an anthology by John S. Miletich entitled *The Bugarštice: A Bilingual Anthology of the Earliest Extant South Slavic Folk Narrative Song* (Urbana and Chicago: University of Illinois Press, 1990).

divided into two parts by a strong caesura, which always occurs after the fourth syllable. This line has a rhythm known to every Serb. It is so familiar, and so charged with association, that—like those written in the *bugarštica*—the poems themselves are identified by their special metrical norm.

The *deseterci* were also transcribed and translated.[18] The earliest extant transcriptions of the *deseterci* songs were set down in Perast (then an aristocratic Venetian community in the Bay of Kotor on the Adriatic) around the end of the seventeenth century, and appeared beside *bugarštice*. Then, around 1720, songs sung by Slav soldiers near Vienna were transcribed—very imperfectly—in a manuscript in which 217 lyrics and epics were collected; this manuscript, the "Erlangen manuscript," was discovered in 1913 in the Erlangen University library and is of great value if one wishes to consider the changes brought about when the presumably courtly songs, having passed to the uses of a bourgeois merchant society, then fell into the hands of Slavic peasants and outlaws under the domination of a foreign power.

Later in the century, in 1774, an Italian traveler and scholar, Alberto Fortis, who had taken an interest in the Italian translations of MacPherson's *Ossian,* traveled to the Dalmatian islands and there translated into Italian two songs, one of which is today known as the *Hasanaginica* or "The Wife of Hasan Aga." They were then translated by Goethe into Ger-

18. Translators of the *deseterci* have over the years remained undecided whether to reproduce the line itself or to suggest its cultural resonance. Over the nearly two hundred years during which English translators have attempted the *deseterac,* very few have agreed upon an appropriate metrical procedure. Some English translators have sought the nearest English equivalent in associative force; they have generally translated into heroic couplet or blank verse, sometimes into ballad stanza. Still others, fearing that the *deseterac* would prove a metrical form too rigidly invariable for the English ear, especially when in translation it must be unaccompanied by the counterrhythms established by the *gusle,* sought complex and variable solutions. The most recent English translations of the heroic songs, the distinguished translations by Anne Pennington and Peter Levi collected in *Marko the Prince: Serbo-Croat Heroic Songs* (New York: St. Martin's Press, 1984), make no attempt to establish a metrical equivalent for the *deseterac.*

The strong caesura has remained a problem for the English translator as well (albeit less so than for translators into other languages). Some leave it unmarked; some space so as to render two half-lines as in Anglo-Saxon; some, especially translators who have recently attempted the *deseterac* itself, have divided the ten syllables into two half-lines organically defined and have broken the lines syntactically, or at breath pauses.

In our own translations we have attempted to conform closely to the syllabic and caesural conventions of the *deseterac* and have at the same time attempted to reduce its monotony, a monotony relieved in the performance of the Serbian poems by conducting the translations in a meter that, especially in the second half-lines, is a highly variable iambic (more natural to the English ear). And we have attempted to conform to a "plain" style, that of the *guslars.*

man and appeared in Herder's *Volkslieder* (1778, 1779), which generated the first enthusiasm among newly romanticized European readers. Walter Scott made an English version ("The Wife of Hasan Aga") of the *Hasanaginica* from the German.[19] Madame de Stael declared herself "ravie"; Prosper Mérimée produced a fraudulent French version of a heroic song; and Pushkin followed Mérimée. But by this time Vuk had begun his collection, which coincided with the first insurrection. And then, as we have said, his *Narodna srbska pjesnarica* caught the attention of Jakob Grimm, then Europe's greatest comparatist.[20]

Grimm and his brother translated nineteen of Vuk's songs for Forster's *Sängerfahrt* in 1818. Then the daughter of a German university professor from Halle, Fräulein Theresa Albertina Luisa von Jacob, an enthusiastic disciple of Goethe, with his encouragement translated slightly less than half of Vuk's first collection into German (using her initials "Talvj" as her nom de plume), beginning in the 1820s. Talvj was the first to translate Vuk's transmissions of the Serbian songs into a major European language.[21] Again there was a spate of retranslation. The first into English seems to have been that of John Gibson Lockhart, Scott's biographer, in an anonymous and privately printed collection of 1826 entitled *Translations from the Servian Minstrelsy: to Which are Added Some Specimens of Anglo-Norman Romances* (Lockhart, the editor of the *Quarterly Review*, acknowledged his role as retranslator in that journal in 1845).[22] But by far more important is Sir John Bowring's *Servian Popular Poetry* of 1827; in it appear English versions of some 107 "songs and ballads," translations made, presumably, from Talvj's German versions but with reference to Vuk's Serbian texts.[23]

So it was Vuk Karadžić who shaped—for his own European literary world, but, more importantly, for many Serbs—a new sense of nationality. He did this in a collection of songs in a language that he had also made it possible to read (through his grammar and dictionary) and that would serve as the vernacular of a newly forming literary tradition. If the im-

19. For a discussion of Walter Scott's translation see D. H. Low, "The First Link Between English and Serbo-Croat Literature," *Slavonic Review* 3 (1924): 362–69.

20. See Koljević's introduction to Pennington and Levi's *Marko the Prince*, xiii–xvii. See also Dragutin Subotić, *Yugoslav Popular Ballads: Their Origin and Development* (Cambridge: Cambridge University Press, 1932), 165ff.

21. See Subotić, *Ballads* 165ff., and his "Serbian Popular Poetry in English Literature," *Slavonic Review* 5 (March 1927): 628–46.

22. See Subotić, *Ballads* 243–44.

23. See Subotić, *Ballads* 225–43.

portance of such an undertaking had been recognized even before its achievement by others, it was Vuk to whom we owe that achievement. There is no person in the cultural history of the Balkans whose work is more entirely beneficent than Vuk. Had its history been different, had Vuk's definition of nationality ultimately obtained, the history of the Balkan people of our own time might well have been more benign than that brought to them by other visions.

1 Songs Before History

HOUSANDS OF YEARS before the birth of Christ, when the Slavic tribes began their first westward stirrings, they presumably bore within their memory the patterned narratives or the formulaic verbalization to which the earliest poetry of the Balkan peoples might be traced.[1] The first Slavs recognized in the west established a habitat in the region between the Vistula and Dnieper Rivers with the Avars, a migrant central Asian people, settled among them. Together the two began to migrate south and west into the Pannonian plain, and there they were joined by other Slavic tribes, among them the Sorbs (or "Serbs"). The various tribes maintained separate identities, and by the sixth century A.D. they had crossed the Danube and entered upon Byzantine lands. In the seventh century they were invited by the Emperor Heraclius (A.D. 610–664) to come south and west, and great numbers of them settled south of the Danube. Two of the larger tribes, the Serbs and Croats, occupied the northwestern lands.[2]

1. Already, according to Svetozar Koljević, these Slav tribes "had a high reputation for singing." See Koljević, Introduction to Pennington and Levi, xiii–xvii.
2. Much of the historical information that follows is set forth in the following works of interest to the student of Serbian history and culture: Marija Gimbutas, *The Slavs* (New York and Washington: Praeger, 1971), and *The Goddesses and Gods of Old Europe 6500–3500 B.C.* (Berkeley and Los Angeles: University of California Press, 1982); Stephen Clissold, ed., *A Short History of Yugoslavia from Early Times to 1966* (Cambridge: Cambridge University Press, 1966); Francis Dvornik, *The Slavs in European History and Civilization* (New Brunswick: Rutgers University Press, 1962), here especially 1–6; Lovett F. Edwards, *Yugoslavia* (New York: Hastings House, 1971); Barbara Jelavich, *History of the Balkans*, 2 vols. (Cambridge: Cambridge University Press, 1983); Josef Konstantin Jirecek, *Istorija Srba* (Belgrade: Slovo ljubve, 1978); Michael Boro Petrovich, *A History of Modern Serbia 1804–1918*, 2 vols. (New York: Harcourt Brace Jovanovich, 1976);

In spite of efforts by Frankish, Roman, Byzantine, and even Irish monks, the Slavs were not converted to Christianity until late in the ninth century, the Serbs by Byzantine missionaries (traditionally in 874), and then only somewhat superficially. Christianity would be incorporated into a rather unstructured nature worship, at times dualistic, anthropomorphic, and monistic in its character. Thus their folk songs preserved elements from pagan religions and mythologies, perhaps brought with them from central Asia and certainly shared with Slavic peoples as far north as Lithuania and even with the Germanic peoples who had preceded them.

Among Vuk's "Women's Songs" are to be found several narrative poems that give evidence of these earlier beliefs. These songs often account for the origins of things and are thus more likely to reflect forgotten mythologies of times long past.[3] Recently some informed readers, Miodrag Pavlović among them, have seen a certain wisdom in the placement of the "Women's Songs" at the beginning of Vuk's chronologically arranged volumes. For perhaps Vuk's four-volume collection should be seen as a form of historical record. Vuk apparently recognized as much, for among his various subdivisions of the women's songs is a group identified as being *Pjesme osobito mitologičke,* or "Of Mythological Interest."[4]

Like Vuk, who placed them in his first volume among the *Najstarije pjesme* (Oldest Heroic Songs), we believe that these songs belong at the beginning, or rather at the beginnings, of the heroic songs, for they contain the fullest evidence of their origins.[5] Because some of these songs are without discernible historical reference, they are difficult if not impossible to date. But often it is these very songs, about which nothing is known of the actual dates of their original composition, that appear to be the oldest. As one can trace in the *guslar* tradition evidence of the conventions of the court singers of the Nemanjić despots or even evidence of those of

Leopold von Ranke, *A History of Servia and the Servian Revolution,* trans. Mrs. Alexander Kerr, 2d ed. (London, 1848; reprint, New York: Da Capo, 1973); Harold W. V. Temperley, *History of Serbia* (London, 1917; reprint, New York: Howard Fertig, 1969); L. F. Waring, *Serbia* (London: Williams and Norgate, 1917; New York: Holt, 1917); Rebecca West, *Black Lamb and Grey Falcon* (New York: Viking, 1968); and the extant volumes of the as yet uncompleted multivolume work edited by Sima Ćirković, *Istorija srpskog naroda* (Belgrade: Srpska književna zadruga, 1981–). Here especially see Sima Ćirković, ed., *Istorija srpskog naroda od najstarijih vremena do Maričke bitke [1371]* (1981).

3. Miodrag Pavlović, in conversation with Milne Holton, Belgrade, 17 September 1980. See also his subsequent collection, *Antologija lirske narodne poezije* (Belgrade: Vuk Karadžić, 1982).

4. See Vuk Stefanović Karadžić, ed., *Srpske narodne pjesme* (Belgrade: Prosveta, 1969), subsequently cited as *Srpske narodne pjesme*), 1: 6; see also Koljević, 106.

5. Koljević, 11–30.

singers among the pre-Christian Slavic tribes of the Balkans, so one can sometimes find in these undated songs elements of a pre-Christian folk-lore that reiterates mythologies common to much of Europe and to the lands and peoples of the Asian continent.

 ## The *Vila* Builds a Town[6]

This song—composed in an eight-beat rhythmic unit shorter than the decasyllables of the heroic songs—tells of a *vila*, perhaps a fairy or a spirit, who is here identified as "white." Often she is associated with building (we will meet her, or her more ominous sister, again in "The Building of Skadar" and elsewhere).[7] The *vila*, who supervises construction, shows respect for the destructive forces of nature—for lightning, whose god, Perun, may have been central to, if not at the very center of, the religion of the pagan Slavs. The result here seems a fortunate one.

The *Vila* Builds a Town
from Montenegro

The white *vila* builds a city,
not on the earth nor in the heaven;
it is built upon the cloud-banks.
For the city there are three gates:
the first gate is made all golden;
the second gate is made of pearl;
the third gate is all in scarlet.
Here is the gate made all in gold;
at this gate her son is married.
Here is the gate of shining pearl;   10
at this gate her daughter weds.
Here is the gate set all in scarlet;
on it the *vila* sits alone.
On it she sits alone and watches.

---

6. "*Vila zida grad*," I, 150, #226. The original title of the song, the volume number, the page number, and the poem number, as listed in Karadžić, *Srpske narodne pjesme*, are provided in the notes throughout this book.

7. For a fuller discussion of *vila*, see Svetozar Koljević, appendix, 347–48.

As the lightning plays with thunder,
so a sister with two brothers,
a bride with her two brothers-in-law.
The lightning overcomes the thunder,
as a sister does her brothers,
as a bride her brothers-in-law.   20

Assisted by Dragana McFadden

 ## The Shepherd Who Was Devoured[8]

In Slavic mythology the forest, the fields, even the herds, have spirits who protect them, and these spirits are not always benign. Also, one can be threatened by the spirits of the dead, especially when they seek to return to life or to live on after the time of their death has come (hence, the vampire). It is from such fears that the following song—again, written in a short line—is generated.

The Shepherd Who Was Devoured

The sky was all sprinkled with stars,
and the field was all sprinkled with sheep,
yet with the sheep was no shepherd,
but only the child Radoje,
and he, the poor boy, was sleeping.
Janja, his sister, awakes him:
"Go, get your self up, Radoje!
Your sheep have gone into the grove!"

"Let them, sister, I can't help it.
I have been eaten by witches;   10
my mother has taken my heart out,
with my aunt holding the candle."

Assisted by E. Toševska

8. *"Izjeden ovčar,"* I, 157, #237.

The Sun and the Moon Woo a Maiden[9]

The Vedic hymns of the Indian subcontinent describe two horsemen of the heavens who capture a maiden. She chooses them for husbands and ascends in their chariot drawn by birds.[10] In Slavic mythology the sun and the moon (perhaps the more important) were significant deities, and both were masculine; they were perhaps related to the ancient Indian horsemen of heaven, as in the song that follows.

The Sun and the Moon Woo a Maiden

from the upper coast

Fog fell upon the Bojana;[11]
light dew fell upon the meadow,
a dew on which no one can walk
except for the barefoot Maria.
Not even she can walk through dew;
her foot has slipped; she's lost her ring.
Maria then asks of Marko:
"Help me find my lost ring, Marko."

Marko then swears unto her:
"Nowhere could I find your lost ring.   10
When last night I left the army,
I let loose the guards and greyhounds;
the greyhounds searched through the meadows,
and the guards looked through the woodland,
until they came to Danube town,
and then they searched in Danube town.[12]

"In that town there are nine brothers,
these nine brothers have a sister,
whom the sun would like to marry,

9. "*Sunce i mjesec prose djevojku*," I, 152, #229.
10. See Maurice Bloomfield, *The Religion of the Veda* (New York and London: G. Putnam's Sons, 1908), 112.
11. A river flowing into the Adriatic near the present Albanian border. Vuk's reference to "the upper coast" is therefore to an area inland, or above the coast.
12. *Dunav* (Danube) is, of course, the name of a river. Vuk notes, "here *Dunav* is thought to be a town. Carinthians call Vienna *Dunaj.*" *Srpske narodne pjesme*, 1: 152 n. 83.

but none will give away their sister   20
except the youngest of the brothers.
So the brothers spoke together,
'Don't, my brother, best of brothers,
for the sun will always burn her;
he will burn away our sister!'

"The moon also woos the sister,
but none will give away their sister,
except the middle of the brothers.
All the brothers listened to him,
for the moon is always changing,   30
and she'll have a large family,
all the stars for sisters-in-law,
and the morning stars for nephews."

Assisted by E. Toševska

 # The Wedding of the Shining Moon[13]

Some of the women's songs seem almost to show an awareness of their diverse heritage. One such song is "The Wedding of the Shining Moon" (of which there are several versions). This song seems to use material common to both the Vedic hymns and Slavic myth and also to incorporate Christian elements into the story; it seems to celebrate a wedding of mythologies as well as of heavenly bodies. This song was composed in a ten-beat unit, similar to the line used in the heroic songs.

The Wedding of the Shining Moon

The bright North Star   of Morning made a boast:
"I'll make marriage   with the shining moon;
I'll ask Thunder   if I can now wed her,
the One True God   will be the sponsor there;
Peter and Paul   will give the bride away,
Saint John will be   the senior of the guests,

13. "*Ženidba sjajnoga mjeseca,*" I, 153, #230.

Saint Nicholas,   he will serve as witness,
good Elijah   will drive away the carriage."

Just as the Morn,   the North Star made her boast,
it was given   to her by the Lord: 10
she made marriage   with the shining moon,
the One True God   did serve as sponsor there,
Peter and Paul   did give the bride away,
and Holy John   was senior of the guests,
Saint Nicholas   did serve as first witness,
good Elijah   drove away the carriage.
The lightning gave   a gift to each of them:
a hot, hot day   was given to Saint Peter,
the freezing ice   and snow for our Saint John.
For Nicholas   the freedom over waters,   20
to the One God   she gives the heights of heaven,
and Elijah   got arrows and the lightning.[14]

Assisted by Aleksandar Prokopiev

 # The Tsar and the Girl[15]

This strange song, in a version sung during the Turkish occupation, seems
to express a wish to return to an ancient past, perhaps a past protected by
the Slavic gods of field and forest. It was composed in a ten-beat line, like
the *deseterac* of the heroic songs, to which it bears a certain resemblance.

The Tsar and the Girl

A pretty girl   once made a proud boast:
"I will not weave,   I will not embroider,
I will not mind   my grandmother's cattle.
Instead I'll build   a church in the forest;

---

14. Ilias, or Elijah, is much revered in the Orthodox Christian tradition; he is associated (because of his miraculous ascent; see Kings 2: 11) with thunder and lightning and is often called *Ilija gromovnik* or "Elijah, the thunderer." It is believed—and indeed, this song may offer evidence—that Elijah is thus the successor to the pagan Slavic god of lightning, Perun.

15. "*Car i djevojka*," I, 155, #234.

its foundation   will be made of marble,
and its roof beams   will be cut from boxwood,
and its rooftrees   will be of the maple."[16]

And then the tsar   heard of her words of boast,
and so the tsar   sent two of his young men,
two noblemen   who were the tsar's own nephews,   10
to go and bring   the beautiful girl to him.
But when they came,   and they caught sight of her,
they dared not go   even before her court,
nor to lead her   to stand before the tsar.
She sat alone   before all of her court,
before her court   upon a golden throne;
she wore a hat,   sable, above her eyes,
and held a sword,   a weapon on her lap.

The men returned   unto the tsar, their uncle:
"Oh, your highness,   oh, mighty shining sun,   20
Oh, your highness,   oh, noble golden crown,
here is the sword,   and here are our own heads,
for we dared not   to go before her court,
much less to bring   her back with us to you."

The mighty tsar   was much shamed by all this;
he called to him   all his powerful army,
a hundred Tartars,   twice as many Arabs,
and yet again   three hundred janissaries.
They were to bring   the famous girl to him.
But when she looked   on these mighty soldiers,   30
she then went out   into the green garden,
and she leapt up   upon her antlered horse.
She mounted him;   she used a snake for harness,
she rode alone   before this mighty army.
With her great mace   she struck down a whole army.
Another band   she struck down with her sword;
the rest she caught   and drove them to the water.
And when the lord,   the tsar, saw all of this,
he fled headlong   straight through his palace court,

16. Traditionally, the *gusle* is made of maple wood.

his loosed turban   trailing after him.   40
He didn't dare   even to look behind,
nor stop to wind   the turban round his head.

But then the girl   cried out and called to him,
"Stand, tsar, because   you cannot run away!"
She caught the tsar   while he was still alive.
She went to him   and then tore out his eyes,
and let him loose   alone in the forest.
And there he went   from fir tree to fir tree,
like a bird from   one branch to another.   50

Assisted by Aleksandar Prokopiev

 ## Jovan and the Leader of the Giants[17]

The *deseterac* was traditionally used for accounts of a historical nature—
"true" stories of "what happened." However, one of the less artful and
more primitive of the decasyllabic poems, "Jovan and the Leader of the
Giants," was sung to Vuk in *deseterci*. Although in it there are several references to the social conventions prevalent during the Turkish occupation, the song is clearly not historical. It abounds in magical and super-
natural elements and draws from mythic sources, sometimes prose
legends, that are obviously Asiatic and Mediterranean as well as Conti-
nental. According to one scholar it may be based on legends of Hercules
and Solomon.[18]

This strange song is one of the oldest of those Vuk collected in his second volume. Although most of the oral poems of the Serbs that describe
mother-son relationships celebrate filial piety or maternal wisdom and
devotion, this song tells the story of a son's revenge for his mother's cru-
elties. "Jovan and the Leader of the Giants," however, is remarkable in
more than this. At times it manifests a sharp psychological realism that,
together with its archaic primitiveness, makes it one of the most disturbing of the folk songs.

17. "*Jovan i divski starješina*," II, 29, #8.
18. See Svetozar Matić, "Beleške i objašnjenja" in V. S. Karadžić, *Srpske narodne pjesme*, ed. Vojislav Djurić et al. (Belgrade: 1953), 634–35; cited in Koljević, 325 n. See also Koljević, 324–25.

Jovan and the Leader of the Giants

There is a tsar   who'd be rid of his queen.[19]
The tsar wants this,   for he has much trouble;
his queen's wronged him   in many, many ways.
Because of this   the tsar feels hate for her.
But the servants   do not wish to lose her,
and so they beg,   plead to the honest tsar,
and by their prayers   they save the tsar's lady.
For the good tsar   listens to his servants,
and he gives her   yet one more year of life.

She has a son,   and his name is Jovan.   10
She speaks to him;   she says this unto him:
"Now where are you,   my son, dearest Jovan?
Do you too wish   to disown your mother?"

The tears fall down   from the eyes of the boy,
and he speaks out;   gives this answer to her:
"Listen to me,   oh, my dearest mother,
I'd flee with you   across this wide, wide world!"

To her own son   the mother says these words:
"Now go you forth,   to the tsar's seraglio;
there you will find   your own white horse called Swan.[20]   20
With him we'll flee   across this wide, wide world!"

Jovan jumps up,   jumps onto his own feet,
and so he goes,   does as his mother says
(for he's a boy   of not yet fifteen years),
and he brings out   his own white horse called Swan.
He throws himself   on the horse's shoulders.
And then Jovan   says unto his mother:
"Now, by God's will,   oh, my dearest mother,
you've taken me   from my very father;

---

19. The "tsar" here is clearly a sultan, who can follow Islamic law in matters of divorce; that is, he can dispose of a wife by simple dismissal.

20. Literally, "fat Labud" (*gojeni labud*) or "trained Labud"; *labud* ("swan"), however, is often a formulaic simile for a white horse.

I'm his one son;   he has no one but me.   30
And so, what next?   wherever shall we go?"

The boy's mother   says unto her own son;
"We'll flee, my boy,   across this wide, wide world,
far from that tsar,   that ruler, mine and yours,
away from him,   thirty full nights away,
so far away   that he cannot hear us,
nor then see us   with his two evil eyes."

Out they go then,   across the wide country,
until they come   to the giants' mountain,
and there they find   a cold and gloomy cave.   40
Within that cave   are seventy giants,
and among them   there, the giants' leader.
When the giants   catch a glimpse of Jovan,
they would kill him,   they would chop off his head.
What a hothead!   What a fool, that Jovan,
for he draws out   his saber at his thigh!
Jovan smites them,   swings his saber freely,
and he kills them,   all seventy giants.
But one escapes;   the giants' leader hides.
With his mother   brave Jovan spends the night.   50

When the day dawns,   when the sun is shining,
the young Jovan,   the boy, cannot keep still.
So he sets forth   to hunt in the mountains
on his proud Swan,   on his white horse called Swan.
Jovan shoots down   a doe and a roebuck.
In afternoon,   when the sun is brightest,
he then returns   to the cave, to mother.
There he gives her   the doe and the roebuck,
to give her cheer,   to feed his banished mother.

Then his mother   speaks these words unto him: 60
"Oh, my Jovan,   go to the cave's entrance,
for you're tired,   and you must now sleep there."
Jovan obeys,   does as his mother says.
As he goes there,   quick, to the cave's entrance,

then his mother   glances at the giant,
deep in the cave,   at the giants' leader.
And that giant,   the leader, calls to her:
"Come unto me,   oh, you, Jovan's mother,
come unto me,   for I want to make love."

Then the mother   speaks these words unto him: 70
"You come to me,   oh, leader of giants,
you come to me,   and kiss me on my face!"

But the giant   answers this unto her:
"But I cannot,   for I fear your Jovan,
he who has killed   some seventy giants.
When Jovan comes   deeper into the cave,
You must ask him,   you must ask your boy,
if he has fear   for any but his God.
And from the first   you must begin a game,
that cursed game   of ring on the finger.   80
And in that game   he will not try to win;
your son's stupid,   and is a bit foolish,
so you'll beat him;   you will win easily.
Then you'll tie him,   tie his hands together.
Then I'll kill him;   I'll kill your son, Jovan.
Then I'll hold you,   and we will make love."

Now when Jovan   comes deeper in the cave
to eat dinner,   to feast with his mother,
his mother speaks,   she then asks her own boy:
"Oh, my Jovan,   my son, dearest Jovan,   90
you who have killed   some seventy giants,
who goes hunting,   who walks across mountains,
whom do you fear   other than your own God?"

And now Jovan   answers to his mother:
"I still fear Him,   fear our God Almighty,
but I fear not   any man or warrior
while I still have   my own white horse called Swan."

Then his mother   speaks to her son, Jovan:
"Oh, my Jovan,   my dear and only son,

we're poor, my son;   the two of us are poor,   100
but let us play   a little game between us."

Jovan agrees,   does as his mother says,
and they begin   to play the game together,
the cursed game   of ring on the finger.
Now he could win;   he could beat his mother;
now he could win;   but he doesn't want to,
so his mother   is the one who wins.
"Now I've got you!   Now I have won, my boy!"
So she binds him,   ties his arms together,
from his elbows   down to his fingernails.   110
Foolish Jovan   now pulls his arms apart
and tears the rope   into seven fragments.

In the morning,   when the sun is shining,
Jovan goes forth   to hunt in the mountains.
When he rides up   to the royal highway,
he encounters   a few hired draymen,
and before them,   is the drayman Rade.
They are leading   sixty loaded wagons,
and these wagons   are filled with wine and wheat.
Jovan blocks them   there upon the highway;   120
he doffs his cap,   and he stands before them:
"If you please, sirs,   friends from across the world,
please sell to me   sixty loaded wagons,
all these wagons   loaded with wine and wheat,
for I need them   to feed my banished mother.
I will pay you,   now, with golden ducats."

So the draymen   sell the wagons to him.
Then asks Rade,   leader of the draymen:
"So, young Jovan,   as you fear the great God,
where's your mother,   your own aging mother?'   130
Jovan tells him   that she is in the cave,
and they set out,   off in that direction.

When they are still   a distance from the cave
and can see it,   there, off in the distance,
the mother, too,   can see her son, Jovan,

and she goes back,   deep into the cave there,
and she utters   these words to the giant:
"Come you to me,   giant; let us think, now.
For he's coming,   here comes my boy, Jovan.
What can we do   to rid ourselves of him,   140
so we're able   to make love together?"

Then the giant   answers her with these words:
"Pretend you're ill,   although you are not so,
and when he comes,   your boy, dearest Jovan,
he will worry,   have fear for his mother;
then he will ask   what to bring his mother:
'Is there, mother,   anything that you need?'
Then you will say   words like these unto him:
'I want, my boy,   an apple from the beech tree,
there in water,   in the Kaladžija.'[21]   150
In the depths there   lives a hungry dragon,
who there devours   both warriors and horses,
and beside her   there are two cruel lions,
who could also   kill a brave warrior.
So that either   the dragon will eat him
or two lions,   cruel, will kill Jovan."

So when Jovan   comes there into the cave,
and he visits   with his ailing mother,
Jovan sits down   near his mother's head;
he weeps for her,   sheds great tears of sorrow: 160
"How sad I am,   oh, my dearest mother!
Is there, mother,   anything that you need?"

So she then says   these very words to him:
"I want, my boy,   an apple from the beech tree,
the tree which grows   in the Kaladžija;
if I eat it,   I think I'll be better."
Jovan jumps up,   up onto his own feet,
he takes his seat   on the white horse called Swan,
and he rides off   into the moonless night.

21. Presumably a fictitious river name.

Quickly Jovan   is beside the water,   170
and now the horse   dives straight in the water.
Jovan takes it,   the apple from the beech.
When he reaches   the edge of the water,
then the dragon,   the hungry dragon, sees him,
and she charges;   she attacks our Jovan.
With his saber   Jovan now awaits her,
and he cuts off   the hungry dragon's head.
Then there leap forth   two ferocious monsters;
they thrash about   in the deep, deep waters,
and they attack   the horse Jovan calls Swan.   180
But the boy now   has a valorous heart,
and he takes them,   both of them, alive,
and he ties them   both to the horse's tail.
He flies with them   across the green mountain,
and he arrives   now, at his mother's cave,
and he gives her   the apple from the beech.

When she sees this,   mother of our Jovan,
she speaks to him,   and she says these words:
"Oh, my Jovan,   let me ask you something:
you have traveled   across the green mountain;   190
if you'd fallen   in the hands of *hajduks,*
what could hold you,   what could restrain your arms?
if they tied them,   what would really hold them?"

And then Jovan   answers thus unto her:
"Nothing holds me,   nothing, my dear mother,
but this cursed string,   cut for *gusle* strumming."

When she hears this,   when his mother hears this,
she then jumps up,   up onto her own feet,
she then quickly   takes that piece of tendon,
and she ties him,   ties his arms together   200
from his elbows   down to his fingernails.
And from his nails   there flows the black, black blood,
so then Jovan   says unto his mother,
"Oh, my dear God!   Oh, my aging mother,
release me now;   free my two white arms,
for, oh mother,   they feel they will fall off!"

Then she jumps up,   up onto her own feet;
quickly she calls   the giant from the cave.
He comes quickly,   he, the giants' leader,
and for Jovan   they have many tortures.   210
They tear from him   both of his two bright eyes,
then toss him down   in the back of the cave
and it is there   that the two spend the night.

In the morning,   when the sun is shining,
this bitch-woman   speaks thus to the giant:
"Do you hear me,   you, the giants' leader?
Take you this boy,   take you this fool, Jovan,
on his Swan's back,   on his horse you put him,
take him away,   across the green mountain,
and there hurl him   into the cold hovel."   220

The giant stands,   then he takes up Jovan.
When the giant   seizes young Jovan there,
the foolish boy   cries out very loudly,
he speaks to them,   in the name of our Lord:
"Do not hurl me   into some old hovel;
at least leave me   beside the mountain road."

But his mother   gives no answer to him;
instead she speaks   these words to the giant:
"Seize him, giant!   Oh, you fiend, you devil!"
So he takes him   across the green mountain,   230
and he finds there   a hovel by the road.
There he hurls him,   deep into that hovel.
But the giant   is moved by misfortune!
This has all been   as the Lord has willed it.
And then he ties   the horse above the hovel,
and he returns,   back again to the cave.

Some time passes,   very little happens,
it's terrible   for anyone to hear
The horse's cry,   for his loud cry lingers.
Then the horse strikes   the hovel with his feet;   240
from that striking   the split logs bound upward,
and he seizes   his master, with his teeth.

All this tumult   resounds below the mountain,
where the travelers,   thirty draymen, now pass;
leading them all   is the drayman Rade.

When he sees them   both beside the road there,
the horse crying,   and the foolish Jovan,
then Rade speaks,   Rade, the first drayman:
"Just look at this,   oh, my dearest brothers;
here is his horse,   the foolish Jovan's Swan!   250
How he cries now,   sadly, on the mountain!
Only God knows   if Jovan has been killed.
Let's look, brothers,   to see if he is here."

When they arrive   at the frigid hovel,
then the horse cries   and clatters with his feet.
Then the drayman,   Rade, jumps from his horse.
He gathers up   thirty bits of rope there;
then he weaves them   all in pairs together.
Now they're fifteen   of them for him to use.
Rade ties them   together round his waist;   260
thirty draymen   lower him down below.
There he finds him,   Jovan, who's still living;
he brings him forth,   brings foolish Jovan out.

He unties him,   releases his white arms.
He would take him   about the wide world with him.
The boy, Jovan,   then cries out to Rade,
"God be with you,   Rade, traveling drayman;
do not take me   about the wide world with you.
Only place me   on my horse, the proud Swan,
and direct me   to Kaladžija's waters,   270
for I'm dying   of a heroic thirst.
Send two or three   to Kosovo's flat field,
to my sister   by blood and by God's grace,
my own sister,   the innkeeper, Jana.
Tell her to come   to Kaladžija's waters;
from there to bear   to Kosovo her brother.
Sister Jana,   she is a clever one.
There's no *guslar*   like her in all the world.
She will teach me   to play on the *gusle*."

Rade hears him,   and this he understands.   280
So he puts him   upon the proud Swan's back,
and directs him   to Kaladžija's waters;
and only then   does he part from Jovan.
He sends his men,   on mission to Kosovo.

Now when Jana   hears from these men the news,
she calls quickly   her two servants to her,
and these servants   bring to her her horses.
She rides on them   straight across Kosovo.

There's just Jovan   by Kaladžija's waters,
and he cries out   like a crazed serpent,   290
and the *vila*   in the mountains hears him,
and she quickly   makes her way to Jovan.
When she sees him,   sees the foolish Jovan,
and when she sees   his eyes have been ripped out,
she washes him   with Kaladžija's waters,
and the *vila*   asks the Lord Almighty
that He help her,   make new eyes for Jovan.

Then when Jovan   has been given new eyes,
he takes his seat   upon the proud Swan's back,
and he plays there   beside the cold water,   300
and there he makes   in his white throat a song:[22]
"Oh, my Dear God,   thanks be Yours for all things,
for the great help   that You have given me,
but no thanks go   to my aging mother,
the one who wants   to murder her own child!"

But now comes there   that Jana of the inn,
riding forth there   upon her stout, strong horse.
When she sees him,   sees the foolish Jovan,
she first weeps tears,   she dissolves in weeping,
then she's laughing,   she shakes with her laughter.   310
"Thanks be to God,   my own dearest brother,
and, by God's will,   are your eyes made better?"
Now they embrace,   now they kiss each other,

22. He is blind, and thus by tradition, a *guslar*—or perhaps fit for nothing else.

and she asks him   about his misfortunes,
those that the boy   received from his mother,
those she has caused,   may her dark soul be damned!
Then together   they drink the cold, cold wine.

Now comes the time   that these two must here part.
Jana returns   to Kosovo's flat field;
Jovan sets out   to find the murderess.   320
But when Jovan   arrives there at the cave,
there's his mother   seated before the cave;
she is combing   the monstrous giant's hair.
Then she looks out,   and she sees her Jovan,
and then she speaks,   says this to the giant:
"Alas, giant,   here is foolish Jovan!"
Then they jump up,   jump onto their feet.
Now you can see   our Jovan's own mother,
that bitch-woman,   she heads for the mountains!
The giant runs   back into the cold cave.   330

Quickly Jovan   captures his own mother.
Then he binds her,   ties her arms together,
and he throws her   on his white horse's back;
for the giant,   Jovan cuts off his head.

And now Jovan   mounts Swan, his noble horse,
and they ride forth   across worlds and kingdoms,
for he would find   the land that is his home.
When he comes near   to the land that is home,
there are many   who seek the tsar's reward,[23]
The first to ask   for reward, for good news,   340
is then given   a horse that is untamed;
the next to ask   for reward, for good news,
is then given   jewels not yet counted;
the third to ask   for reward, for good news,
he is given   green baize as yet uncut.[24]

---

23. A reward was traditionally given to the bearer of good news.
24. Green baize—forbidden by Turkish law to the *raja*—was by tradition the cloth from which the clothing of the Muslim upper classes was made.

Now when Jovan   arrives there on his horse,
the courtiers there   are so pleased to see him
that they then say   these words unto the tsar:
"So here he is,   our young lord and master!"

The tsar jumps up,   he rises from his throne,   350
for now he meets   before him his dear child,
and sadly there,   he embraces his son,
and to Jovan   he speaks these very words:
"Oh, my Jovan,   all is forgiven, son;
what have you done   to your own dear father?
For I have said   that you would never come."
And they begin   celebrating for him.

And then the boy   tells the tsar everything,
tells everything   his mother's done to him,
and they jump up,   and they take hold of her,   360
and they force her   to put on a thin shirt;
they cover her   with gunpowder and tar.
They come to her   from all four directions.

Then she cries out,   the mother, to Jovan:
"Do not do this   to your mother, Jovan!
Your mother burns!   She's burning with live fire!"

And our Jovan   answers his mother thus:
"So let it be,   and curses on your soul!
May you burn up;   may your soul burn in hell!"

Assisted by Dragana McFadden

The Brothers and Their Sister[25]

One of the older songs that considers the obligations of family members
to one another within the context of traditional patriarchal norms, "The
Brothers and Their Sister" seems also to reach even further back in time.

25. "*Braća i sestra*," II, 37, #9.

As Koljević has it, what happens, in fact, in the story is that the brothers disregard the mother's advice to marry their sister to "a neighbor in the village" and give her instead to "a ban beyond the sea." Koljević says,

This means that the brothers have not only disregarded their mother's wise advice, but also sinned against a time-honoured patriarchal norm by marrying their sister into an alien world. The sister is obviously innocent: her duty was to obey the males who always have and should have the last word in such matters. This is why God punishes the brothers by death, but when the innocent sister claims her patriarchal right to be visited by one of them, when she comes to "shriek bitterly" in an alien world, God is moved.[26]

Of course, at the end the sister and mother also die, but central to the tragedy here is the assumption that they are inevitably tied—by blood and thus by fate—to the consequences of their men's actions.

The Brothers and Their Sister

A mother rears   her dear sons, nine of them,
and a tenth child,   the best loved, a daughter.
She cares for them   until they all grow up,
till the time comes   for the sons to marry,
till the time comes   for the daughter's marriage.
Many suitors   wish to marry the girl;
one is a ban,[27]   another a general,
and a third man,   a neighbor from the village.
To this neighbor   her mother would give her;
the brothers choose   the ban beyond the sea.

So the brothers   further advise the girl: 10
"Go to the ban,   our most-loved sister,
go to the ban,   the ban beyond the sea,
and we will come,   there on visits often.
We'll come each month,   each month in every year.
We'll come each week,   each week in every month."
So the sister   does her brothers' bidding,
and she marries   the ban across the sea.

26. Koljević, 112–13.
27. A *ban* is a regional governor, an Ottoman title.

But now there comes   a wondrous miracle!
God allows Death   to go now forth from Him,
and now Death takes   each of the nine brothers   20
and leaves behind   mother to keep herself.
And so three years,   three long years slowly pass.

Now Jelica,   the sister, speaks sharply:
"Dear God above,   it is such a wonder!
What have I done   to offend my brothers,
that they do not   yet wish to come see me!"

The ban's sisters   often scold Jelica:
"You're a bad girl,   Jelica, our sister,
and your brothers   must strongly dislike you,
for they never   wish to come to see you."   30
And Jelica   answers them quite sharply
every morning,   also every evening.

But the dear God   has mercy upon her,
and he sends forth   a pair of His angels:
"Go out to her,   you, my two dear angels.
Go to the grave,   the white grave of Jovan,
Jovan's gravesite,   Jovan, the youngest brother.
Breathe upon him   your own sweet angels' breath.
From the grave there   make a sound horse for him.
From the earth there   make some sweet cakes for him.   40
From the shelter   make some fine gifts for him.
Make him ready   to visit his sister."

So they set forth,   two of God's own angels,
forth to the grave,   the white grave of Jovan.
From the grave there   they make him a sound horse.
They breathe on him,   breathe their breath into him.
From the earth there   they make sweet cakes for him.
From the shelter   they make fine gifts for him,
make him ready   to visit his sister.

Quickly he goes,   Jovan, strengthless brother.   50
When he sees it,   the mansion looms in view.

From far away   the girl also sees him,
and quite quickly   she comes out to meet him,
and she weeps there,   from sorrow does she cry.

They embrace there,   hug and kiss each other.
Now the sister   speaks to her dear brother:
"Did you not say,   not promise me, brother,
when you gave me,   gave my hand in marriage,
that you would come   here to visit often?
You'd come each month,   each month in every year?   60
You'd come each week,   each week in every month?
And yet today   three full years have now passed,
and you've not come,   not once, to visit me!"
And the sister   says more to her brother:
"Why, my brother,   are you so gray of face?
You look all gray,   like one who's been buried!"

Now he answers,   the poor, strengthless Jovan,
"Silence, sister,   if you honor your God!
I have suffered;   yes, I've seen great trouble.
I had, before,   eight brothers, all married;   70
I served, before,   my eight sisters-in-law.
And when all eight,   my eight brothers had wed,
nine white houses   were ours; we cared for them.
And by such work   my skin has blackened, sister."
And he stays on;   he visits three white days.

Now Jelica   prepares herself to travel,
prepares her gifts,   gifts which are quite proper,
for her brothers,   also for her sisters.
For her brothers   she sews fine shirts of silk;
for her sisters   are jewels, wedding rings.   80
But her brother,   Jovan, tries to stop her;
"Stay here, sister;   stay home, my dear sister,
till more brothers   come to make their visits."
But Jelica   does not wish to stay there;
she brings rich gifts,   ready for her journey.
So he sets out,   Jovan, from the mansion;
with him travels   his sister, Jelica.

Now when these two   arrive near a mansion,
near that mansion   they approach a white church.
He speaks to her,   Jovan, strengthless one: 90
"Now you stay here,   my beloved sister;
I'll go behind   that white church standing there.
When he married,   the middle of our brothers,
I lost a ring,   a ring made of pure gold.
I'll look for it,   my beloved sister."
And to the grave   strengthless Jovan returns.
So Jelica   waits for strengthless Jovan.
She waits and waits   there for strengthless Jovan.
She waits for him,   then she goes to fetch him.

Near the white church   there is a new graveyard;   100
there the sister   feels sad and grief-stricken;
there her brother,   strengthless Jovan, has died.
Now she hurries   toward the great, white mansion.
As she comes near   to the great, white mansion,
from the mansion   she hears a cuckoo's cry.
But what she hears   is not a cuckoo's cry;
it is, rather,   her old mother crying.
When Jelica   arrives at the threshold,
from her white throat   she calls to her mother,
"Oh, my mother,   open the door for me!"   110

The old mother   answers from the mansion,
"Go away! Hence!   You, God's own angel, Death![28]
You who killed them,   my own, dearest, nine sons!
Do you wish now   to kill their old mother?"
Then Jelica   answers to her mother,
"Dear, poor mother,   open the door for me,
for I am not   God's mighty angel, Death,
but Jelica,   your own, your dear daughter."

Now the mother   opens the door for her.
The two cry there;   like cuckoos, they cry there,   120

28. In Serbian mythology and grammar, *smrt* (death) is feminine.

embrace and hold   each other with their arms,
fall together,   down to the earth, and die.

Assisted by Dragana McFadden

 ## God Leaves No Debt Unpaid[29]

This crude but powerful song of filial loyalty and betrayal seems the very
embodiment of the patriarchal values of the Serbs. Its opening anthesis,
which implicitly compares a sister and two brothers to a fir tree between
two pines, is certainly one of the most celebrated figurations of the heroic songs.[30] Indeed, motifs of natural analogy for human actions mark the
poem—to its extension in the highly elaborated fantasy at the poem's
end. And the curious dualities, of pine and fir, of sister and wife, of two
brothers, and finally of *immortelle* and basil and thorns and nettles, seem
somehow to restore a natural order, or at least a natural symmetry, to re-
solve the opposition of seeming and being, of the ideal and the actual,
which this dark poem laments. Certainly such a poem gains much from
its links to a pre-Christian past.

God Leaves No Debt Unpaid

Two pine trees grew   one beside the other
and between them   a fir with narrow top.
But it was not   pine trees that grew up there
and it was not   a fir with narrow top,
they were brothers   born of the same mother.
One was Pavle,   the other Radule.
Between the two,   their sister Jelica.
The two brothers   loved their sister dearly
and showered her   with many loving gifts,
and among them   a finely forgéd knife,   10
silver-plated   and gold-plated also.

---

29. "*Bog nikom dužan ne ostaje,*" II, 20, #5.
30. This is the classic example of Slavic antithesis, a rhetorical device that opens many of the
songs and will frequently recur throughout. See Koljević, 38 n, 113–15 et passim.

When Pavle's wife   saw what they've given her,
she was jealous   of her sister-in-law,
and so she said   to Radule's dear wife:
"Sister-in-law,   my dear sister in God,
do you know of   an herb that brings forth hate,
that brings forth hate   between brothers and sister?"

She answered her,   the wife of Radule:
"So help me God,   my dear sister-in-law,
I do not know   an herb that brings forth hate.   20
E'en if I knew,   I would still not tell you:
Both my brothers   always loved me dearly
and showered me   with many loving gifts."

When Pavle's wife   heard her sister-in-law,
she went away   to the field of horses,
and she stabbed there   a black horse in the field.
She then said this   to her master Pavle:
"To evil end   you loved your dear sister,
and even worse,   you showered her with gifts:
She stabbed your horse,   your black horse in the field."   30

Pavle then asked   his sister Jelica:
"Why, O sister,   why, in the name of God?"
And his sister   thus swore to her brother:
"Not I, brother,   I swear by my own life,
by my own life   and by your life also."
And her brother   believed his dear sister.

When Pavle's wife   realized what happened,
she went at night   to her husband's garden,
she cut the throat   of his beloved falcon.
And then she said   to her master Pavle: 40
"To evil end   you loved your dear sister,
and even worse,   you showered her with gifts:
She cut the throat   of your beloved falcon."

Pavle then asked   his sister Jelica:
"Why, O sister,   why, in the name of God?"
And his sister   thus swore to her brother:

"Not I, brother,   I swear by my own life,
by my own life   and by your life also."
And her brother   believed his dear sister.

When Pavle's wife   realized what happened,   50
she went at night,   after the dinner feast,
and then she stole   her sister-in-law's knife
and cut the throat   of her child in its cradle.
When the next day   the bright morning had dawned,
she ran quickly   to her master Pavle,
while wailing and   disfiguring her face:
"To evil end   you loved your dear sister,
and even worse   you showered her with gifts:
She cut the throat   of your child in its cradle.
If what I say   you do not believe me,   60
draw out the knife   from her belt and you'll see."

Pavle jumped up,   as possessed by a fiend,
and he ran up   to the high tower's chambers,
but his sister   was still in peaceful sleep.
Under her head   was still her gilded knife.
Pavle snatched it,   the knife from her pillow
and drew it out   from its own silver sheath.
Indeed the knife   was all covered with blood.

When he saw that,   Pavle, her dear master,
he pulled the hand   of his sleeping sister: 70
"O my sister,   may God's wrath strike you dead!
It's bad enough   you killed my grazing horse
and my falcon   in my green garden too,
but why killed you   my child in its cradle?"

And his sister   thus swore to her brother:
"Not I, brother,   I swear by my own life,
by my own life   and by your life also.
If you do not   believe me and my oath,
then take me out   into the wide green field,
there tie me up   to the tails of horses,   80
tear me apart   and throw me to all winds."

But her brother   did not believe her words.
He took her up   by her tender white hand,
he took her out   into the wide green field,
he tied her up   to long tails of horses,
and whipped them off   across the wide green field.

Where any drop   of her blood had fallen,
there grew basil   and the *immortelle*.
Where her body   had fallen on the ground,
there a small church   has risen by itself.   90

After some time,   a short time, had passed by,
Pavle's young wife   suddenly became ill.
For nine long years   she pined away in bed,
all through her bones   the grass began to sprout,
and in the grass   deadly snakes were breeding,
sucking her eyes   while hiding in the grass.

Pavle's young wife   lamented bitterly
and then she spoke   to her master husband:
"Listen to me,   O my dearest master!
Please do take me   to your dear sister's church,   100
so that the church   might forgive me my sins."

When her husband   Pavle had heard her words,
he carried her   to his dear sister's church.
But as they were   near the holy white church,
they heard a voice   speaking from the white church:
"Do not come here,   you, young wife of Pavle,
for this church here   will not forgive your sins."

When the young wife   of Pavle heard this voice,
she then implored   her husband and master:
"For love of God,   O my dearest master,   110
do not take me   back to our white manor,
but just tie me   to the long horses' tails
and let them run   across the wide green field.
Let the horses   tear me apart alive."

Pavle heeded   his wife's last desire:
And he tied her   to the long horses' tails,

and let them run   across the wide green field.
Where any drop   of her blood had fallen,
there grew the thorns,   there grew the wild nettles.
Where her body   had fallen on the ground,   120
there a wild lake   has made its appearance.
In the same lake   a black horse is swimming,
and behind him   a small golden cradle.
On the cradle   a gray falcon stands guard.
In the cradle   a small boy is sleeping,
under his throat   rests his mother's white hand,
and in her hand   lies his aunt's gilded knife.

2 Before the Battle of Kosovo

*M*ANY IF NOT MOST of the poems in Vuk's collection recount historical events, and of these many, especially the early songs, recount the deeds of the nobility in the years of grandeur of the Serbian feudal state of Sclavonia, or Rascia, in what is now southern Serbia and Macedonia, ruled by the Nemanjićes in the thirteenth and fourteenth centuries, and in Zeta to the west, today's Montenegro.[1]

The area, protected from the Byzantines by its mountains, had long been occupied by Slavs, organized in collective families known as *zadruge,* who had flooded the area between the Danube and the Peloponnesus between the seventh and the ninth centuries. In the mountains of Zeta and the highlands of Rascia they preserved their predominantly Slavic identity and their pagan traditions, perhaps more fully than the Slavs in Bulgaria and Macedonia to their east and south, who were closer to Byzantium. In the ninth century, when the Bulgarians defied the Byzantines, the Serbs sought the protection of the Byzantines against the Bulgarians. Vlastimir, the first king of the Serbs, resisted the Bulgarians and established himself as a Byzantine dependency. So when, in the later years of that century, the brothers Constantine (later Cyril) and Methodius, armed with a papal concession permitting a vernacular liturgy, set out

---

1. The kingdom was variously identified—as *Sclavonia* (from Latin, *sclavorum gens,* a generalized term for Slavs found in Latin documents of Ragusa/Dubrovnik and referring to the peoples living in the valleys of the Raška and Bosna rivers), and as *Rascia* (a toponymic used in foreign sources, sometimes pejoratively). The kingdom was first centered on the lands of the valley of the Raška River, near the present city of Novi Pazar; its court was located presumably at a *Stari Pazar,* or *Pazarište,* or *Ras,* somewhat north of the present city.

north from Salonika on their mission to the Slavs of Moravia, they left behind disciples who brought Christianity to the Slavs of the Balkans, including the Serb state, together with a written liturgical language and a
degree of civilization.

In the eleventh century, after the destruction of the confederation of
pre-feudal states assembled under Tsar Samuil of Ohrid by Basil II, the
area fell into a kind of anarchy, which came to an end with the unification
of Rascia and Zeta under a single feudal principality, achieved at the
hands of the man with whom the Serbs associate their origins as a nationality, Stefan Nemanja.[2] Nemanja came from a family of petty chieftains of Zeta, situated near the Adriatic in a fortress not far from the present location of Podgorica. His father, the Grand Župan Uroš II, had fled
there after his own failure to unify the Slavic tribes under the authority of
Serbia. After his succession to his easternmost lands in 1167, Nemanja, by
means of alliances first with Venetians and later with Hungarians, was
able to gain control of the territories of his brothers, to expand his authority as far north as Niš, and finally to gain control over the rapidly de-
clining feudal principality of Dioclea in Zeta and on the coast. Nemanja
even made overtures to Holy Roman Emperor Frederick Barbarossa, who
was contemplating a new crusade, and in 1189 received him at Niš. But the
next year Frederick drowned, and Nemanja was without his protection.
Then Nemanja was defeated in battle by the Byzantine emperor and
forced to sue for peace. Nemanja lost some territory but received in return
the Byzantine emperor's niece, Eudokia, as wife for his son and heir, Nemanjić, and for himself the highest Byzantine title of sebastocrator. By
these means, a kind of Serbian autonomy was assured.

A wise politician and devout Christian, Nemanja maintained cordial
relations with both the Orthodox churches of the East and the Holy See
at Rome. He encouraged his youngest son, Rastimir, or Rastko (1175–
1234), in his wish to study to become a priest in the monastery of Vatope-

2. *Stefan* was at the time a designation of royalty, not a name. Thus, "King Nemanja" might
be a more accurate translation. The term *Serbia* as descriptive of a specific political or geographical area—although it seems to have been immediately derived from Sorbia, a Roman
name identifying a small district at the headwaters of the Drina River, near the present city of
Srebrenica, which meant "silver country" (there were Roman mines nearby)—was not used until the time of Nemanjić, whose brother in 1202 identified himself as "the King of the Serbs."

After Lazar Hrebeljanović had lost the Nemanjić Empire to the Turks at Kosovo and after
three hundred years of Turkish domination, the descendants of the Slavs who had been ruled by
the Nemanjićes made their long trek north to Hungary and settled in territories later called Hungarian "Serbia," bringing their history with them. Only then did they come to identify Rascia and
Zeta, the heart of the Nemanjić lands, as "Old Serbia."

di on Mount Athos. And in 1196, after he had been forced to accept Byzantine suzerainty, Nemanja resigned his throne in favor of his middle son, Nemanjić, and retired to Studenica, a monastery he had founded, to take holy orders and the name of Simeon. Later he joined his son, Rastko, who had taken the name of Sava (and would come to be revered as Saint Sava, the founder of the Serbian Orthodox Church), and founded the great monastery of Hilandar, on the Holy Mountain at Athos. Simeon died there in 1200.

The country Stefan Nemanjić undertook to rule was quite different from that of his father. Byzantium, fallen into anarchy, was no longer a serious threat. But Stefan Nemanjić was challenged by his older brother, Vukan, who, with papal support, drove Nemanjić from his lands. Vukan was challenged in turn for his Roman Catholic crown by his former ally, the king of Hungary. Seeing his chance, Nemanjić returned in 1204 and regained authority in a devastated Serbia. Meanwhile, Constantinople had fallen to the Crusaders, who established there a Latin kingdom, while the Byzantine patriarch retired with the emperor to Nicaea. Nemanjić accordingly repudiated his Byzantine wife, began negotiations with the pope at Rome, agreed to accept papal authority, and in 1217, some sources say, he received a crown from the pope. The next year Sava journeyed to Žiča to crown his brother in the Orthodox rite, however (thus, rather ironically, to the Orthodox he became known as "Stefan the First Crowned").

The Bulgarian Tsar Ivan Asen II's defeat of Nemanjić's successor Radoslav's Epirot allies at Marica in 1230 made Bulgaria for a time the dominant power in the Balkans. But soon there came out of the east a Golden Horde of Tartars, who swept over Russia, pursued the Hungarians across Croatia and, on to the Adriatic coast, reduced the Bulgarians to tributaries for half a century, swept through Bosnia and Zeta to the sea, then retired across Rascia, driving the people into their hills. Vladislav, Radoslav's successor, passed his crown to his other brother, Uroš I, who proved a vigorous warrior and the real king of Serbia from the moment of his accession in 1243.

The Tartar invasions and the bloodless recapture of Constantinople by the Epirot Greeks had changed the order of things in the Balkans. The Byzantine Greeks were a power again, and Bulgaria, in a state of serious disorder, would in 1257 find a Nemanjić, Konstantin Tikh, on the throne. Hungary relaxed its hold on its Balkan and Adriatic territories and turned away from the Slavs to more western alliances. The Angevin king of Sicily, the ambitious Charles, began to emerge as the dominant Catholic power in the east. His daughter, the devoutly Catholic Helen of Anjou, was married in 1250 to Uroš, who, as the leader of a prosperous state and a pillar of stability amid shifting winds and wandering mercenary armies, established the Nemanjićs once again as a major power in the Balkans.

When he grew older, Uroš lost his throne to his son, the ascetic Dragutin, who reigned for only six years, from 1276 until 1282, when he surrendered the majority of his territory to his brother Milutin and retired to the north and west to establish himself in Hungarian territory at Belgrade.[3] A leader of extraordinary prowess, Milutin ruled for nearly forty years (until 1321), married four wives, the last being a six-year-old Byzantine princess, Simonida, and presided over a period of expansion and economic prosperity in Serbia.[4] It was Milutin who captured Skopje and established his court there in 1282, who pressed westward to the Adriatic, who built the great monastery at Gračanica, who even had dreams of a reunited Byzantine Empire. In these years Serbian mines and fields gave up great riches—precious metals, wheat, cattle, oil—and Serbia was on her way to becoming a rich and important European state.

Simonida bore Milutin no children, but there were already sons by his renounced second wife, Elizabeth. One of them was given a principality of his own, but he fell into struggle with his father, was defeated by him, and suffered the Byzantine punishment of blinding before being exiled to Constantinople. The blinding seems not to have been permanent. As legend has it, on the evening of the blinding on Kosovo field (where the sentence was carried out) St. Nicholas appeared to the prince and said, "Fear not, for your eyes are in my hands." In any event, at the monastery of Christ Pancrator in Constantinople, miraculously or not, the prince regained his sight.

Serbia in the thirteenth and fourteenth centuries was literate as well as powerful. Like the Bulgarian, the Old Serbian texts were written in a variety of Old Church Slavic (there were some differences that accommodated differences in the vernaculars), and both were based upon a Byzantine literary inheritance. Many liturgical works were composed, and the

---

3. Belgrade (Beograd), called Beligrad ("the white city") by the Bulgarians who controlled it in the ninth century, was built around the old Roman fortress of Singidunum.

4. Serbian coins had been first minted under Milutin, and since some were debased imitations of Venetian ducats, their appearance in Italy caused some consternation, at least for Dante, who immortalized poor Uroš as a forger and cheered on his Hungarian enemies in the *Paradiso*, Canto xix. See David H. Higgins, intro., commentary, notes, and biblio., *The Divine Comedy*, trans. C. H. Sisson (Chicago: Regnery Gateway, 1981) 435, 660 n. 140.

Bible itself was translated into Old Church Slavic in monastic centers in Bulgaria and then transmitted or adapted, often by the clerics at Ohrid, to the western vernacular. Many liturgical works were apocryphal: "The Descent of the Virgin into Hell," "The Discussion of the Patriarch Methodius" on the end of the world, and "The Vision of Isaiah." But secular works appeared as well, romances, like the *Aleksandrida* (which turns the world conqueror into a Christian knight). The story of Troy is preserved in a Bulgarian translation, and the stories of Tristram and King Arthur were told by the South Slavs. There is even a version of a Greek translation of "Stefanit and Ichnilat," from the Indian *Panchatantra,* as well as historical and scientific works—a *Physiologus,* or bestiary, and a "Synopsis of peoples and languages" setting forth various tongues and alphabets. In addition to all of these are the original works, the hagiographies, secular and holy. Many motifs, themes, and characterizations of historical figures from this body of writing found their way into the heroic songs.

In Milutin's reign a monk named Theodosije, writing at Hilandar, produced several secular hagiographies in Old Serbian that prefigure—and perhaps provide indirect sources for—the heroic songs. In his narratives one finds the kind of "Providential moral interference," the crusading fervor, and the representation of character that is to be found in the songs. But Theodosije also gave direct evidence in his work of the presence of singers in Serbia, for he indicated, in his *Life of Saint Sava,* his disapproval of the "indecent and harmful" songs and praised Sava for avoiding them. And from other accounts we can be sure that in Milutin's time the singers were to be seen in the courts of the Serbs.[5]

The prince married the Byzantine emperor's daughter and after five years and the intercession of Danilo, archbishop of Serbia, was reconciled to his father. After Milutin's death in 1321 there was a struggle for the throne among three brothers—Konstantin, supported by the Bulgarians; Vladislav, the candidate of the Hungarians; and the prince, who had the support of the Greeks. The prince bribed Konstantin's army (which crucified Konstantin, sawed him in half, and tossed the remains into a river), drove Vladislav back into the arms of his Hungarian friends across the Sava River, occupied Belgrade, and gained the crown for himself.

These struggles were not without cost. In Bosnia a newly independent

---

5. See Koljević, 13–16. Koljević also tells us of the *Chronicle* of Father Dukljanin, written in the aristocratic city of Bar on the Montenegrin Adriatic sometime between the twelfth and fifteenth centuries, in which parallels to many elements of the heroic songs are to be found. Koljević, 16–21.

and Bogomil[6] king seized the opportunity to wrest Hum (Hercegovina) from the newly crowned Serbian king, thus dashing his ambitions for access to the Adriatic. But the new king turned south and east. He gained control of the fortress of Prilep and of the Vardar valley by a famous victory over the Bulgarians and Byzantines at Kustendil in 1330 (the victory was celebrated by the building of the magnificent church of Dečani, and thus he was to be *Stefan Dečanski* to all Serbs).

For some time thereafter Bulgaria ceased to exist as a significant presence in the Balkans. Dečanski himself lost his power the following year (he was supplanted by his son, Dušan, the warrior-hero of Kustendil), and died soon thereafter, probably not of natural causes. In popular legends this son is known as *Tsar Dušan* or *Dušan Silni* (Dušan the Mighty). But he was the only Nemanjić monarch not canonized by the Serbian church.

Dušan seized the Albanian coast from the Angevins; he took advantage of the dynastic struggles of the Byzantines to extend his dominion to Epirus, Aetolia, Thessaly, and as far south as Athens. He married Helen, the sister of Ivan Alexander, tsar of Bulgaria, and thus formed an alliance with that weakened state. In 1346, recognizing the opportunity of gaining the imperial throne of Byzantium for himself and thus reestablishing the old empire, he had himself crowned tsar, or emperor, at Skopje by Joanikije, the bishop of Ohrid. Joanikije was appointed Serbia's first patriarch for the purpose, and then assumed his throne at Peć, a monastery high in the mountains in the center of the kingdom, which had been the seat of her archbishops since 1269.

Tsar Dušan's empire was indeed glorious. He ruled from the city of Skopje, from a magnificent court shaped in imitation of that of Byzantium. His mines produced great quantities of Europe's silver and gold, and much was shipped west out of Ragusa (Dubrovnik). He endowed his many monasteries—especially Dečani—generously, and the most accomplished of artisans adorned them with magnificent frescoes, woodcarvings, and other rich treasures. His *Zakonik,* or legal code, published shortly after he assumed the imperial crown, gave evidence of the enlightenment of his society and civil government.

But a danger imperiled this civilization and others like it in the Balkans and elsewhere in Europe, a danger that Dušan was the first to recognize. For a Byzantine general, John Cantacuzenus, one of the parties to the

6. The Bogomils were a Manichaean and heretical Christian sect that rejected the sacraments and all church organization. The heresy spread widely throughout the Balkans, especially in Bosnia, and further westward, in the twelfth, thirteenth, and fourteenth centuries.

Byzantine dynastic struggle, had allied himself with the Ottoman Turks and had invited them onto the European mainland to assist him. Dušan, who finally entered the struggle and sided against Cantacuzenus, saw a detachment of his own forces defeated by Turks in 1343. He saw Cantacuzenus and his Turks enter Constantinople in 1347, Cantacuzenus proclaiming himself emperor; he saw the Great Plague sweep eastern Europe in 1348 and bring with it the seeds of economic devastation. Even as Serbian and Bulgarian forces defending Cantacuzenus's Byzantine opponents were being cut to pieces by the Turks at Dimotika in 1353, Dušan pleaded for alliance with the Venetians in order that he might establish himself as emperor at Constantinople and thus unify Christian opposition to the Muslim Turks. He also appealed to Pope Innocent VI, at Avignon, and even offered to accept papal authority over the Old Serbian church. At first the plan seemed promising; the Holy Roman Emperor Charles IV, himself a Bohemian, welcomed Dušan as a fellow Slavic ruler. But in 1354 the avaricious Hungarians invaded Nemanjić land. Dušan drove them back (it was then that he recaptured Belgrade), and then set out for Constantinople, relying solely upon his own not inconsiderable power to conquer the imperial city. Dušan had a fair chance of success, but he died suddenly in 1355 in an obscure village along the way.

Dušan's successor was Uroš IV, nineteen at the time of his father's death and not the man his father had been. He was never able to establish authority over his vassals. Two brothers of the Mrnjavčević family, Vukašin of Prilep and Uglješa, who ruled in the valley of the Vardar, ignored him, as did his uncle, Simeon, who ruled in Epirus, and the Balša family in Zeta. Bulgaria seceded and immediately broke apart. And in the midst of all this the Turks continued inexorably to advance.

The Turks occupied Adrianople in 1363. They defeated and killed Vukašin and Uglješa on the banks of the Marica River in 1371, the year of Uroš's death. Vukašin's son, Marko, who succeeded him at Prilep and became a vassal to the Turks in 1385, was to become in song and legend a fantastic and sometimes comic hero. But he was in fact never to be more than a minor Turkish vassal; he died in their service in 1394, fighting against Christians in Wallachia, although he kept his Christian faith, and, it is said, on the eve of his last battle prayed for a Christian victory.

Uroš did have vassals who showed somewhat more loyalty, albeit of an independent-minded kind. One of these was Vuk Branković, Uroš's brother-in-law, who had been given the Kosovo; another was Lazar Hrebeljanović, who ruled in Serbia in the north and was married to another of Uroš's relatives. Lazar contested with another vassal, Tvrtko, who had declared himself king of Bosnia, and he emerged from these battles as "Prince" Lazar, the titular leader of what was left of Dušan's empire, although he never claimed the imperial, or even the royal title for himself. The vassals under Lazar did come together long enough to defeat the Turks at Pločnik in 1387 and to drive them back upon Niš, the strategic crossroads of the Balkans occupied by the Turks some time earlier. Even the quarrelling Bulgarians came together long enough to join in this alliance. But as Lazar and Tvrtko knew, Niš had to be recaptured, as well as the Vardar valley (which opened upon Salonika), if the region were to be free of the Muslim Turks. The Turks, in their turn, continued their advance into Serb lands. With Dušan's death, the Nemanjić dynasty came effectively to an end, and, we are told, the course of Christian civilization in the Balkans found a new and darker destiny.

Such a history—of a lost glory—would certainly have an appeal to a people occupied by a foreign power, and would as well quite naturally attract the attention of European readers caught up in the Romanticism and nationalist aspirations of the first half of the nineteenth century. So it is no surprise that many of the earliest of the heroic songs recount events taking place during these centuries. It is also no surprise that many of these songs recount the beginnings of things. "The Building of Skadar," "The Building of Ravanica," "The Wedding of Tsar Dušan," "Uroš and the Mrljavčevićes," three of the five songs collected here, are all examples. As we shall see, all of these songs concern building—of families (through marriage) or of fortifications. Most concern actual places and historical families, but there are many mythic elements remaining to be found in these songs.

 ## The Wedding of Tsar Dušan[7]

"The Wedding of Tsar Dušan," a parodic, anti-heroic song, was recited—not sung—to Vuk in 1815 by Tešan Podrugović, his usual deadpan scowl masking its comedy. The representation of a passive and dependent Dušan, of the noble shepherd become shepherd-champion, of a series of accidents—not heroic exploits—that determine victory in the almost uninterrupted adventures recounted make "The Wedding of Tsar Dušan" a

7. "*Ženidba cara Dušana*," II, 102, #29.

departure from the usual celebration of heroism and nobility and give it an ironic quality that prefigures the songs of the Marko Kraljević cycle. And the song is ironically patriarchal as well. Historically, Miloš Vojinović was a captain in the service of Dušan, not a relative, but the feudal relationship is here transformed to a familial one. And the song itself has a traditional plot, of a bride sought in a foreign land, of the journey there to fetch her among treacherous strangers, of the tests imposed before she may be taken away. These elements, and the bride's name itself, suggest remote antecedents; "Roxana" is a name occurring in the *Aleksandrida,* the medieval Old Slavic romance of Alexander the Great and his love.[8]

The Wedding of Tsar Dušan

When the Serbs' tsar,   Dušan, thought of marriage,
he wooed a girl   in a far, distant land,
a far city,   Latin town of Ledjan,[9]
of King Michael,   a Latin over there,
a pretty girl,   whose name is Roxana.
The tsar proposed   to wed, the king agreed.
The tsar wooed her,   following the custom.
And so the tsar   called Todor the Vizier:
"O my servant,   O Todor, my vizier,
go to Ledjan   that far-off white city,   10
to my cousin,   the Latin, King Michael
so we can now   arrange things for the wedding,
when we should go   to fetch the pretty bride,
and the number   of guests that we should bring.
And have a look   at the girl Roxana,
if she will be   a good wife for a tsar.
Go look at her   and give her this gold ring."

The answer came   from Todor, the vizier:
"I shall obey,   O my tsar, my dear lord."   20
He got ready,   and set out for the Latins.

---

8. See "Marko the Prince," 70.
9. The identity of "Ledjan" is uncertain, although it is presumably Italian, or Venetian.

When he arrived   in white Ledjan city,
he was welcomed   quite warmly by the king.
They drank red wine,   the two, for a full week.
Then that Todor,   the vizier, spoke these words:
"O my good friend,   Michael, great Latin king,
my tsar did not   send me to your household
to drink red wine   in the town of Ledjan.
He sent me here   to plan the wedding with you,
when he should come   to fetch the pretty bride,   30
and at what time   of year that it should be,
and the number   of guests that he should bring,
to see for him   the girl Roxana here,
see and give her   the tsar's betrothal ring."

Michael, the king,   spoke then in his answer:
"O my good friend,   O Todor, the vizier,
what the tsar asks   about the wedding guests,
let him bring here   as many as he likes.
When should he come?   whenever he might wish.
But take to him   this message in greeting: 40
He should not bring   his two nephews with him,
his two nephews,   the two Vojinovićes,
Vukašin and   his brother Petrašin,
because they are,   both of them, heavy drinkers
and in quarrels   very savage fighters.
They will drink much   and start an ugly fight,
and it is hard   to put up with their fighting
in this city,   the white town of Ledjan.
As for the girl,   you will see her quite soon
and give her then   the ring, as is the custom."   50

And when the night,   the dark night had fallen,
they did not bring   the candles made of wax,
but brought her forth,   the girl in the darkness.
When he saw her,   Todor, Dušan's vizier,
he presented   a ring made of pure gold,
set with a pearl   and many precious stones.
The room was lit   by all the precious stones,
and in that light   the girl appeared to him

more beautiful   than any white *vila*.
He gave the ring   to the girl Roxana,   60
and he gave her   a thousand gold ducats.
And her brothers   led away Roxana.

When the morning   of the next day dawned,
Vizier Todor   prepared for his trip home
and he set forth   for the town of Prizren.[10]
When he arrived   at Prizren, the white town,
the Serbian tsar   Stefan began to ask:
"O my servant,   O Todor, my vizier,
did you see her,   the fair girl, Roxana?
Did you see her   and give her the gold ring?   70
What did the king,   Michael, say unto you?"
Todor told him   everything that happened:
"I saw the girl,   and gave to her the ring.
What a beauty   this girl Roxana is!
There's no such girl   in all the Serbian lands.

"And King Michael,   he spoke such pleasing words:
'Come for the bride   whenever you desire.
Bring as you will   however many guests.'
But then the king   in sending greeting asked
that you not bring   your two nephews with you,   80
the two nephews,   the two Vojinovićes,
because they are,   both of them, heavy drinkers
and in quarrels   very savage fighters;
they will drink much   and start an ugly fight,
and it is hard   to put up with their fighting
here in Ledjan,   this white Latin city."

When he heard that,   the Serbian tsar, Stefan,
he slapped his hand   firmly against his knee:
"Woe unto me,   and may God be my help!
How far has spread   news of misbehavior   90
of my nephews,   the two Vojinovićes!
But so firm is   my true faith in the Lord,

10. Prizren was a large city in Kosovo, where Dušan built his beautiful memorial church, later totally destroyed by the Turks.

as soon as this,   this merriment is over,
I'll have them hanged,   both of those mean scoundrels,
above the gates   of Vučitrn city,[11]
then neither one   will shame me ever more."

The tsar began   to gather wedding guests;
he invited   some twelve thousand people
and assembled   them all at Kosovo.
When they approached   the town of Vučitrn,   100
they were observed   by those Vojinovićes,
who wondered long   among themselves, those youths:
"Why's our uncle   so furious with us;
he won't take us   there as his wedding guests?
Someone did speak,   did slander us before him,
may all the flesh   of that vile slanderer melt!
The tsar sets forth,   goes to the Latin country,
but no warrior   goes to accompany him,
not a brave man,   none of his own kinsmen,
to protect him   if trouble arises,   110
to give him help,   aid in some misfortune.
Latins are sly,   deceivers, as we know,
And they will kill   the uncle that we love;
uninvited,   howe'er, we dare not go."

Their old mother   spoke to them this advice:
"My dear children,   you two Vojinovićes,
you've a brother   up in the high mountain,
who keeps the sheep,   young Miloš the shepherd.
He's the youngest,   but the bravest of you
and of Miloš   the tsar has no knowledge.   120
Send him a page,   a letter in your hand,
tell him to come   to Vučitrn city.
Do not tell him   the whole truth about it,
but you tell him,   your mother is dying,
and she wishes   to give him her blessing,
so that no curse   shall remain upon him,
and that quickly   he should come to the court
if he wishes   to find his mother living."

11. Vučitrn, a town between Priština and Kosovska Mitrovica.

The two brothers   did as their mother said.
Quickly they wrote   a letter on their knees,   130
and dispatched it   straight up the Šar Mountain[12]
to their brother,   to the shepherd, Miloš.
"O our Miloš,   our own last-born brother,
gallop quickly   to Vučitrn city.
Our old mother   lies sick on her deathbed.
And she calls you   to give you her blessing,
so that no curse   will remain upon you."
When Miloš read   the letter of his brothers,
while he read it   his tears flowed heavily.

Thirty shepherds,   his comrades, then asked him: 140
"O our Miloš,   our head man and leader,
often you used   to get many letters,
but you did not   read them with tears flowing.
In God's good name,   where's this letter come from?"

Miloš jumped up   onto his nimble feet
and he spoke thus   to his shepherd comrades:
"O my shepherds,   my dear, loyal brothers,
this letter here   is from my home and court.
My old mother,   dear mother, is dying,
and she calls me   to give me her blessing,   150
so that no curse   shall remain upon me.
You take good care   of our mountain sheep here
while I am gone,   until I come back here."

Miloš traveled   to Vučitrn city.
When he was near   his own white home and court,
his two brothers   walked out to welcome him,
and behind them   came their dear old mother.
Shepherd Miloš   told them all, in wonder:
"Why, O brothers,   if God is dear to you,
make you trouble   where there is no trouble?"   160
Then his brothers,   his dear brothers, told him:

12. Šar Mountain (*Šar-Planina*) is a high plateau above the town of Tetovo, today in western Macedonia. It is a traditional grazing land, and is therefore associated with shepherds.

"Come, O brother,   there is great misfortune."
Right there they kissed   each other's white faces,
and Miloš kissed   his mother's sweet, white hand.
And they told him   everything in order:
how the tsar went   to fetch his promised bride,
far, far away,   in the Latin country,
but he did not   invite his own nephews.
"And so, Miloš,   our own brother by blood,
will you, brother,   go there with our uncle   170
as wedding guest,   e'en if uninvited?
If any kind   of misfortune befalls him,
you should be there   as his aid and comfort.
If he suffers   no trouble whatever,
you can return   without telling your name."

Miloš could not   wait to hear what they said:
"I will, brothers,   yes, I will, my brothers!
If not for him,   my uncle, for whom then?"
Then the brothers   began to prepare him.
Petrašin went   to prepare his dun horse,   180
and Vukašin   readied Miloš himself:
he put a shirt,   thin, next to his body,
woven with gold   all the way to his waist,
and from the waist   woven with pure white silk.
Over the shirt   he placed three light waistcoats,
then a tunic   having thirty buttons;
on the tunic,   discs made of beaten gold,
those heavy discs   weighing seven gold okes;
and on his legs   trousers with worked metal;
on top of it   a heavy Bulgar's coat,   190
and on his head   a Bulgar's black fur hat,
so that Miloš   looked like a dark Bulgar,
e'en his brothers   could not recognize him.
Then they gave him   a deadly battle lance
and the green sword   of old father Vojin.
Then Petrašin   brought forward the dun horse
all covered up   with embroidered bear skin,
so that the tsar   would not recognize him.

And his brothers   gave him this good advice:
"When you, Miloš,   come to the wedding guests,   200
they will ask you   who you are and where from.
Tell them you are   from the Karavlaška:[13]
'I was servant   of the bey, Radul-Bey.
But he refused   to pay my earned wages,
and so I left   for the wide, unknown world,
to look around   for a better service.
And then I heard   about the tsar's wedding,
and so I came   as uninvited guest
to earn a piece   of the white daily bread
and earn a cup   of good red wine as well.'   210
Keep tight the reins   of your dun-coated horse,
because the horse   has grown much accustomed
to travel much   with horses of the tsar."
At that Miloš   spurred on his horse, away,
went to join   the good tsar's wedding guests.

At Zagorje[14]   Miloš caught up with them.
The wedding guests,   well dressed, kept asking him:
"Where are you from,   O young Bulgarian?"
Miloš told them   in roundabout ways,
as his brothers   instructed him to do.   220
The wedding guests   received him with friendship:
"You are welcome,   O young Bulgarian.
One more guest   makes the wedding merrier."
As they traveled,   all of them, down the road,
Miloš, somehow,   who acquired the habit
while guarding sheep   high on the Šar Mountain
to have a nap   every day around noon,
he would doze off   riding on his brown horse.
And as the reins   loosened on his brown horse,
the horse pranced out   and pushed among the guests,   230
pushed them about,   along with their horses,
till he came up   to the tsar's fine horses.
As he came up,   put himself in their rank.

13. An area in northeastern Serbia, close to Romania; therefore people from this area would look like strangers to Dušan's company.
14. A mountainous area north of the Adriatic Coast between Split and Šibenik.

The guests, angered,   sought to thrash the Bulgar,
but Tsar Stefan   would not let them do it:
"Do not strike him,   that young Bulgarian,
for he has learned   to sleep, that young Bulgar,
while guarding sheep   high up in the mountains.
Don't strike at him   but wake him up instead."

The tsar's courtiers,   his dukes, tried to wake him: 240
"Wake up, you hear,   you young Bulgarian!
May the good Lord   punish your old mother
for giving birth   to such a dunce as you,
for sending you   to the tsar's wedding party."
When he woke up,   Miloš Vojinović,
and when he saw   the dark eyes of the tsar,
and his own horse   walking beside his horses,
he pulled the reins   of his dun-coated horse,
and rode him out   from the wedding party;
he dug his spurs,   sharp ones, into his flanks.   250
Then the horse jumped   three lances' lengths sideways,
and jumped even   four lengths up in the air,
and jumped ahead   so far you couldn't count.
From his mouth spewed   a stream of burning fire,
and from his nose   a bluish flame flared forth.

The wedding guests   stopped, all the twelve thousand,
and watched the horse   of the young Bulgarian,
looked at the horse   wondering to themselves:
"Merciful God,   O what a great wonder!
What a good horse   and what a poor rider!   260
We have not seen   such a fiery horse yet,
except for one,   owned by Vojinović,
he, the husband   of Dušan's sister, has him."

There were also   three merchants who watched it.
And one of them,   called Vuk Djakovica,
the other was   Janko Nestopoljče,
the third merchant,   a Prijepolje[15] lad.
They all watched him   and spoke among themselves:

15. Prijepolje is a town in southwestern Serbia.

"What a good horse   the young Bulgarian has!
There's no other   like him among the guests'.   270
Even our tsar   has not so fine a horse.
Why don't we stay   behind a little bit,
perhaps we'll lure   that horse away from him."
When they came close   above Klisura gorge,
these three merchants   stayed behind a little,
and then they spoke   to Miloš the shepherd:
"Do you hear us,   O young Bulgarian,
how would you like   to make a trade with us?
We will give you   a horse better than yours,
and moreover   we'll pay a hundred ducats,   280
in addition,   a plough and two oxen,
so you can plough   and feed yourself and yours."

But he tells them,   Miloš Vojinović:
"You three merchants,   please pass by me in peace.
I do not wish   a better horse than this.
I cannot tame   even the one I have.
What do I need   a hundred ducats for?
I don't know how   to weigh them on a scale,
nor to count them;   I haven't yet learned how.
What do I need   a plough and oxen for?   290
My good father   did not plough land either,
and yet he fed   his family with bread."

To that replied   the three clever merchants:
"Do you hear us,   O young Bulgarian?
If you don't give   us your horse in a trade,
we shall take him   away from you by force."
He spoke to them,   Miloš Vojinović:
"If force can take   away lands and cities,
it can surely   take away my one horse.
But I don't mind   exchanging my dun horse,   300
for I cannot   continue the trip on foot."
He then halted   his dun-coated brown horse
and put his hand   underneath the bearskin.
They thought he was   taking off his saddle,

but he brought forth   his gold six-pointed mace
and struck with it   at Vuk Djakovica.
He hit him so,   lightly and tenderly,
spun him 'round   three times with that one blow.

Miloš then said   to Vuk Djakovica:
"May your vines bear   so many grape clusters   310
in your own town,   fertile Djakovica."[16]

Nestopoljče,   that Janko, ran away.
Miloš caught him,   on his dun-coated horse,
and he hit him   between his two shoulders,
spun him around   four times with that one blow.
"Hold on firmly,   Janko Nestopoljče.
May your fruit trees   bear so many apples
in your own field   of fertile Nestopolje."

And the poor lad   from Prijepolje fled.
Miloš caught him,   on his dun-coated horse,   320
and he tapped him   with his six-pointed mace,
spun him around   seven times with one blow:
"Hold on firmly,   youth from Prijepolje,
and when you come   to your Prijepolje,
do some boasting   among your pretty girls
that you have seized   a horse from a Bulgar."
And then he turned   his horse to the party.

When they arrived   at white Ledjan city,
they pitched their tents   in the fields around it.
There were some oats   left for the tsar's horses,   330
but there were none   for Miloš's dun horse.
When he saw that,   Miloš Vojinović,
he took with him   a bag in his left hand,
from one oat bag   he went to another,
till he filled up   his own bag full of oats.
And then he went   to find an innkeeper:
"O innkeeper,   give me some wine to drink."

16. A town in Kosovo, northwest of Prizren and near the Albanian border.

The innkeeper   answered him with these words:
"Get out of here,   you dark Bulgarian!
If you had brought   a Bulgarian trough,   340
I would give you   some good red wine to drink.
But the gold cups   are not for you to use."
Miloš gave him   an angry, scowling look
and he slapped him   on his cheek with his hand,
hit him lightly   and just so tenderly,
he drove three teeth   of his right down his throat.

The innkeeper   then begged and implored him:
"Please don't hit me   any more, you Bulgar.
There is enough   of wine for your pleasure,
even if there   is no more for the tsar."   350
Miloš did not   ask any more of him,
but took himself   and drank his fill of wine.
And so Miloš   drank his fill of wine.

Then came the dawn;   the sun shone all around.
From the ramparts   a Latin lad shouted:
"Do you hear me,   Serbian tsar, Stefan?
You there, O tsar,   beneath Ledjan's ramparts,
a prisoner   of the king has come forth.
He challenges   your worship to a duel.
You must fight him   in a single combat,   360
Or you won't leave   this Ledjan town alive,
nor take with you   one of your wedding guests,
and not to speak   of your betrothed, Roxana."

When Tsar Stefan   of Serbia heard those words,
he sent his man   before his wedding guests.
The man announced   aloud, for all to hear:
"Has a mother   borne a valiant warrior
and sent him here   among the wedding guests,
who can come out   and fight the tsar's combat?
For then the tsar   would reward him with honors."   370

Such a warrior   could not be found at all.
The tsar then struck   his hand down on his knee:
"Woe unto me   and may God be my help!

If my kinsmen,   my nephews were with me,
my two nephews,   two Vojinovićes,
they'd have come forth   to do combat for me."

But e'en before   the tsar finished speaking,
Miloš came up   with his dun-coated horse
to the white tent   of the Serbs' tsar, Stefan:
"Is it all right,   my esteemed tsar and lord,   380
if I go forth,   fight in combat for you?"

The Serbs' own tsar,   Stefan, then said to him:
"It is all right,   O young Bulgarian.
It is all right,   but the task's not easy.
If you can kill   the strong young prisoner,
I'll reward you   with many great treasures."

Miloš mounted   his spirited dun horse
and rode away   from the tsar's white tent,
holding his lance   aimed downward from his hand.
Then Tsar Stefan   offered a word to him: 390
"Youth, do not hold   your lance downward that way,
turn it around,   here, this is the right way,
or the Latins   will surely laugh at you."

To that replied   Miloš Vojinović:
"I'll tend to it,   your majesty, my Lord.
If I come up   onto any trouble,
I'll turn the lance   in the right way quickly.
If I don't come   onto any trouble,
I will return   holding it thus, my lord."
And he rode forth   onto Ledjan meadow.   400

The Latin girls   looked at him and wondered,
they looked at him   and said to each other:
"Merciful God,   O what a great wonder!
Is such a man   the champion of a tsar?
For he does not   have the proper clothing.
That prisoner   of our king can rejoice.
For there is none   for him to lift a lance with,
nor any man   to blood his lance against."

In the meantime   Miloš came to the tent.
The prisoner   was sitting in the tent.   410
He had tied up   his bay horse to his lance.
To him then spoke   Miloš Vojinović:
"Get up, you boy,   you white-faced Latin boy,
and let us have   a real single combat."

The Latin boy,   all white-faced, spoke to him:
"Out of this tent,   you dark Bulgarian!
I see nothing   to dirty my sword on,
you don't even   have the proper clothing."

This angered him,   Miloš Vojinović:
"Get up, you boy,   you white-faced Latin boy!   420
Yes, it is true;   you have the proper clothing.
I'll now seize it   from you, and I'll wear it."
The Latin boy   then leaped up to his feet
and he mounted   his spirited bay horse,
and it began   to prance in hope of combat.
Miloš stood there   as a target for him.
The Latin boy,   all white-faced, heaved his lance
straight at Miloš,   there at his manly chest.
Miloš then held   his six-point gilded mace,
parried with it   the Latin boy's sharp lance   430
and he broke it   in three separate pieces.

The Latin boy,   white-faced, then said to him:
"Wait a moment,   you dark Bulgarian!
I was given   the wrong kind of lance.
Let me go off   and select another."
And he galloped   off across the flat field.

But then cried out   Miloš Vojinović:
"Wait a minute,   you white-faced Latin boy!
I know you'd like   to run away from here."
And he chased him   straight across the flat field.   440
And he chased him   to the gates of Ledjan,
but the main gates   of Ledjan had been closed.
Miloš let fly   his battle-lance at him
and he struck him,   the white-faced Latin boy,

nailed him right there   to the gates of Ledjan,
and he cut off   his head with bright red hair,
and he threw it   in his horse's feed bag.
And then he caught   the Latin boy's bay horse
and led the horse   to the glorious tsar:
"Here, my dear tsar,   is the prisoner's head."   450

The tsar gave him   the many great treasures.
"Go on, my son,   and drink your fill of wine.
I'll reward you   with many great honors."

Just as Miloš   sat down to drink his wine,
from the ramparts   a Latin lad shouted:
"Look there, O tsar,   beneath the walls of Ledjan,
in the meadow,   are three noble horses,
under saddles,   under heavy armor,
and above them   three steel swords set aflame,
with the sword tips   pointing toward the sky.   460
Now you must leap   over these three horses.
If you don't leap   over these three horses,
you won't leave here,   nor take away the bride."

The tsar's own man   spoke to the wedding guests:
"Has a mother   borne a valiant warrior
and sent him here   among the wedding guests,
who can well leap   o'er three noble horses
and above them   three steel swords set aflame?"
Such a hero   couldn't be found at all.

But there he comes,   the young Bulgarian,   470
to the white tent   of the Serbs' tsar, Stefan:
"Is it all right,   my esteemed tsar and lord,
if I go forth,   leap over three horses?"
"It is all right,   my Bulgarian youth.
But do take off   that Bulgarian cloak.
May God punish   the unskillful tailor
who made for you   that heavy shepherd's cloak."

Then he replied,   Miloš Vojinović:
"Not to worry;   just drink your cool red wine,

and don't worry   about my shepherd's cloak.   480
For when there is   a big heart in a warrior,
the shepherd's cloak   will not be in his way.
For if the sheep   is troubled by its own fleece,
there is neither   sheep nor fleece to speak of."
And he rode forth   onto Ledjan meadow.

When he came up   to the three fine horses,
he took his horse,   his dun-coated, brown horse,
he said to him,   his dun-coated, brown horse:
"Wait for me here,   my dun-coated, brown horse."
He went around   to the far side of them,   490
and came running   across the green meadow,
then leaped over   the three noble horses,
and o'er the swords   set aflame above them,
landed again   upon his own dun horse.
Then he took hold   of the three fine horses
and led them there   to the Serbs' tsar, Stefan.

A little time   did pass, then once again
from the ramparts   a Latin lad shouted:
"And now, O tsar   of the Serbs, you must go
to the tower   the highest tower of Ledjan.   500
On the tower   there's a lance jutting out,
and on the lance   there's a gilded apple.
You must strike it,   the apple, through a ring."

Miloš was now   too impatient to wait,
he asked again   the honorable tsar:
"Is it all right,   O my dear tsar and lord,
for me to shoot   at the golden apple?"

"It is all right,   O my Bulgarian youth."
And Miloš went   to the high, white tower,
set an arrow   in a bow made of gold,   510
and then he shot   the apple through the ring,
took the apple,   fallen in his white hands,
and carried it   to the glorious tsar.
And the great tsar   gave him many treasures.

Some time did pass,   but then once more again
from the ramparts   the Latin lad shouted:
"There, O tsar,   under the white tower,
there have walked out   the two sons of the king.
They have led out   three beautiful maidens,
three lovely maids,   all three looking alike,   520
and they all wear   identical dresses.
Go, O you tsar   and pick out Roxana,
and if you choose   any but Roxana,
you won't come out   of this contest alive,
and surely you   won't take away the bride."

When the tsar heard   and understood these words,
he called his man,   Todor the tsar's vizier:
"Go, my servant,   and pick out the right bride."

Then Todor begged,   swore to his honesty:
"O my dear lord,   I have never seen her,   530
for they brought her   forth in the black darkness
when I gave her   your betrothal ring."

The tsar then struck   his hand down on his knee:
"Woe unto me,   and may God be my help!
We outwitted,   and then we outfought them,
and yet this girl   will be our greatest shame."

When he heard this,   Miloš Vojinović,
he came forward   to the Serbs' noble tsar:
"Is it all right,   O my dear tsar and lord,
if I could choose   the young girl Roxana?"   540

"It is all right,   my Bulgarian youth,
yet how can I,   my youth, depend on you?
How will you now   recognize the maiden,
for you've not seen   that lovely girl before?"

He spoke these words,   Miloš Vojinović:
"Don't be afraid,   O my dear tsar and lord.
During my time   on the high Šar Mountain,

I guarded there   almost twelve thousand sheep,
three hundred lambs   born in a single night.
I recognized   each one by its mother.   550
By her brothers   I can tell Roxana."

Then the Serbs' tsar,   Stefan, said this to him:
"Then go you forth,   my Bulgarian youth.
And if God grants   that you pick out Roxana,
I will give you   the Skenderija land,[17]
and it's all yours   as long as you do live."

Miloš rode out   across the wide meadow.
When he rode up   to where the girls were standing,
he threw away   his Bulgarian hat,
and he took off   his Bulgarian cloak.   560
Scarlet velvet   and purple gleamed on him,
and the gold discs,   heavy there on his chest,
and on his legs   shone the gold ornaments.
Miloš glittered   there in the green meadow,
like the bright sun   behind the mountain peaks.
And he spread out   his cloak on the green grass,
and he scattered   on it jewels and rings,
tiny white pearls   and many precious stones.
Then he drew out   his green sharp battle sword,
and then he spoke   to the three pretty girls: 570
"Who among you   is the girl Roxana,
let her lift up   her skirt and roll her sleeves,
let her pick up   all these jewels and rings,
these tiny pearls   and shiny precious stones.
If another   reaches out for any,
so help me God   and my true faith in Him,
I will cut off   her arm to her elbow."

When the three girls,   three pretty girls heard this,
the two beside   looked at the middle one,
and Roxana   looked down at the green grass.   580
She lifted up   her skirt and rolled her sleeves,
and she picked up   the jewels and the rings,

17. Northern Albania.

the tiny pearls　　and shiny precious stones.
The other girls　　wanted to run away,
only Miloš　　would not let them escape.
He caught them both　　quickly by their white hands
and led all three　　before his tsar Stefan.
Miloš gave him　　the young girl Roxana,
and another　　the second, with Roxana,
but the third girl,　　he kept her for himself.　　　　　590
The tsar then kissed　　Miloš upon his brow,
he did not know　　who he was or from where.

Then the master　　of the party shouted:
"You wedding guests,　　you adorned ones, ready,
the time has come　　for us all to go home."
The wedding guests　　then prepared and set off,
taking with them　　the young bride Roxana.

When they had left　　Ledjan city behind,
then Miloš came,　　and he began to speak:
"O my good lord,　　O Serbian tsar, Stefan,　　　　　600
there is right there,　　there in Ledjan city,
there is a duke,　　the name of Balačko.
I know him well,　　and he knows me also.
The king fed him　　right here for seven years,
to drive away　　any wedding party
and to abduct　　the young girl Roxana.
The king will now　　dispatch him after us.
Balačko has　　three heads on his body.
From the one head　　a blue flame is streaming,
from the other　　a cold wind is blowing.　　　　　610
When the two winds　　leave their heads together,
it is easy　　then to kill Balačko.
You go ahead　　and take the girl with you,
I will wait here　　for the duke, Balačko,
to stop him here　　somehow and in some way."

The wedding guests,　　all garlanded, rode on,
taking with them　　the lovely Roxana.
Miloš remained　　in the great green forest,
and there with him　　about three hundred friends.

When the tsar's guests   had left Ledjan city,   620
the king summoned   the fierce duke, Balačko:
"O Balačko,   my good, faithful servant,
are you quite sure,   confident in yourself,
to drive away   this tsar's wedding party
and to abduct   the lovely Roxana?"

Balačko then   asked the king in return:
"O my dear lord,   you good king of Ledjan,
who's the warrior   among the wedding guests
that did show you   such enormous courage?"

The queen then spoke   to Balačko, the duke: 630
"O Balačko,   our good and faithful servant,
there's no warrior   among the wedding guests
except for one,   a black Bulgarian,
who was so young   he could not grow a beard."

And Balačko,   the duke, replied to her:
"Ah, that was not   a black Bulgarian,
that was, indeed,   Miloš Vojinović.
Even the tsar   does not recognize him,
but I've known him   for quite a few years now."

Then the queen spoke   to Balačko, the duke: 640
"Go, Balačko,   duke and faithful servant,
take our daughter   from all those Serbians,
and I'll give her   to you as a present."
Then Balačko   prepared his swift bay horse
and galloped off   after the wedding guests
with six hundred   horsemen from Ledjan town.

When they arrived   in the great green forest,
where the dun horse   stood there in the wide road,
behind him stood   Miloš Vojinović.
Then Balačko,   the duke, shouted to him: 650
"O my Miloš,   were you expecting me?"
And he let go   a blue flame from one head,
setting a fire   in Miloš's bearskin.
But when he saw   that he did not harm him,

he blew a wind,   cold, from the other head.
The dun horse then   went head o'er heels three times,
but to Miloš   no great harm was done.

Miloš shouted   loudly from his white throat:
"This is for you,   something you don't expect!"
And he let fly   his great six-pointed mace.   660
And it hit him,   the duke, oh so lightly,
he was struck off   his saddle with the blow.
Then he took out   his pointed battle-lance
and he nailed him,   the duke, to the green grass,
and he cut off   all of Balačko's heads,
and he tossed them   in his horse's feed bag.
Then he attacked   the horsemen of Ledjan
with his comrades,   with his three hundred men,
and they cut off   three hundred Latin heads.
Then they rode forth,   after the wedding guests.   670

When they caught up   with the tsar and his guests,
Miloš threw down   Balačko's heads before him.
The tsar gave him   a thousand gold ducats,
and they rode on   to the white Prizren town.
As they traveled   through the Kosovo field,
Miloš wanted   to turn toward Vučitrn,
and so he spoke   to Stefan, the Serbs' tsar:
"God be with you,   O my dearest uncle,
O my uncle,   Serbian tsar, Stefan!"
And only then   did the Serbs' tsar know him,   680
as his nephew,   Miloš Vojinović.

Then the tsar spoke   to his brave young nephew:
"Is that you there,   my dear youth, O Miloš?
Is that you there,   O my dearest nephew?
Blessed the mother   that brought you to this world
and the uncle   whose luck is to have you!
Why did you not   reveal yourself before?
On the journey   I have caused you hardships
with your sleeping,   with your food and your drink."

Without one's kin   it is hard everywhere.   690

Uroš and the Mrljavčevićes[18]

"Uroš and the Mrljavčevićes" (often in histories and in songs identified as "Mrnjavčević") addresses itself to the disorder in the empire after the death of Stefan Dušan and to the legitimacy of the succession of Uroš. Its protagonist is Marko Kraljević, so the song could really take its place in the Prince Marko cycle, if one did not consider its political realism and its sense of foreboding tragedy. For there is no irony here; Marko in his honesty (the product of his mother's teaching) is the agent of legitimacy, who restores the Nemanjić line and thus brings an end to the violence and anarchy always attendant—in the Balkans and elsewhere—on the death of a strong leader.

Uroš is the legitimate but passive heir. Svetozar Koljević tells us that the earlier fresco paintings of the monarch show him to be a large man, but that the image gradually diminishes in the work of later artists until the late frescoes picture him as a dwarf;[19] certainly here, though he is no dwarf, neither is he a great hero. His three adversaries, Vukašin (Marko's father), Uglješa, their fictional brother, Gojko, and their "fiery heralds," who whip a priest and threaten to do each other in, are certainly the agents of disorder. At the end Marko—always the pragmatist, in spite of his honorable and self-effacing act—takes to his heels to be chased around the church. But, of course, he survives. It is only an angel who is killed. But even more ominously, at the end, Marko must bear his father's curse, a curse that, as the hearer knows, will prove to be a prophecy.

Like many of the medieval songs, "Uroš and the Mrljavčevićes" was sung to Vuk by Old Raško.[20]

Uroš and the Mrljavčevićes

Four warriors' camps   are set there all together,
there on the field,   the lovely flat Kosovo,
by the stately   church of Samodreža:[21]
one is the camp   of old King Vukašin,

---

18. "*Uroš i Mrljavčevići*," II, 141, #34.
19. Koljević, 136–41, 138.
20. See Koljević, 186–87, 318.
21. A church in northern Kosovo, northwest of Priština, between Priština and Kosovska Mitrovica.

one is the camp   of Despot Uglješa,
the third the camp   of the lord, Duke Gojko,
and the fourth camp   of the young Prince Uroš.
The four great lords   fight over the kingdom,
among themselves   they want to start a war,
kill each other   there with their golden knives,   10
for they don't know   whose is the royal crown.
Vukašin says: "The kingdom is all mine!"
and Uglješa,   the despot: "It is mine!"
and Duke Gojko: "No, it is truly mine!"
But young Uroš,   the young prince, is silent;
the silent child,   the young lad, says nothing,
for he's afraid   of three older cousins,
of three cousins,   three Mrljavčevićes.

King Vukašin   writes an urgent letter,
writes a letter,   sends his emissary,   20
sends to Prizren,   the city of white stone,
to Nedeljko,   the archpriest of Prizren,
for him to come   to Kosovo's flat field,
to tell the truth   to whom the land belongs.
He has given   the king the communion.
He has taken   his holy confession.
He has with him   the ancient books of laws.

And Uglješa,   the despot, writes also,
writes a letter,   sends his emissary,
sends to Prizren,   the city of white stone,   30
to Nedeljko,   the archpriest of Prizren.
And Duke Gojko   writes another letter.
He too sends off   his quick emissary.
A fourth letter   is written by Prince Uroš,
He sends his own,   sends his emissary.
All four lordships   write their urgent letters,
and they send them   by their fiery heralds,
all in secret   one from all the others.

And so there meet   all four fiery heralds,
meet in Prizren,   the city of white stone,   40

there in the home   of the priest, Nedeljko.
They do not find   Nedeljko at his home.
He is in church   saying his matins there,
the first matins   and the liturgy.
So power drunk   are the fiery heralds,
feeling stronger   than others of their kind,
that they do not   dismount from their horses,
but they ride them   straight up into the church,
and they draw forth   their woven leather whips,
and they begin   to strike at Nedeljko: 50
"Hurry and go,   you, archpriest Nedeljko!
Hurry and go   to flat Kosovo field,
to tell the truth   to whom the land belongs.
You have given   the king his communion.
You have taken   his holy confession.
You have with you   the ancient books of laws.
Hurry and go   or you'll pay with your head."

He sheds some tears,   the archpriest, Nedeljko.
He sheds some tears   and starts to speak to them:
"Get out, and wait,   you men drunk with power,   60
until the end   of God's holy service.
It will be known   then whose kingdom it is.
They leave the church,   the four fiery heralds.

After the end   of God's holy service,
they all come out   in front of the white church.
And then he speaks,   the archpriest, Nedeljko:
"O my children,   you four emissaries,
I have given   the king his communion,
I have taken   his holy confession,
but I've never   asked him of his kingdom,   70
just of his sins,   which he has committed.
But all of you,   go to Prilep city,[22]
to the manor   of Marko Kraljević,
to Prince Marko,   one of my best pupils.
I have taught him   both reading and writing.

---

22. A city in central Macedonia, the seat of Marko's princedom.

He's been a scribe   to the high emperor.
He has with him   the ancient books of law
and sure he knows   to whom the land belongs.
Go and summon   Marko to Kosovo.
He will tell you   rightly and honestly,   80
for Marko is   afraid of nobody,
but of the one   and only truthful God."

And so they leave,   the four fiery heralds.
They set out straight,   straight to Prilep city,
to the manor   of Marko Kraljević.
When they arrive,   in front of the manor,
they strike iron   before the tall gateway.

Marko's mother,   Jevrosima, hears them,
and she summons   her valiant son Marko:
"My son Marko,   my dearest child, Marko,   90
who could that be   knocking at our tall gate,
as if they were   father's fiery heralds?"
Marko stands up   and opens the tall gate.

The four heralds   all bow before Marko:
"God be with you,   O our master, Marko!"
Marko touches   all their heads in kindness:
"Welcome, welcome,   my dear, good children!
Are the Serbs well,   all the Serbian knights,
and all the tsars   and honorable kings?"

The four heralds   bow before him humbly: 100
"O our master,   O Marko Kraljević,
they're all healthy,   but they are not at peace.
The lordships there   have fallen quarrelling
there on the field,   lovely flat Kosovo,
by the stately   church of Samodreža.
And these four lords   fight over the kingdom;
among themselves   they want to start a war,
kill each other   with their golden knives,
for they know not   whose is the royal crown.
They call you forth   to the flat Kosovo   110
to tell the truth   to whom the land belongs."

Marko then goes   to his stately manor
and there he calls   his mother, Jevrosima:
"Jevrosima,   O my dearest mother,
the lordships there   have fallen quarrelling
there on the field,   lovely flat Kosovo,
by the stately   church of Samodreža.
And these four lords   fight over the kingdom;
among themselves   they want to start a war,
kill each other   with their golden knives,   120
for they know not   whose is the royal crown.
They call me forth   to the flat Kosovo
to tell the truth   to whom the land belongs."

Although Marko   always is for justice,
Jevrosima   still pleads with her son:
"My son Marko,   my only son, Marko,
so that my milk   may not bring curse on you,
do not, my son,   ever speak a falsehood,
for your father's   nor for your uncles' sake,
but just the truth   of the God Almighty.   130
Do not, my son,   lose your God-given soul.
It is better   that you lose your own head
than to burden   your soul with mortal sin."
So Marko takes   the ancient books of law
and he prepares   himself and his Šarac.[23]
He then leaps up,   upon his faithful horse
and they ride forth   to Kosovo's flat field.

When they arrive   at the king's spacious tent,
King Vukašin   speaks the words which follow:
"May God be praised   and His boundless kindness!   140
Here is Marko,   my princely son, Marko.
He will say now   that it is my kingdom,
and it will go   from father to his son."
Marko listens   and does not say a word,
nor does he turn   his head toward the tent.

23. The legendary dapple horse of Marko, who could perform tremendous feats befitting the exploits of his master.

When Uglješa,   the duke, sees this Marko,
he speaks these words   to Marko Kraljević:
"May God be praised,   here is my dear nephew!
He will say now   that it is my kingdom.
Please say, Marko,   that it is my kingdom;   150
we will then rule   together like brothers."
Marko listens   and does not say a word,
nor does he turn   his head toward the tent.

When Duke Gojko   catches sight of him,
he speaks these words   to Marko Kraljević:
"May God be praised,   here is my dear nephew!
He will say now   that it is my kingdom.
When Marko was   still an infirm young lad,
I had Marko   very close to my heart,
I held him close   to my silken bosom   160
like a pretty   apple all made of gold.
Wherever I   rode on my faithful horse,
I took Marko   to ride out beside me.
Please say, Marko,   that it is my kingdom,
and you, Marko,   will be the first ruler,
and I will be   your servant by your knee."
Marko listens   and does not say a word,
nor does he turn   his head toward the tent.

He then goes up   straight to the small white tent,
to the white tent   of the infirm Uroš.   170
He rides his horse   Šarac up to the tent,
and there Marko   dismounts from his Šarac.
Just as Uroš   sees him enter the tent,
he then jumps up   nimbly from the mattress,
jumps up nimbly   and greets Marko warmly:
"May God be praised,   here is my godfather,
my godfather,   my Marko Kraljević!
He will say now   that it is my kingdom."
They spread their arms   and they warmly embrace,
and then they kiss   each other on the cheek,   180
they inquire   about each other's health,
and they sit down   on the silken mattress.

So time passes,   a little time goes by;
the day is done   and now the night descends.
When in the morn   the next day has dawned bright,
and from the church   the bells begin to peal,
all the nobles   come to the liturgy.
When the service   of liturgy has ended,
they all come out   from the stately white church,
and they sit down   at the tables in front,   190
eating sugar   and drinking cool *raki*.[24]
Marko then takes   the ancient books of law.

Seeing the books,   Marko begins to speak:
"O my father,   O my King Vukašin!
Is all the land   you hold too small for you?
Is it too small?   May it be deserted!
You want to seize   someone else's kingdom.
And you also,   my uncle Ugleša,
is all the land   you hold too small for you?
Is it too small?   May it be deserted!   200
You want to seize   someone else's kingdom.
And you also,   my uncle Duke Gojko!
Is the dukedom   you hold too small for you?
Is it too small?   May it be deserted!
You want to seize   someone else's kingdom.
If you don't see,   may God never see you,
that the book says   it is Uroš's kingdom.
It has come down   from father to his son.
The son has thus   inherited the land.
The tsar has willed   the kingdom to Uroš,   210
at his deathbed   before he passed away."

When he hears that,   the old King Vukašin
leaps quickly up   from the earth to his feet,
and he draws out   his long gilded dagger
to stab his son,   his own dear son Marko.
Marko runs fast   away from his father,
for it's not fit   nor proper, my brother,

24. *Raki* is the strong drink of the Balkans, a kind of *grappa*. The service of sweets seems an obligation of hospitality in the region.

to make a fight   against your own father.
Marko runs fast   around the stately church,
the stately white   church of Samodreža.   220
Marko runs fast,   the king is chasing him,
until they run   three times around the church,[25]
round the white church   of stately Samodreža.
The king almost   catches up with Marko,
but a faint voice   is then heard from the church:
"Into the church,   O Marko Kraljević!
Don't you see that   you'll lose your head today,
and at the hands   of your own dear father,
just for the sake   of our Lord God's justice."

The church's doors   there open by themselves.   230
Marko runs fast   into the stately church
and after him   the doors shut by themselves.
King Vukašin   runs quickly to the doors;
he strikes the post,   the door post with his dagger.
From the door post   blood begins to trickle.

King Vukašin   then repents his action
and he cries out   bitter words of lament:
"Woe unto me,   by one and only God,
for I slay here   my own dear son, Marko!"
But a faint voice   speaks from inside the church: 240
"Do you hear me,   O you King Vukašin!
You did not slay   your own dear son, Marko,
but you did slay   an angel of your God."

King Vukašin   is enraged at Marko,
and he utters   bitter curses at him:
"My son Marko,   may God smite you dead now!
And may you have   neither a grave nor offspring!
May your own soul   never leave your body
until you serve   the Turkish tsar as slave!"

The king hurls oaths,   the tsar sends his blessings: 250
"Godson Marko,   may God help you always!

---

25. Three circuits of an Orthodox church has liturgical significance.

May your face shine   at *divan* like the sun!²⁶
May your saber   cut swiftly in battle!
May there be no   greater hero than you!
May your bright name   be remembered always,
as long as there   are the sun and the moon!"

What they said then,   it came to pass later.

 ## The Building of Skadar²⁷

"The Building of Skadar" has long been regarded as one of the most interesting of the poems collected by Vuk. It is set in the period well before the Battle of Kosovo, when, in an effort to stem the tide of the advancing Turks, a fortress was erected at Skadar, an important crossroad on the coastal route east of Kotor on Lake Skadar near the present Albanian border. The antagonists here are the Mrnjavčević (here Mrljavčević) brothers, Uglješa and Vukašin (the father of Prince Marko), traditional villains of the songs. The third, the youngest of the brothers in the song, Gojko, is fictitious. Historically, the Mrnjavčevićes had nothing to do with the building of the fortress, which was occupied by Stefan Dušan for a time. But this disturbing poem is obviously highly mythic and perhaps its historical interest is only to reflect the difficulties inherent in the attempt to establish this fortification on its swampy land.

"The Building of Skadar," was greatly admired by Jakob Grimm, who sent his own German translation of it to Goethe in 1824. Goethe, however, found its assumptions, and perhaps the providential interference on which it turns, "superstitious and barbaric."²⁸ Certainly he was in part right, for the poem is darkly primitive; central to it is the pagan Slav belief that the gods will not allow the raising of a fortification, or of any building, unless they are appeased by human sacrifice. Even today in Macedonia the laying of a cornerstone is traditionally accompanied by the slaughter of a lamb. And the presence of the *vila*, the ambiguously good and evil mountain spirit, always female and often with misshapen

---

26. The *divan* is the sultan's court.
27. "*Zidanje Skadra*," II, 90, #26.
28. See Wilson, 366. Wilson's excellent translation of the poem, published in the biography, is much to be admired. See also Koljević, 147, and J. W. Goethe, "Serbische Lieder," in his *Schriften zur Literatur* ii (Berlin, 1972), 278, cited in Koljević, supra, 147 n. 7.

or bestial legs as a female Pan figure, is hardly unique here, for the *vila* appears often in the songs, especially, as we shall see, in the Prince Marko cycle.[29]

What may be more remarkable in the poem is the curiously realistic and peasantlike behavior and relationships of the three noble wives. Obviously such a presentation is a reflection of the origins and audience of the singer. Such presentation is a noticeable element—albeit often more subtly handled—in other poems, even in the poems of the Kosovo cycle.

Vuk collected several poems about the building of the fortress at Skadar, one from Filip Višnjić, another from the Blind Stepanija. The one that follows was sung to him after 1816 in Serbia by Old Raško, the singer of several of the finest poems on medieval themes, who had come from Kolašin in Montenegro to live in Serbia after it was freed of the Turks.[30]

The Building of Skadar

Three blood-brothers   build a fortified town;
the three of them   are all Mrljavčević.
King Vukašin   is the oldest of them;
Duke Uglješa   is the second oldest;
the youngest one   of the three is Gojko.
They build the town,   Skadar, on Bojana.[31]
They are at work   each day for three long years.
For these three years   three hundred masons work,
but they cannot   even lay foundations,
much less can raise   the fortress walls themselves.   10
What the masons   build in a single day
the *vila* wrecks   and tears down in one night.

When the fourth year   of the building begins,
the *vila* calls   down from the high mountains,
"King Vukašin,   give up, stop your suffering.
Suffer no more;   waste no more of your gold.
You cannot lay   foundations, mighty king,

29. See Koljević, 147–50 and Appendix 3, 347–48.
30. Koljević, 318.
31. Today located in Albanian territory, Skadar (*Shkoder* in Albanian, *Scutari* in Italian) is near the southeastern shore of Lake Skadar, some twenty miles east of a Montenegrin town, Bar. Skadar stands on the banks of the Bojana River, a tributary of the Drim.

or even raise   the walls of Skadar's fort
until you find   two twins with matching names.
You must first find   a Stojan and a Stoja—[32]   20
Stojan, the twin   to his sister, Stoja—
and bury them   within the tower wall.
Then the groundwork   will retain all its strength
and the fortress   can rise up with its walls."

When Vukašin,   the king, has heard these words,
he calls his man,   the servant, Desimir:
"O Desimir,   you're like a son to me,
you've always been   my dear, faithful servant.
Now be loyal   just once more, my dear son!
Go, Desimir,   go harness our horses,   30
and take with you   six bags of precious gold.
Then go you forth   across the wide, wide world;
go search for twins,   two twins with matching names.
Find them for me,   Stojan and a Stoja,
Stojan, the twin   to his sister, Stoja,
and if for gold   they refuse to come here,
then seize the two,   and bring them back by force;
we'll bury them   within the tower wall,
so the groundwork   can retain all its strength
and the fortress   can rise up with its walls."   40

Once Desimir   has heard Vukašin's words,
with all due haste   he harnesses horses.
He takes with him   six bags of precious gold,
and he goes forth   across the wide, wide world
to search for twins,   two twins with matching names,
for he must find   Stojan and a Stoja.
Desimir goes   and searches three long years,
but he can find   no twins with matching names,
and no Stojan   with Stoja can be found.

So he returns   to Skadar on Bojana.   50
He gives the king   the royal harnessed steeds.

---

32. Stojan and Stoja ("Constantine" and "Constance") are, respectively, the masculine and the feminine given names derived from *stojati*: to stand, to be erect, to be immovable.

He gives the king   the six bags of bright gold.
"Here, O my king,   are your harnessed horses,
and here as well,   your six bags of bright gold.
I found no twins,   no twins with matching names;
I did not find   Stojan and twin, Stoja."

When Vukašin,   the king, has heard these words,
he summons forth   Rade, the master mason,[33]
and Rade calls   his three hundred masons.
The king still wants   to raise Skadar's fortress.   60
All day they build,   and in the night all falls.
And so they fail   again to build groundwork,
much less to build   the entire high fortress.

The *vila* calls   down from the high mountains,
"King Vukašin,   you hear what I have said?
Suffer no more;   waste no more of your gold;
you cannot lay   foundations, mighty king,
nor ever raise   the walls of Skadar's fort.
But you are three   close brothers of one blood,
and each of you   has a faithful woman.   70
On the morrow   no matter which wife comes
to bring the men   food for their midday meal,
you bury her   within the tower wall.
Then the groundwork   will retain all its strength,
and the fortress   can rise up with its walls."

When Vukašin,   the king, has heard these words,
he right away   sends for his two brothers:
"My dear brothers,   have you heard what she said?
The *vila* cries   down from the high mountains,
we waste our gold;   all our work is in vain.   80
She won't let us   lay down the foundation,
much less let us   complete the fortress here.
But, listen now,   the *vila* tells us more,
for we are three,   close brothers of one blood,
and each of us   has a faithful woman.

33. Rade, the master mason, may well have been a historical person, a noted architect-builder of the time; he appears in several of the songs of building.

On the morrow,   no matter which wife comes
to bring the men   food for their midday meal,
we'll bury her   within the tower wall.
Then the groundwork   will retain all its strength
and the fortress   can rise up with its walls.   90

With faith in God   let each of us now swear
to keep the plan   a secret from his love,
to leave to chance   on whom the doom will fall
to come at dawn   to Skadar's building site."
With faith in God   each brother now does swear
to keep the plan   a secret from his love.
After the oath   the fall of night does come,
so each returns   unto his own white hall,
and takes his meal,   a supper set for lords,
and goes to rest,   each one beside his love.   100

But you should see,   a wonder of wonders!
When Vukašin,   king, tramples on his oath,
he is the first   to warn his faithful wife:
"Take care, take care,   my dear and faithful wife.
On the morrow,   don't come to Bojana,
nor bring the men   food for their midday meal,
for if you do,   my love, you'll lose your life;
they'll bury you   within the foundation!"

Then Uglješa,   also defies his oath,
when he too tells   his wife the awful plan: 110
"Don't fool yourself,   my dear, my truest love.
On the morrow,   don't come to Bojana;
don't bring the men   food for their midday meal.
For then you'll die,   you'll die before your time.
They'll bury you   within the foundation!"

But young Gojko   would never break his oath.
To his dear wife   he does not tell the plan.

At the sunrise   on the morrow morning,
three brothers rise,   three Mrljavčevićes,
and they go forth   to Bojana's fortress.   120

Then the time comes   to take the midday meal.
Today the queen   was to bring food by turn.
She'd gone to see   Uglješa's wife early
and said to her,   her young sister-in-law:
"Uglješa's wife,   O my own true sister,
My head aches so!   The pain is terrible.
I wish you health;   I am too ill to go.
Go take the men   food for their midday meal!"

Uglješa's wife   then answers to the queen:
"O sister mine,   O Vukašin's dear queen,   130
my arm is hurt;   the pain is terrible!
I wish you health;   this arm of mine won't heal.
Go out and find   our dear youngest sister."

So she goes out   to their youngest sister:
"O Gojko's bride,   my dear sister-in-law,
my head aches so!   The pain is terrible!
I wish you health;   I am too ill to go.
Go take the men   food for their midday meal!"

Gojko's young bride,   her sister, answers her:
"Vukašin's queen,   my sister, hear me now.   140
I'll take the meal;   with pleasure I will go.
Before I go,   I must bathe my baby,
and I must wash   his clothes so fine and white."

Vukašin's queen   then answers quite quickly:
"My dear sister,   don't tarry; go at once,
and take the men   food for their midday meal,
and I will wash   your baby's fine, white clothes,
and bathe with care   your noble infant son."

Young Gojko's bride   neither waits nor tarries;
she takes the men   food for their midday meal,   150
and when she comes   to Bojana's fortress,
young Gojko's eyes   soon catch the sight of her.
The brave lad's heart   is quickly filled with pain.
His faithful wife!   His grief is deep for her.
He sorrows, too,   for his dear, cradled son,

soon an orphan,   alive just thirty days.
Down Gojko's face   his tears do freely flow.

His slender bride   looks shyly up at him;
with slow, shy steps   she stands there beside him,
and then she speaks   to him in a soft voice: 160
"Why are you sad,   my own and dearest lord?
Why do your tears   run freely down your cheeks?"

Then young Gojko   gives answer to his bride:
"Such a sad day,   my dear and faithful love,
for in my hand   I held a golden apple
but let it fall   into Bojana's depths.[34]
I weep for it,   and the sharp pain won't go!"

The slender girl   cannot understand him,
and so she speaks   again to her dear lord:
"Ask God, instead,   to give you your good health,   170
and you will find   another, better apple!"
The hero then   feels a yet deeper grief,
and in that pain   he turns his face away
and looks no more   upon his own dear love.

Now Vukašin   and Duke Uglješa come,
brothers-in-law   of Gojko's faithful wife.
They take his bride   by her white, slender hand,
and lead her off   to where she will be buried.
They call Rade,   the deft master mason,
and he calls forth   all his three hundred men.   180
Yet still she smiles,   this fair and slender bride;
she thinks it all   must be some sort of jest.
They set her down   to build her in the wall.

Three hundred men   now cut the stakes of wood;
they set the stakes;   they lift the stones in place
and build a wall   which reaches to her knees.
And still she smiles,   this fair and slender bride,
for she believes   this all to be a jest.

---

34. As we often observe, *jabuka* (apple) is a term of endearment in Serbian.

Three hundred men   now cut more stakes of wood;
they set the stakes,   they lift more stones in place,   190
and build the wall   to reach up to her waist.

Now, when she feels   the weight of wood and stone,
she sees, poor girl,   what they intend to do,
and like a snake,   she cries out in anger.
She starts to beg   her two brothers-in-law:
"Don't bury me,   if you know God at all!
Don't bury me,   a young and tender bride!"
She pleads and pleads,   but all to no avail.
They see her not,   refuse to look at her.

Now all her shame,   her modesty, is gone;   200
to her young lord   she now directs her plea:[35]
"Do not let them,   my own and dearest lord!
They'll bury me,   so young, inside this wall!
Go find Mother,   my dear, aged mother.
She is quite rich;   she has great stores of gold,
and she will buy   a slave girl for this space,
to be buried   here in Skadar's tower!"
She pleads and pleads,   but all to no avail.

And when she sees,   this young and slender bride,
that all her pleas   cannot bring any change,   210
she turns to speak   to the master mason:
"Brother in God,   Master Rade, hear me!
Leave a small space,   a window for my breasts,
and draw them out,   draw my white breasts both out,
so when my son,   my little Jovo comes,
when he comes here   he still can nurse from them."

Like a brother,   Rade now grants her plea.
He leaves a space,   a window for her breasts.
He draws her breasts,   her white breasts, to the light,
so when her son,   her infant son will come,   220
when he comes here,   he still can nurse from them.

35. In medieval Serbia it was considered improper and immodest for a married woman publicly to accost her husband.

Now once again   the poor girl speaks to him:
"Brother Rade,   hear me out in God's name,
and leave a space,   a window for my eyes,
so I can see,   can look on my white hall,
can see my son,   when they bring him to me,
and when he leaves,   when they take him away."

Like a brother,   Rade again grants her plea.
He leaves a space,   a window for her eyes,
so she can see,   can look on her white hall,   230
can see her son,   when they bring him to her,
and when he leaves,   when they take him away.

The work is done;   they've closed her in the tower.
They bring her son,   her tiny infant son.
She nurses him;   he feeds for a whole week.
After a week   they no more hear her voice.
But milk still flows;   she still gives him to suck.
She nurses him;   gives suck for a whole year.

As it was then,   so it remains today.
The milk still flows   today as it did then.   240
That milk is charmed;   it works miraculous cures
for all women   who have no milk to nurse.[36]

 # The Wedding of King Vukašin[37]

In the remarkable song that follows Vukašin is again the villain, a cruel, inconsistent, dwarflike creature. In "The Wedding of King Vukašin" he provokes acts of violence to steal another nobleman's wife.

The characters are historical: Duke Momčilo was a nobleman of the fourteenth century who lived in Rodopa and died in 1361—at Peritheorion—in a battle against the Turks. There was conflict in the last half of the fourteenth century between aggressive and exploitive central Serbian no-

---

36. Witnesses report that a chalky liquid oozes from Skadar's walls today—from the holes through which Gojko's wife nursed her son. Peasant women are said to mix this chalky substance with water and to drink it, for it is believed that this mixture will restore milk to women who cannot nurse and will relieve the pain associated with full breasts.

37. "*Ženidba kralja Vukašina,*" II, 83, #25.

bles and independent Montenegrin princes. But the plot here is fictitious, or at least in part derived from literary sources; the magic sword and the winged, Pegasus-like horse are to be found in an Italian chivalric romance, *Buovo d'Antona,* available in Serbo-Croatian translation from the sixteenth century.

An earlier and less interesting version of the song was recorded in Dubrovnik in the eighteenth century. But Vuk heard the song in 1820 from Stojan the Outlaw, in prison for the murder of a woman whom he regarded as a witch. Stojan was apparently a remarkable artist, if one assumes that it was he who manipulated the elements of the earlier song into the rich interplay of ironies and the stunning and extended—and subtly allusive—conclusion with which this song is provided. For Momčilo's dream of the separation in the mist is here told not to his kinsmen, but to the wife who has already betrayed him, and thus the rich dramatic irony of her response that "only God is truth" is prepared.

In another song, *Bolani Dojčin* (Dojčin the ill one), a Serbian girl saves her brother to fight again by binding his wounds with "a rag of linen," but in "The Wedding of King Vukašin" such treatment will be less efficacious. The *denouement,* with the unexpected advice from the dying Momčilo, generates complex psychological ironies of motivation. Yet all of this high drama is again ironically subverted in the final scene, in which Vukašin's smallness is offered as an emblem of his diminished value. Certainly "The Wedding of King Vukašin" must stand as one of the most remarkable of the heroic songs.[38]

The Wedding of King Vukašin

King Vukašin,   a small man, wrote a letter
from white Skadar   by Bojana's river,
and he sent it   to Hercegovina,
to a white town,   the town called Pirlitor,
to Pirlitor   by the Mount Durmitor,[39]
to Vidosava,   the wife of Momčilo,
wrote in secret   and sends it in secret.
In that letter   it is this which he wrote:

38. Our discussion here is derived from that of Koljević, 126–32.
39. "Pirlitor" is, as Koljević points out (ibid., 127), the now destroyed coastal city of Peritheorion, the *locus* of Momčilo's death. Durmitor (named presumably after Pirlitor) is a magnificent mountain some one hundred fifty miles to the north.

"Vidosava,   O Momčilo's great love,
why waste your life   in all that ice and snow?   10
When you look up   from Pirlitor city,
you have nothing   of beauty to observe,
nothing but this,   the white Mount Durmitor,
and it's covered   with cold ice and white snow
all the summer   as well as in winter.
If you look down   steeply from the city,
the Tara flows   muddy, stormy river,
in its rushing,   it tumbles trees and rocks;
there is no ford   nor bridge standing o'er it,
and around it   pine trees and marble rock.   20

"You should poison   your husband, Momčilo,
either poison   or betray him to me,
and come to me,   on flat land by the sea,
to white Skadar   on Bojana River.
I will take you   to be my faithful wife,
so you will be   th'exalted Lady Queen.
You will spin silk   on a golden distaff,
you will spin silk   sitting on a silk seat,
you will be dressed   in velvets and brocades
and all adorned   with refined gold pieces.   30
What a city,   Skadar on Bojana!
When you look up   at the mountains above,
they are covered   with fig and olive trees
and with vineyards,   luscious, full of red grapes.
When you look down   steeply from the city,
there the white wheat   grows neatly all around
and around it   lies the greenest meadow,
through all this flows   green Bojana River,
all kinds of fish   are there swimming in it,
for you to eat,   fresh, any time you like."   40

The letter came   to Momčilo's dear love.
Momčilo's love   looks long at the letter.
She looks at it   and she writes another:
"My esteemed lord,   O my King Vukašin!
It's not easy   to betray Momčilo,
to betray him   or to give him poison.

Jevrosima,   sister of Momčilo,
prepares for him   food fit for a high duke,
she tries the food   before Momčilo eats.
And Momčilo   has nine loyal brothers   50
and twelve cousins,   all on his father's side.
They serve him wine,   red wine when he wants it,
and they try it   before he is to drink.
And Momčilo   has a horse, Jabučilo,
Jabučilo,   a horse that flies on wings,
that can fly o'er   whatsoe'er he wishes.
Momčilo has   a sword with its own eyes.
He is afraid   of none but God Himself.

"Listen to me,   my dear King Vukašin.
You must go forth,   gather a strong army.   60
Take the army   to level Jezera,[40]
and lie in wait   in the verdant forest
for Momčilo;   he has a strange habit;
every morning   on each holy Sunday
he goes hunting   on level Jezera.
He takes with him   his nine loyal brothers,
and takes with him   his twelve loving cousins,
he takes also   forty ablest soldiers.
When the time comes   on the eve of Sunday,
I will then burn   Jabučilo's strong wings,   70
and I will dip   that swift saber in blood;
I will dip it   into that salty blood,
so that it can't   be drawn out from its sheath.
Then you can come   and destroy Momčilo."

When Vukašin   received her dear letter,
and when he saw   what there was within it,
he was most pleased   with that written message.
He then gathered   to him a strong army
and marched with it   to Hercegovina.
He led his men   to level Jezera,   80
prepared ambush   in that verdant forest.

---

40. *Jezera* (literally, "lakes") presumably refers to the lakes in the region.

When the time came   on the eve of Sunday,
Momčilo went   to sleep in his chamber.
There he lay down   on the soft bed pillows.
In a short time   his dear wife came to him.
She did not wish   to lie down beside him,
but she shed tears   standing above his head.
Duke Momčilo   then inquired of her:
"Vidosava,   O my good, faithful wife,
what are the cares   that trouble you so now   90
that you're weeping,   and tears fall on my head?"

Vidosava,   his love, gave her reply:
"O my good lord,   my dear Duke Momčilo,
there are no cares   which trouble me at all,
but I have heard   about a great wonder,
I have heard it   but I have not seen it,
that you've a horse   that's named Jabučilo,
Jabučilo,   a horse that flies on wings.
I have not seen   any wings on your horse,
I can't believe,   as youthful as I am,   100
and I'm afraid   that you will soon be killed."

Duke Momčilo   was a clever person;
he was clever   but he made an error,
when he spoke thus   to his belovéd wife:
"Vidosava,   O my belovéd wife,
it is easy   to set your mind at peace.
It is easy   to see my horse's wings.
When the cocks crow   early in the morning,
you go alone   to our new-made stables.
Jabučilo   will then extend his wings,   110
you will then see   his great extended wings."
And he lay down   to take his needed rest.

Momčilo slept   but his love did not sleep.
On her pillows   she listened, wide awake
for the cock's crow   early in the morning.
At break of dawn,   when cocks begin their song,
the young woman   started from her pillows,
she set alight   a lantern, a candle,

she took with her   some tallow and some tar
and she went straight   to the new-made stables.   120

What Momčilo   predicted came to pass:
Jabučilo   spread forth his mighty wings,
extended them   all down to his own hooves.
Vidosava   then tarred his mighty wings,
she tarred the wings   with tallow and with tar,
and then she lit   the wings with the candle,
and thus she burned   Jabučilo's great wings.
What of the wings   she could not burn in fire,
she tied tightly   beneath the saddle-girth.
Then the young wife   went to the armory,   130
and there she seized   Momčilo's best saber,
she dipped it in   a dish of salty blood,
and she returned   to her own soft pillows.

In the morning,   when the dawn had whitened,
Duke Momčilo   rose early, as always,
and he then spoke   to his Vidosava:
"Vidosava,   O my dear faithful love,
last night I dreamed,   I dreamed the strangest dream:
a patch of fog   wound itself all the way
from the dark land   of the Vasojević.   140
It wound itself   around the Durmitor.
I made my way   through that patch of dense fog.
And I was there   with nine loyal brothers,
and with all twelve   of my loving cousins,
and with forty   of my ablest soldiers.
And in that fog   our ways parted, my love,
our ways parted   and never met again.
God knows, no good   can come of such a dream."

His faithful wife   answered him lovingly:
"Don't be afraid,   my dear lord, Momčilo.   150
A good warrior   has dreamed an awesome dream.
A dream deceives,   but only God is truth."

Duke Momčilo   then made preparations.
He descended   from his tall white tower.

And he was met   by nine loyal brothers,
and by all twelve   of his loving cousins,
and by forty   of his ablest soldiers.
His own dear love   led out his piebald horse.
They all mounted   their fine, lively horses
and all went forth   to hunt at Jezera.   160

When they arrived   at level Jezera,
a strong army   was closing upon them.
When Momčilo   caught sight of that army,
he tried to draw   his saber from scabbard,
but the saber   could not be drawn at all;
it was as if   t'were grafted to its scabbard.

Duke Momčilo   then said to his companions:
"Can you hear me,   my dear, loyal brothers?
Vidosava,   the bitch, has betrayed me.
But give you me   the best sword that you have."   170
His dear brothers   then quickly obeyed him,
and they gave him   the best sword that they had.

Duke Momčilo   spoke to his dear brothers:
"Can you hear me,   my dear loyal brothers?
You must attack   that army at its flank,
and I will strike   at them toward the center."

O my dear God,   what a wondrous marvel!
What a great sight   for anyone to see,
how Momčilo   the duke turned left and right,
how he carved out   a road down that mountain!   180
Jabučilo   trampled more of the foes
than Momčilo   cut down with his saber.
But good fortune   turned against him just then:
When he came forth   down into Pirlitor,
he was met there   by nine jet-black horses,
not one brother   rode on any of them.

When he saw that,   Momčilo, the brave duke,
the hero's heart   broke in two from sadness,
from his great grief   for his loving brothers.

His two white arms   fell, weak and exhausted;   190
he no longer   could strike out at the foe.
Then he spurred on   his horse Jabučilo,
he spurred him on   with his boot and stirrup,
that he should fly   to Pirlitor city,
but his good horse   could no longer fly forth.

Duke Momčilo   began to curse his horse:
"Jabučilo,   may the wolves devour you!
We used to fly   away only for play,
for no reason,   simply for amusement,
but on this day   you now refuse to fly."   200

Then his good horse   answered him with a neigh:
"O my dear lord,   my dear Duke Momčilo,
do not curse me,   and do not spur me on,
for no longer   can I fly forth today.
May God strike down   your love, Vidosava!
For it was she   that set my wings on fire.
What of my wings   she could not burn in fire,
she tied up tight   under my saddle girth.
But you must run   where'er your legs take you!"

When he heard that,   Momčilo, the brave duke,   210
his tears flowed down,   all down his warrior's face,
he dismounted   from his valiant piebald.
In three long leaps   he reached his own city,
but the tall gates   of the city were shut,
the gates were shut   and they were bolted tight.

When Momčilo   saw himself in trouble,
he called his dear   sister, Jevrosima:
"Jevrosima,   my dear loving sister,
hang down for me   some old rag of linen,
so I can climb   to refuge in our town."   220

His sister wept,   answering her brother:
"O my brother,   my dear Duke Momčilo,
how can I hang   down a rag of linen,
when my sister,   your wife, Vidosava,

my own sister,   your unfaithful wife,
she has tied me   by my hair to the beams."
Yet the sister   had pity in her heart,
pity for him,   her own brother, the Duke.
She let a cry   like a snake in trouble,
she drew her head,   and with all her power   230
she pulled the hair   right out of her own head,
leaving her hair   hanging on the beams there.
And then she seized   an old rag of linen
and she threw it   over the city wall.

Momčilo seized   that old rag of linen
and he began   to climb over the wall.
He was about   to leap down in the town,
but then she came,   his own unfaithful love,
with a sharp sword   borne high in her two hands.
She cut in two   the rag above his hands.   240

Momčilo fell   back down the city wall.
The king's soldiers   waited and greeted him
with sharp sabers   and with battle-lances,
with sharp axes   and with heavy maces.
King Vukašin   ran quickly up to him
and he struck him   with his long battle-lance,
he pierced him there   directly in the heart.

Then Momčilo,   the duke, spoke thus to him:
"King Vukašin,   this is my testament.
Do not marry   my love, Vidosava,   250
Vidosava,   my own unfaithful wife,
for she'll cost you   your head as she did mine.
Today she did   betray me for your sake,
and tomorrow   she will betray you too.
Take in her stead   my kind, loving sister,
my dear sister,   loving Jevrosima.
She will always   be faithful unto you,
she will bear you   a son as brave as I."
Thus spoke to him   Momčilo, the brave duke.
He spoke to him   struggling for very life;   260
he spoke those words,   gave up his very soul.

Thus Momčilo,   the duke, did lose his life.
Pirlitor's gates,   they then were opened wide,
and she stepped forth,   the bitch Vidosava,
and she then bid   King Vukašin welcome.
She took him up   to the great white tower,
she sat him down   at the golden table,
and she offered   the red wine and *raki*
and other things,   great and royal presents.
She then went out   to the duke's treasury,   270
and she brought back   Momčilo's belongings,
all his clothing   and Momčilo's weapons.

What a wonder   was there for all to see:
the coat that hung   just to Momčilo's knees,
on Vukašin   it trailed along the ground;
the cap that fit   neatly on Momčilo,
on Vukašin   it fell on his shoulders;
and in the boot   that fit Momčilo's foot,
poor Vukašin   could place both of his feet;
in the gold ring   that fit Momčilo's finger   280
King Vukašin   could place three of his fingers;
the sword that hung   rightly on Momčilo,
on Vukašin   it dragged upon the ground;
and the armor   that once fit Momčilo,
was so heavy   Vukašin could not stand.

Then Vukašin,   the king, began to speak:
"Woe is to me,   in the name of dear God!
Behold this whore,   this young Vidosava!
If she betrayed   such a valiant hero,
the likes of which   you'll not find again,   290
then she'll betray   me, for sure, tomorrow."
And he summoned   his good, faithful servants.
And then they seized   the bitch Vidosava.
They tied her up   to the horses' long tails,
they drove horses   out below Pirlitor
and the horses   tore her apart alive.

King Vukašin   looted Momčilo's court
and then he took   Duke Momčilo's sister,

his dear sister,   lovely Jevrosima.
He then took her   to Bojana's Skadar,   300
he married her   and made her his own love.
And she bore him   fine and handsome children,
for she bore him   Marko and Andrija.
Marko later   grew up like his uncle,
his own uncle,   Momčilo, the brave duke.

 ## The Wedding of Prince Lazar[41]

"The Wedding of Prince Lazar" is a much more foreboding song than "The Wedding of Tsar Dušan" or even "The Wedding of King Vukašin." Sung to Vuk by Old Raško, it tells of "Lazo," Lazar Hrebeljanović (1374–1427), historically lord of north Serbia and not a vassal of Stefan Dušan (Dušan died before Lazar was born) but of his son and successor, Uroš IV. Central to the story is the arrangement of the marriage of Lazar to Milica, historically a Nemanjić and not a Jugović (that name is apparently fictitious, for it is not recorded among the noble families of the time).

Milica was one of the remarkable women of her epoch. After the battle of Kosovo and the death of her husband, Prince Lazar, she accepted the new sultan, Bayazid, as her overlord (she married her daughter, Mara, to him) in order to assure that her son, Stefan Lazarević, would maintain control of Serbia. Then she retired to the monastery of Dečani where, under the name of Jevgenija, she wrote, among other important and surviving works, a eulogy to Prince Lazar.

Also present is old Jug Bogdan (Bogdan Jug, or Bogdan Jugović), the independent and truculent nobleman—by whom even Dušan seems intimidated in this song. Jug Bogdan was apparently fictitious, but he repeatedly appears in the songs, always headstrong and independently powerful, accompanied by his sons, the nine Jugovićes. It is Jug Bogdan who here searches the texts to find prophecy of the coming "last days," a recurrent theme in the medieval songs and central here, for it is the coming of "the last days" that, it is hoped, will bring him to see the wisdom of the marriage.[42]

41. "*Ženidba kneza Lazara*," II, 135, #32.
42. See Koljević, 125–26.

The song again takes on a patriarchal and rural setting. The vassal is presented simply as Lazo the servant; evidence of the coming of the "last days" is supported by natural analogies. But it is the retrospective sadness of the song—Stefan Dušan's apologies and intimidation, Jug Bogdan's sense of a predestined future, Lazo's strange look and his sense that even marriage to the beautiful Milica will come somehow too late—that gives something of an atmosphere of the decline of things and a loss of central control among the Nemanjićes, a dark foreboding of what is to come.

The Wedding of Prince Lazar

The mighty lord,   Tsar Stefan drinks red wine
in his city,   the lovely white Prizren.
The wine is poured   by the faithful Lazo.
He overfills   the tsar's cup with red wine,
and then he looks   upon the tsar strangely.

The tsar then asks   his servant, faithful Lazo:
"Now, in God's name,   my own faithful Lazo,
tell me frankly   what I am asking you:
Why do you keep   filling my cup o'erfull?
Why do you look   upon your lord so strangely?   10
Is it your horse   that has gone lame on you?
Is it your clothes   that have become too old?
Is it your pay   that is displeasing you?
What do you find   lacking at my court here?"

To him answers   then the faithful Lazo:
"Thank you, my lord,   for kind and gentle words.
Since you ask me,   I will tell you frankly:
No, it is not   my horse that is gone lame,
nor is it clothes   that have become too old,
nor is my pay   too meager to please me;   20
everything is   in plenty at your court.
Thank you, my lord,   for kind and gentle words.
Since you ask me,   I will tell you frankly:
all those servants   who arrived after me,
all those servants   built houses for themselves.
You have given   to each one a good wife,

but I, my lord,   could not build a good house.
You did not find   a good young wife for me
despite my youth,   despite my handsome looks."

The powerful   Tsar Stefan speaks to him:
"In God's own name,   O my faithful Lazo,   30
I cannot make   a good marriage for you
with a woman   that tends to pigs and cows.
I am seeking   a gentle girl for you
and for a good   relation for myself,
who would make me   a decent company,
with whom I'd drink   a good well-chilled red wine.
But hear me out,   O my faithful Lazo,
I have now found   a gentle girl for you,
and for myself   a good relationship,   40
for I have found   of the old Jug Bogdan,
the dear sister   of nine Jugovićes,
that Milica,   the favorite of all,
but no one dares   to approach Jug Bogdan.
It's not easy   to mention it to him—
Jug Bogdan comes   from a high family.
He would not give   his child to a servant.

"But hear me out,   O my faithful Lazo.
Today's Friday,   Saturday tomorrow,
day after that   the glorious day of Sunday.   50
We shall go forth   hunting in the mountain;
we shall invite   old Jug Bogdan as well.
With him will come   the nine Jugovićes.
But you, Lazo,   don't go to the mountain;
you stay at home   at the white court instead.
And you prepare   a dinner fit for lords.
When we return   from the mountain hunt there,
I will invite   the old Jug for dinner,
and you'll invite   the nine Jugovićes.
When we sit down   at the lordly table,   60
you start serving   the sweets and the *raki,*
and you offer   the well-chilled red wine too.
After we've had   our fill of chilled red wine,
then old Bogdan   will talk of everything,

of all brave lads   and of all their exploits.
He will bring out   the glorious old books,
and he will speak   of the last days to come.

"When you hear that,   O my faithful Lazo,
you run quickly   atop the slim tower
and bring with you   the cup that's made of gold,   70
the very one   I have bought recently
in the bright town,   city of Varadin,
from a young girl,   a beautiful goldsmith,
for which I paid   a load-and-half of goods.
You fill it up   with the well-chilled red wine,
give it as gift   to the old Jug Bogdan.
Jug Bogdan then   will begin to ponder
what gift to give   to Lazo, in return.
Then I will speak,   will mention, in passing,
of Milica,   his fair beloved daughter."   80

So Friday passed   and Saturday also,
after which came   the glorious day of Sunday.
The tsar set forth   to hunt on the mountain.
He invited   old Jug Bogdan as well,
and with him came   the nine Jugovićes.
And so they went   hunting in the mountain.
They hunted long   in the deep green forest,
they killed nothing   but they enjoyed themselves,
and they returned,   all to their white castle.
Lazo came out   to meet and welcome them.   90

And there the tsar   invited Jug for dinner,
and then Lazo   invited his nine sons.
When they sat down   at the lordly table,
there at the head   of table sat Stefan.
Next to him sat   the revered Jug Bogdan,
and next to Jug   the nine Jugovićes,
and they were served   by the faithful Lazo.
He offered them   the sweets and the *raki,*
And he offered   the well-chilled red wine too.

After they've had   their fill of chilled red wine,   100
they then began   to talk of many things,

of the brave lads   and of all their exploits.
Old Jug brought out   the glorious old books,
and he then talked   of the last days to come.
"Do you see here,   my wonderful brothers,
O do you see   what the Good Book says here:
that the last days,   they now await us soon.
For there'll be sheep   and golden grains no more,
nor will there be   busy bees and flowers.
Sworn brother then   will take brother to court,   110
and brother then   will challenge his own brother."[43]

When he heard that,   faithful servant Lazo,
he ran quickly   up the slender tower,
brought back with him   the cup made all of gold,
And filled it up   with the good chilled red wine,
Gave it as gift   to the old Jug Bogdan.
Jug Bogdan took   the golden cup of wine,
he took the cup   but did not drink the wine.
Bogdan pondered   the meaning of all this,
and how he would   return Lazo in kind.   120

Jugovićes,   the nine, speak to Bogdan:
"O our father,   respected Jug Bogdan,
why don't you drink   the wine from the gold cup
given to you   as a gift from Lazo?"

Old Jug Bogdan   answered to them this way:
"O my children,   my nine Jugovićes,
I'll easily   drink from the golden cup, ·
but I'm thinking,   dear belovéd children,
what gift should I   give to faithful Lazo."

To Bogdan spoke   the nine Jugovićes: 130
"It is easy   to repay him, father.
We have many   good horses and falcons;
we have enough   of long spears and *calpacs*."[44]

---

43. The *pobratim,* the relationship of brotherhood created by an exchange of blood and mutual oath, was of overweening importance in the patriarchal culture of the south Slavs.
44. A *calpac* is a large cap of sheepskin or felt, common in the Balkans and Turkey.

To these words spoke   the mighty tsar, Stefan:
"Lazo's equipped   with horses and falcons,
just as he has   enough spears and *calpacs*.
Nor does Lazo   have want in any things,
Lazo would love   the fair girl, Milica,
that Milica,   the favorite of all,
the dear sister   of nine Jugovićes."   140

When they heard that,   the nine Jugovićes,
they all jumped up   on their swift, nimble feet,
and they quickly   drew their sharp daggers out
to make an end   of the tsar sitting there.
But Jug Bogdan   pleaded with his dear sons:
"If you love God,   please don't do it, my sons!
If you today   do away with the tsar,
a curse will rest   on your name forever.
But let me search   deep in the glorious books,
and let me see,   my sons, if the books say,   150
that Milica   is preordained for him."

He studied books,   the wise old Jug Bogdan,
he studied books,   with large tears on his face.
"If you love God,   please don't do it, my sons!
For Milica's   preordained for Lazo.
And he will soon   inherit the kingdom,
and together   with her he will then rule
in Kruševac   by Morava River."[45]

When he heard that,   the mighty tsar, Stefan,
he reached into   his deep silken pockets,   160
and he pulled out   a thousand gold ducats,
together with   an apple made of gold.
In the apple   there are three precious stones,
a wedding gift   for the fair Milica.

---

45. Kruševac, a town in central Serbia on the Morava River, was Prince Lazar's capital. The Morava here is actually the Western Morava that, together with the Southern Morava, forms the Great Morava flowing into the Danube.

The Building of Ravanica[46]

Dečani, situated in the southwestern corner of Kosovo, is only one of the monasteries of Serbia that are perhaps to be her ultimate cultural achievement. At Studenica, Gračanica, Žiča, Peć, Ravanica, and elsewhere are still to be found the brilliant church buildings with their magnificent frescoes containing portraits of heroes, kings, and holy men that still move the visitor—and that certainly in Vuk's time and earlier moved the *guslari*. For they must have visited these places and seen (those who could see) the images of their heroes. And the singers themselves, as well as the chroniclers, recognized that the crowning glory of a Balkan king was often to be achieved in the building of a church, for it would be in that achievement that he would be remembered in history and perhaps in eternity as well.

Yet this song sets against that quest through building for a victory over time that same dark foreboding that so marks many of the medieval songs, that awareness that the "last days" of glory are at hand. For the singers, and their audience—and even the characters of the songs themselves (here especially the honest Miloš Obilić, who will die at Kosovo)—seem to sense what is coming next, seem aware here quite specifically that the pagan Turks are on their way to destroy their high Christian culture, that even in building great monuments there can be no final victory over time.[47]

"The Building of Ravanica" perhaps has its origins in a Byzantine text, the *Narration of Saint Sophia,* of the eighth or ninth century, which concerns itself, among other matters, with the building of St. Sophia. The song was traditionally sung before Saint Sophia itself on the monastery grounds after the celebration of the liturgy. There are two versions of "The Building of Ravanica"; the shorter version translated here (Karadžić ii, 35), sung to Vuk by Old Raško, and a longer, anonymous version, which is often regarded as the superior version. Among other things, the longer version (Karadžić ii, 36) identifies the site of the future church as the place where Lazar fell from his horse (the modern place name suggests as much).[48] We prefer the purity of Raško's version, in which the principal theme of the song seems to be more clearly established.

46. "*Zidanje Ravanice,*" II, 147, #35.
47. See Koljević, 103, 143–47.
48. See Koljević, 18.

The Building of Ravanica

On the *slava*[49]   of glorious Prince Lazar,
in Kruševac,   brightly colored fortress,
on his *slava*,   the day of St. Amos,
he invited   all of his noblemen
by letters and   with greeting flasks also.
All Serbia's lords   came there at his request.
Lazar placed them   at the feasting table
according to   nobility and age.
At the head sits   glorious Prince Lazar.

So they sat down   to drink the cool red wine.   10
Just as the feast   was at its liveliest
and they were all   talking of many things,
there among them   came Lady Milica.
She walked lightly   in the tsar's dining hall.
She had on her   nine priceless woman's belts,
and on her neck   nine shining necklaces,
and in her hair   nine lovely ornaments,
and on her head   rested a golden crown,
and in the crown   three precious jewels too;
they shine at night   as the sun shines on days.   20

And then she spoke   to glorious Prince Lazar:
"O my master,   my glorious Prince Lazar,
I am ashamed   even to look at you,
let alone have   a word or two with you.
I have no choice,   I will speak to you now:
The old rulers,   the old Nemanjićes,
they had their reign   and time has passed them by.
Never did they   pile up riches in heaps.
They built churches,   all in their memory.
They built many   stately monasteries: 30
They ordered built   high Dečani, the church,
high Dečani   above Djakovica;

49. In Serbia the *slava* is an annual celebration of the day of the saint chosen as patron to the family when it first accepted Christianity. Slava is still celebrated in Serbia today, the most important of family anniversaries. See Koljević, Appendix 4, 348–49.

above flat Peć   built a patriarchate,
and white Devič   in Drenica region,
and Peter's Church   near Pazar, the city,
and higher up   Djurdjevi Stupovi;
Sopoćane   above the cool Raška,
and Trinity   in Hercegovina;
And Janja's church   in Stari Vlah also;
and Pavlica   below Mount Jadovnik;   40
Studenica   below Brvenik town;
the church Žiča   above Karanovac;
and in Prizren   the church of St. Petka;
Gračanica   in level Kosovo.[50]
All these churches   are in their memory.
And you now sit   upon their glorious throne,
and you've piled up   much riches in great heaps,
but you've not built   one church in your honor.
All the riches   you have piled up in heaps
but not for health   nor for our souls' goodness,   50
neither for us,   nor for our children's souls."

And then he spoke,   the glorious Prince Lazar:
"Are you listening,   Serbian lords and masters,
what the lady,   Milica, is saying
that I've not built   my own memorial church?
Now I will build   a church called Ravanica
in Resava   by the river Ravan.[51]
I have riches   as my heart would desire.
and I will set   its foundations in lead,
I will build up   its walls high all around,   60
I will build it   out of shining silver,
I will cover   its roof with burnished gold,
I'll decorate   the church with little pearls,
and fill my church   full of precious jewels."

All the high Lords   rose nimbly to their feet
and bowed deeply   to the prince in respect:

---

50. All these churches and monasteries are located in and around Kosovo, the heart of the Rascian territories.

51. Ravanica is located in central Serbia, about seventy-five miles north of Kruševac.

"Build it, O Prince,   it will be for your soul
and for the health   of Visoki Stefan."
But all alone   sat Miloš Obilić.[52]
He sat afar,   at the end of table.   70
He sat alone,   and uttered not a word.

When Prince Lazar,   the glorious, saw there
that Obilić   said not a single word,
he raised his cup   of red wine to Miloš:
"This to your health,   O valiant Duke Miloš!
Why don't you say   something to me also,
for I do plan   to build my own fine church."

Miloš then rose   nimbly to his two feet,
and he took off   his sable, feathered hat,
and he bowed down   in honor of the Prince.   80
They gave him then   the golden cup of wine.
Miloš took it,   the golden cup of wine.
He didn't drink,   but began with these words:
"Thank you, my Prince,   for the words you just spoke.
As for your wish   to build a holy church,
the time's not right   nor can it now be right.
Look up, my Prince,   the ancient books of law,
and have a look   at what they here tell us:
This is the time   of the Last Judgment Day.
The Turks will take   your kingdom by brute force.   90
The Turks will start   their own reign very soon.
They will tear down   all our own fine churches.
They will tear down   our monasteries too.
They will tear down   your Ravanica church.
They will dig out   its foundations of lead
which they will melt   to make their cannon balls,
with which to break   our cities to the ground.
They will tear down   the walls of your white church;
they will use them   to make of it a stable.

52. Miloš Obilić, one of the most exalted of the Serbian heroes and a loyal knight out of favor with Lazar, would in the battle of Kosovo kill Sultan Murad and then die at the hands of the Turks. Miloš will thus prove his loyalty, questioned by Lazar, in his death. See Koljević, 23–24 et seq.

They will tear down   the roof of your white church;   100
and make from it   necklaces for their wives.
They will unstring   all the pearls from your church
and string them out   in women's necklaces.
They will pluck out   all those precious jewels
and hammer them   into the hilts of swords
and into rings   of gold for their women.

"But hear me out,   O glorious Prince Lazar!
Let us dig out   marble from the quarries,
and let us build   your church out of marble.
Let the Turks take   your kingdom by brute force,   110
but our churches   will last forevermore,
now and ever   until the Judgment Day,
for from stones none   can take any profit."

When he heard that,   glorious Prince Lazar,
he spoke these words   to Miloš Obilić:
"Thank you so much,   my faithful duke, Miloš;
thank you so much   for your wise oration.
What you have said   is no more than the truth."

 ## Banović Strahinja[53]

Banović Strahinja, a song with a curious title, for its protagonist is identified as a *ban* (a governing lord during the Turkish occupation) and never a *banović* (the future inheritor of that title), is one of the longest and most admired of the heroic songs. For it is developed around a conception of value that transcends the motives of honor, of revenge, or of patriotism informing so many of the other songs. The poem is curious in its genre as well, for beneath its apparently comic surface lies a tragic awareness of the misfortune of the human condition that gives it a darkness perhaps of an order of that of Shakespeare's *King Lear.*

The song was sung to Vuk in Kragujevac in 1822 by Old Milija, a farmer and refugee from Kolašin in eastern Montenegro, who at the age of fifty still had his head "scarred with cuts" at their meeting (as Vuk tells us) and

---

53. *"Banović Strahinja,"* II, 191, #44.

was ravaged by age and drink and near death (he would die a year later). Milija had not been easy for Vuk to locate; it took Prince Miloš Obrenović, ruler of the new kingdom of Serbia, to have him brought to Vuk, and special arrangements were made to accommodate his agricultural responsibilities during his absence from his land.[54]

Milija, constantly fortified by *slivovic,* sang his long songs clumsily and presented many difficulties for his transcriber, so fifteen days were expended in transcribing Milija's four songs. And the songs he sang, full of misfortune, mirrored his own history of suffering. Certainly here the drunken old dervish, who recognizes Strahinić Ban in the Turkish camp but generously repays the ban's courtesies by preserving his anonymity, seems a character autobiographically conceived—and possibly even the embodiment of the conception of value that the ban embraces at the poem's end.

Again the poem mirrors a patriarchal culture. Village customs and attitudes are everywhere—the constant reference to drinking, the condemnation of the daughter for infidelity, the oaths—and the theme of the poem is generated out of such a culture. For in *Banović Strahinja* the central conflict of values is not a conflict centering around wifely infidelity but between the assumptions of Jug Bogdan and his son-in-law, the ban. For Jug Bogdan, the brave and independent old man in the Kosovo poems, is here seen as a canny and cynical lord, carefully and selfishly negotiating his position as father and vassal to the sultan, protecting his family and his position by refusing aid to the emotional and generous ban in the recovery of his wife from the Turk. Yet, in the poem's magnificent ending, when the unfaithful wife has been recaptured, it is the forgiving and generous ban who stays the vengeful hand of the father and her brothers, and who—in spite of his joy in drinking with his friends—finds himself alone.[55]

In spite of its patriarchal qualities the poem has its origins in history. Strahinić Ban seems to be identifiable as Djuradj Stratcimirović Balšić, a member of the Balšić family, lords of Zeta in the middle ages. And an identity of Old Jug Bogdan (Bogdan Jugović) as a member of the Jugas, another noble family of the time, has also been suggested, although it is still probable that the Jugovićes are legendary and fictitious.

54. See Koljević, 314–16.
55. See Koljević, 132–38, 335–36.

Banović Strahinja

Strahinić Ban   was a mighty hero,
a great hero   in the little Banjska,[56]
little Banjska,   there near Kosovo field.
No such falcon   could be found anywhere!
One bright morning   the ban got up early.
He calls his men,   good servants, to himself:
"My good servants,   make haste, do not tarry,
and saddle up   my faithful battle horse,
and fit him out   as nicely as you can,
and girdle him   as tightly as you can.   10
For, my children,   I must now go away
and leave behind   our dear town of Banjska,
for I must test   my good old battle horse
and, my children,   visit my dear old friends,
my dear in-laws   in the white Kruševac,
old Jug Bogdan,   my dear father-in-law,
and his brave sons,   the nine Jugovićes.
My dear in-laws   all await my visit."

The servants then   paid heed to his command
and saddled up   his faithful battle horse.   20
Strahinić Ban   then made himself ready,
attired himself   in his festive garments,
most beautiful   and most resplendent clothes;
they're more crimson   than the sunset waters,
they are brighter   than the warm sun itself.
Thus attired,   this proud Serbian falcon[57]
mounted his horse   his swift, true battle horse
and soon arrived   at the home of in-laws,
at his in-laws   in the white Kruševac,
where a kingdom   had recently been founded.   30

There he was met   by the old Jug Bogdan
and by his sons,   the nine brothers-in-law,

56. A village about ten miles northwest of Kosovska Mitrovica.
57. "Falcon" is a formulaic expression for a young brave lad, appearing throughout Serbian epic poetry.

the nine falcons,   nine brave Jugovićes,
eager to greet   their dear brother-in-law.
They embraced him,   their dear brother-in-law.
Faithful servants   took care of the guest's horse,
the guest himself   was led to the tower.
There they sat down   at the dinner table
and soon engaged   in the talk of nobles.
Male and female   servants sped to and fro,   40
some assisting,   others serving red wine.
All who were there,   those Christian gentlefolk,
sat together   and drank the chilled red wine.
Jug Bogdan was   at the head of table
and to his right,   close to his right arm, sat
Strahinić Ban,   his dear, brave son-in-law,
and there also   were the nine Jugovićes,
and other lords   along the table's sides,
and noble youths   serving the mighty lords.

Daughters-in-law,   all nine of them, were there,   50
all served the lords   with the other servants.
They brought the food   to their father-in-law,
and to their men,   their lords, they served them, too,
most of all they   served their brother-in-law.
One of the wives   served the chilled red wine,
she poured it forth   from a golden chalice,
a bright chalice   holding nine full liters.
There were also   other tasty dishes,
dishes worthy   of the noble diners,
and in all things   the meal befit the kingdom.   60

For a long time   the ban was their dear guest.
But in a time   the ban began to tire.
Yet he was proud   being with his in-laws.
The noble lords   that were in Kruševac
all insisted,   every morn and evening,
they all implored   the mighty Jug Bogdan:
"Our gracious lord,   O mighty Jug Bogdan,
we kiss your robe,   your precious silken robe,
and your right hand,   your fatherly white hand,

just be so kind   and use your noble means   70
to bring your guest,   your charming son-in-law,
bring him, your guest,   the dear Strahinić Ban,
to our own homes,   to our stately places,
so that we, too,   can show him our respect."

Jug Bogdan heeds   each noble lord's request.
But by the time   they all had had their wish,
much time had passed,   much precious time indeed.
Strahinić Ban,   he wearied of it all.
Then suddenly,   woe would come from nowhere.

One bright morning,   when the sun was rising,   80
a messenger   came with a white letter
straight from Banjska,   the ban's small native town;
the letter came   from his dear old mother.
The letter came   directly to the ban.
When he read it,   it became clear to him:
the letter brought   disturbing news to him.
For in its words   his mother chided him:
"O where are you,   Strahinić Ban, my son?
Woe to you and   to the Kruševac wine;
woe to the wine   and to all your in-laws!   90
Read this letter   of our unknown troubles.
Upon us fell   suddenly the great might
of that Turk tsar,   the tsar from Jedrene.[58]

"That tsar swooped down   on our Kosovo field,
the tsar swooped down   and brought his viziers,
brought viziers,   those evil-bearing men.
From all the lands   that Turkish tsar commands
he has gathered   all the Turkish power,
he gathered them   here on Kosovo field,
he filled the field,   the field of Kosovo,   100
he also filled   the two rivers nearby,
the river Lab   and river Sitnica.[59]
All Kosovo   is weighed down with their might.

58. Edirne, or Adrianople, a city in western Turkey.
59. The Lab empties into the Sitnica near the Kosovo field.

People say, son,   they tell all kinds of tales
that all those Turks   have covered Kosovo
from marble rocks   to the maple forests,
from the forests,   son, to the Sazlija,
to Sazlija   and its arched, stony bridge,
from the bridge, son,   to the fort of Zvečan,[60]
and from Zvečan   to the fort of Čečan,[61]   110
and from Čečan   right to the mountain top.

"In numbers, son,   if you were to count them,
the tsar commands   a hundred thousand men
along with some   *spahis*[62] of the sultan,
who got their land   from that very sultan,
who earn and eat   their bread from that sultan,
and who all ride   on their battle horses,
and who carry   hardly any weapons
except for one   sharp saber at the belt.

"And the same Turk,   that mighty Turkish tsar,   120
has another   mighty army, my son,
full of the fire   of Turkish janissaries,
who now hold firm   in the white Jedrene.
They say there are   a hundred thousand men.
The people, son,   tell also such stories,
that these same Turks   have yet a third army,
the mighty force   of Tuka and Mandžuka.
O what a din,   how horribly they strike!

"The sultan has   many kinds of armies.
But those same Turks   have one unusual force,   130
a headstrong man,   Vlah Alija, leads it;[63]
he does not fear   the honorable tsar,

60. A town and fortress northwest of Kosovska Mitrovica, mentioned in the eleventh century already.

61. Another fort, west of Kosovo field.

62. A *spahi* is a Turkish term for cavalry officer, and during the occupation was a person provided a horse in return for military service.

63. As his name implies, Vlah Alija is a Wallachian, traditionally a separate people in the Balkans, itinerant, mercenary, often merchants or fighters who serve the highest bidder and are loyal only to themselves. Vlah Alija is, then, to be trusted by neither ban nor sultan.

he does not mind   all the mighty viziers,
nor all the rest   of the tsar's great army;
he cares for them   no more than for the ants.
That is how strong   the strength of this Turk is.
He won't pass by   without trouble, my son.
He followed not   the tsar to Kosovo.
He took the road   that turns off to the south,
and then he struck   at our town of Banjska,   140
and he lay waste,   my son, to Banjska here
and burned it all   with a living fire,
and did not leave   a single stone unturned.

"He chased away   all your faithful servants,
and so he brought   grief to your old mother,
he broke her bones   under his horse's hooves,
and took away   your faithful wife, he did,
and he took her   off to Kosovo field.
There he kisses   your wife beneath his tent,
and I, my son,   wail in the burned-out home   150
the while you drink   red wine in Kruševac.
May that cursed wine   bring the wrath upon you!"

When the ban read   and thought of the letter,
he was stricken   with sorrow and remorse.
His face was flushed   with sadness and with grief,
his moustaches   hung low on his dark mouth,
his moustaches   dropped upon his shoulders,
and his dark face   showed a threatening scowl,
and the great tears   were just about to flow.

When Jug Bogdan   saw his sad son-in-law,   160
his son-in-law   in the morning's bright dawn,
he burned with rage   like a hot, living fire.
He then spoke out   to that Strahinić Ban:
"O son-in-law,   may the Lord be with you!
Why did you, son,   get up so soon today?
Why is your face   so dark and so distraught?
My son-in-law,   what has made you so sad?
And who has brought   such anger to you, son?
Did they mock you,   your own brothers-in-law?

Or did they say   unpleasant things in jest?   170
Sisters-in-law,   did they fail to serve you?
Or did you find   some fault with your kinsmen?
Speak, son-in-law,   what is bothering you?"

Strahinić Ban,   angered, answered thusly:
"Leave me in peace,   my dear old Jug Bogdan.
I find no fault   with my brothers-in-law.
Sisters-in-law,   they're all of noble birth.
They all speak well   and serve me even better.
I find no fault   with any kinsman here.
But it is this   which makes me so unhappy: 180
This letter came   from my little Banjska,
from none other   than my dear old mother."

And he told him   of his great misfortune:
How all his courts   had been greatly plundered,
how his servants   had been driven away,
how his mother   was trampled by a horse,
and how his wife   was taken as a slave.
"Yes, Jug Bogdan,   my dear father-in-law,
although she is   my lawful wife today,
she is my wife   and she is your daughter.   190
Yet disgrace falls   on both together.
But Jug Bogdan,   my dear father-in-law,
if you have grief   for me when I am dead,
feel pity now   while I am still alive.
I beseech you,   I kiss your honored hand,
allow your sons,   nine sons, to go with me,
your sons indeed,   and my brothers-in-law,
thus can I leave,   depart for Kosovo,
to seek him out,   my deadly enemy,
that loathsome beast,   traitor to the sultan,   200
who took from me   my wife in slavery.

"But do not fear,   my dear father-in-law,
do not worry   about your children, sir.
I will take care   of my brothers-in-law.
I will alter   their usual attire,
I will dress them   all in Turkish clothing,

around their heads   a proper white turban,
upon their backs   and chests a green tunic,
around their legs   violet wide trousers,
and on their belts   sabers breathing fire.   210
I'll call servants,   I will give them orders,
I will tell them   to saddle our horses,
saddle them up   and gird them really tight,
and cover them   over with dark bearskin.
I'll make all them   like the janissaries,
and I'll teach them,   my good brothers-in-law,
when they all ride   with me through Kosovo,
through the sultan's   army at Kosovo.
I will pretend   to be a stern captain,
and they'll pretend   to be shy and frightened,   220
frightened indeed   of their awesome leader.

"Whichever one   of the sultan's soldiers,
whoever starts   to talk with one of us
in Turkish tongue   or any of their tongues,
I'll answer him,   I shall speak with the Turks,
for I can speak   Turkish and the others,
I understand   the Arab tongue as well
and can mumble   some Albanian words.
I will lead them   across Kosovo field.
There I will spy   on the Turkish army   230
until I find   my deadly enemy,
that enemy,   mighty Vlah Alija,
who took my wife,   my wife in slavery.
Brothers-in-law,   let them come to my aid,
for, by myself,   I would be quickly killed,
but I won't die   with my brothers-in-law,
nor suffer wounds   with them all around me."

When Jug Bogdan,   the old man, heard all that,
he burned with rage   like a living fire,
and then he spoke   to that Strahinić Ban: 240
"Strahinić Ban,   my dearest son-in-law,
I see this morn   that you have lost your wits,
because you ask   that my nine children go,
that you take them   to the Kosovo field,

to be killed all   by Turks at Kosovo.
My son-in-law,   no more talk about this.
I won't permit   my sons to go with you
though I no more   will see my daughter's face.

"My son-in-law,   valiant Strahinić Ban,
why are you thus,   torn apart by sorrow?   250
Don't you know, son,   may all men forget you,
that if she spends   only one night with him,
one night alone   with him in his field tent,
she cannot be   dear to you any more.
May God smite her,   it is His awful curse.
She loves him more   than she loves you, my son.
So let her go,   may the Devil take her!
I will find you   a better wife to wed.
I'd like to drink   cool wine with you always,
you to remain   here with friends forever,   260
but my dear sons   won't go to Kosovo."

The ban was red   in face like a hot fire.
In his anger   and his frightful heartache,
he was ashamed   to summon his servant,
to send this news   to his faithful servant,
he himself went   to his horse in the stall.
And he set to,   he saddled his own horse,
and he firmly   girted his gray horse,
and he set tight   the bit made of cold steel
and led the horse   to the open courtyard,   270
to the white stone   that is used for mounting.
And he mounted   in his horse's saddle.
He looked at each   of his brothers-in-law,
and each of them   looked down upon the ground.

The ban looks down   at his wife's sister's spouse,
a youthful lad   with the Nemanjić name,
but Nemanjić   too looks down at the ground.
Together they   had drunk wine and *raki*,
together they   boasted of being heroes,
boasted and swore   by God to their in-law: 280
"Strahinić Ban,   we love you more dearly

than all the land   that is in our empire!"
But when it came   to the real misfortune,
on this morning,   the ban has found no friend.
It's not easy   to go to Kosovo!

When the ban saw   that he had found no friend,
he left alone   by wide Kruševac field.
As he went forth   down the desolate space,
he turned his eyes   back toward white Kruševac,
looking for those   who might have changed their mind,   290
or who might feel   some pain to see him go.
But when he saw   that on this sad morning
his one best friend   was nowhere by his side,
he remembered,   thought all of a sudden
of his greyhound,   Karaman is his name,
whom he loved more   than his own gray stallion.
So he called him   from his mighty white throat.

The greyhound too   had stayed in the stable.
When the greyhound   heard him, he swiftly ran
till he caught up   with the ban's good gray horse.   300
The greyhound ran   and leaped all round the horse,
his gold collar   jingling around his neck.
The ban was pleased   that he had company.

And so the ban   rode on his battle-horse,
he rode over   plains and fields and mountains.
When he arrived   on flat Kosovo field,
when he sized up   the force at Kosovo,
the spectacle   frightened the ban somewhat.
And so, calling   the name of the true God,
he then plunged forth   into the Turkish hordes.   310
So rode the ban   onto Kosovo field.
He rode in all   four directions of it,
in search of him,   the mighty Vlah Alija.
But he could not   find the man anywhere.

The ban went down   to the Sitnica stream,
and there he saw   a wondrous spectacle.
There on the bank   of the Sitnica stream

he saw set out   a green, wide, spacious tent,
a spacious tent   covering the whole field,
and on its top   was perched a golden apple.   320
The apple shone   like the fiery bright sun.
Before the tent   a lance stood in the ground,
a crow-black horse   was tied onto the lance,
and on its head   there was a huge feed-bag.
It beat the ground   with right, then left foreleg.
When he saw this,   the brave Strahinić Ban,
he thought of it,   then came to recognize:
this must be sure   the tent of Vlah Alija.
He led his horse   straight up before the tent.

The hero took   a lance from his shoulders   330
and opened up   the flap of the green tent,
to see who sat   within the great green tent.
But it was not   mighty Vlah Alija;
an old dervish   was sitting there instead.[64]
His long white beard   flowed down below his waist.
No other soul   was with him in the tent.

That old dervish   was a tipsy fellow,
for the old Turk   drank wine from a large cup,
he poured alone   and drank his glass alone.
And this dervish   was blood-soaked to his eyes.   340

When Strahinić,   the ban, saw the dervish,
he greeted him   in the Turkish fashion.
Turning his eyes,   the drunken dervish saw him,
and he answered   with these unfriendly words:
"Good health to you,   valiant Strahinić Ban
from Banjska town,   small town near Kosovo."

The ban showed rage,   but he was frightened too.
Yet he answered   the dervish in Turkish:

64. A *derviš* or "dervish" is an Islamic monk, or member of a monastic order, taking vows of poverty and austerity (although in the Balkans during the Turkish occupation the life of a dervish was often considered comfortable) and wandering as a friar or living in compounds similar to monasteries. Of course, a drunken dervish suggests a certain degeneration, or at least lapse of faith, although such were not uncommon.

"You old dervish, woe be to your mother,
why do you drink, why do you get so drunk,   350
and when you're drunk, why talk all that nonsense
to a good Turk whom you call a *giaour*?[65]
Who is this ban of whom you now babble?
I'm not the ban, that same Strahinić Ban,
rather I am a brave sultan's soldier.
Our lord's horses have just broken away
and have galloped into the Turkish hordes.
All the brave men quickly ran after them,
to catch again and fetch the sultan's horses.
If I should tell our lord or his vizier   360
what you called me just a short time ago,
you would, old man, then have many problems."

But the dervish broke out in loud laughter.
"You are that ban, the brave Strahinić Ban.
Do you know, ban, may the troubles spare you,
if I were now there on Goleč Mountain,[66]
if I saw you in the sultan's army,
I would know you and your good battle horse
and your greyhound, the nimble Karaman,
whom you love more than your good battle horse.   370
Do you not know, O ban of small Banjska,
that I can tell the look of your forehead
and beneath it the color of your eyes,
and I can tell both your black moustaches.
Do you know, ban, may the Devil spare you,
I was taken a prisoner one time,
it was your men who took me in their thrall
in Suhara, on top of the mountain.
They then put me, prisoner, in your hands.
You then threw me in the deepest dungeon,   380
a prisoner; I suffered that dungeon.
I pined away for more than nine long years.

"So nine years passed, and then came the tenth year,
and you, the ban, took pity on me then,

---

65. *Giaour* is a Turkish term for an infidel—a nonbeliever, or Christian.
66. Goleč is a small, bare mountain southwest of Priština.

and you called out   to Rade, the warden.
Your chief warden   right through the dungeon gates
led me to you   I stood there in the yard.
Know you, then, ban,   remember, Strahinić,
when you asked me   a question, mocking me:
'My little slave,   you mighty Turkish serpent,   390
how you've rotted   away in my dungeon!
Can you ransom   yourself, like the heroes?'

"You asked me that;   I answered forthrightly:
'I could ransom   my life quite easily
if I could go   to my home and my courts,
to my birthplace   and my inheritance.
I used to have   some treasure of my own,
a lot of land,   land which could be rented.
I could gather   a ransom together.
But you, my ban,   do not have faith in me   400
to let me go   to my white court, my home.
I will leave you   reasonable hostage,
One best of all,   Almighty God Himself,
a guarantee,   my strong faith in true God,
that I will bring   means to buy my freedom.'

"And you, my ban,   did accept my good word
and let me go   to my white court, my home,
to my birthplace   and my inheritance.
And when I came   to the place of my birth,
evil fortune   met me at my portal,   410
in my own house,   in the place of my birth.
The plague had struck,   had struck my house and court,
had killed them all,   men as well as women.

"No one was left   there at my place of birth,
and my good house   and court had gone to ruin,
the walls apart,   the arches fallen in,
and elder trees   were growing in the walls.
And what had been   my land, my land to rent,
the Turks had seized,   stolen them in their greed.

"When I saw then   my house and court destroyed,   420
my treasure gone   and all my friends departed,

I thought a while,   and then I decided.
So I mounted   a horse, a local post-horse,
and thus I reached   the town of Jedrene.
I visited   sultan and vizier.
The vizier heard   and he told his master
that I was sure,   battle-proven warrior.

"The tsar's vizier   gave me decent clothing,
gave me clothing   and a fine large new tent.
And he gave me   a raven-black horse too,   430
and he gave me   glittering new weapons.
The tsar's vizier   signed me on the records,
and now I am   the sultan's forever.
And so today   you came to me, my ban,
to take from me   that ransom I owe you.
But, my dear ban,   I have not a dinar.
Ban Strahinić,   you have come to trouble;
you have come here   to lose your head for naught,
on Kosovo,   'mid the sultan's army."

The ban just then   recognized the dervish.   440
He dismounted   from his gray battle-horse
and he embraced   the old man, the dervish.
"Brother in God,   my old man, my dervish!
I'm giving you   a gift of what you owe
and I now seek   not a dinar from you,
I don't demand   that you should pay what's owed.
But I here seek   the strong Vlah Alija,
who has laid waste   to all my house and court,
who took my wife,   my wife in slavery.
And so tell me,   O dervish, good old man,   450
where I can find   my deadly enemy.
And I'll call you   my brother once again.
Don't reveal me   to the sultan's army,
so that they don't   surround me, and seize me."

Then the dervish   swore on his faith in God:
"Strahinić Ban,   you falcon of a man,
my faith is strong,   stronger than hardened rock.
If you were now   to draw your sharp saber,

and massacre   half of sultan's army,
I will not break   the faith I have with you,   460
nor desecrate   the bread you then gave me.
Even though I   was locked in your dungeon,
you did give me   enough of the red wine
and did feed me   with a good white bread,
let me go out   to warm myself in sun,
you let me free   on my word of honor.
I did not then   betray you nor pay you;
I would have done,   but had naught to pay with.
But have no fear   at all on my account.

"As for your quest,   and your question, my ban,   470
about the Turk,   mighty Vlah Alija,
he has now pitched,   spread out a big white tent
on that high mount,   the great Goleč Mountain.
But I'll give you,   ban, a word of warning:
Mount your horse now   and run from Kosovo,
or else you will   lose your own head for naught.
Do not presume,   be too sure of yourself,
nor of your arm,   nor of your sharp saber,
nor of your lance,   your lance tipped with poison.
You will go there   to the Turk on the mount,   480
you will arrive,   but there you'll not fare well.
E'en with your arms,   e'en with such a good horse,
you will fall sure   into his hands alive,
he will surely   break both of your white hands
and he will gouge   both of your burning eyes."

Strahinić Ban   laughed at dervish's words.
"Brother in God,   good old man, my dervish,
have you no care   for me, my dear brother,
just don't betray   me to your brother Turks."

Then the Turk spoke   more words to Strahinić: 490
"Strahinić Ban,   brave lad, do you hear me?
My faith is strong,   stronger than hardened rock.
If you were now   to make mad your brave horse,
if you were now   to draw out your sharp saber,
and massacre   half of sultan's army,

I will not break   the faith I have with you,
nor will betray   you to the Turkish army."

So the ban spoke,   made ready to depart.
He spoke again   mounted there on his horse:
"O my brother,   good old man, my dervish,   500
here you water   your horse morn and evening,
water your horse   in the Sitnica stream.
Try to recall,   and tell me straight away
where I can ford   the Sitnica River,
so that my horse   will not sink in the sand?"

And the dervish   answered him directly:
"Strahinić Ban,   you Serbian falcon,
your horse is fine,   as is your bravery,
so there's no place   you can fail to ford it."

The ban set out,   he forded the river,   510
and on his horse,   the good gray battle-horse,
he then set forth   to climb Goleč Mountain.
He is below;   the sun shines above him,
the sun that shines   on all of Kosovo
and all the men   of the mighty army.

But you should see   the strong Vlah Alija!
All night that Turk   kisses Strahin's true love
under his tent   high on Goleč Mountain.
Yet this same Turk   has a troubling habit,
he likes to sleep   too late in the morning,   520
so each morning   while the sun heats the earth.
He shuts his eyes   and floats off in his dream.
How dear she was   to him, how much he loved
that slave of his,   Strahinić's love and wife!
He puts his head   tenderly on her lap,
and there she holds   strong Vlah Alija's head.
She then opens   the flap of his white tent,
and she looks out   over Kosovo field,
and she looks out   at the Turkish power.
She then judges   the kind of tents they have,   530

she then judges   the heroes and horses.
By her bad luck   her eyes then turn from this,
and as she looks   down the side of Goleč,
her eyes see there   a soldier on a horse.

And as she sees   them with her very eyes,
she strikes the Turk   with the palm of her hand
on his right cheek,   she strikes him while he sleeps,
she strikes him there   and she begins to speak:
"O my master,   mighty Vlah Alija,
raise up your head   or never raise it more,   540
and gird yourself   with that great belt of yours,
and dress yourself   in your shiny armor.
Now comes to us   that Strahinić, the ban.
He comes to us   to cut your head off, now,
he comes to us   to put out both my eyes."

The Turk leaps up   in his rage like a fire,
the Turk leaps up,   sees him with his own eyes,
and then the Turk   laughs his roaring laughter:
"My darling slave,   wife of Strahinić Ban,
he frightens you,   that funny little Vlah?   550
Does he really   give you such a big shock?
When I take you   to white Jedrene town,
you will there, too,   imagine Strahinić.
But this, my dear,   is not Strahinić Ban;
this is, instead,   one of sultan's captains.
Sultan sends him   now directly to me,
either sultan   or Mehmed, his vizier.
Sultan calls me   to surrender to him,
so that I don't   take apart his army.
The tsar's viziers   are all worried greatly   560
that I may strike   at them with my saber.
But if, my dear,   you happen to see it,
do not fear it,   do not have fear for it,
when I draw out   my sharp, my quick saber
and cut him down,   this captain of the tsar,
then he won't dare   send another captain."

But Strahin's wife   speaks to Vlah Alija:
"O my master,   O strong Vlah Alija,
don't you see him?   May your eyes fall away!
This man is not   a captain of the tsar,   570
but my husband   and lord, Strahinić Ban.
I recognize   the look of his forehead,
and beneath it   the color of his eyes,
and I can see   both his black moustaches,
and beneath him,   his good gray battle-horse,
and Karaman,   his yellow, swift greyhound.
O my master,   do not play with your life!"

When he hears this,   the Turk, Vlah Alija,
oh how he burns,   how he becomes enraged!
He jumps upright   quickly on his light feet,   580
he girds himself   with that great belt of his,
and in the belt   he thrusts his sharp daggers,
and on the belt   he attaches his sword,
and he searches   for his raven black horse.

At that moment   the ban comes upon him.
The ban is wise,   but now his wit fails him.
It is morning,   he says not good morning,
nor does he make   greeting in Turkish tongue,
but he utters   cruel words to the Turk:
"Ah, there you are,   you old Turkish bastard,   590
Turkish bastard,   traitor to the sultan!
Whose house and courts   have you plundered? tell me!
And whose servants   have you taken prisoner?
And whose dear wife   do you kiss in your tent?
I call you out!   Come, we'll fight like warriors!"

The Turk jumps up   as if touched by madness.
And with one leg   he bounds up to his horse;
with the other   he vaults on his stallion.
He draws up tight   both of his horse's reins.
Ban Strahinić   does not waste a moment.   600
He rides his horse   straight toward Vlah Alija,
and lets his lance   fly toward Alija.
Warriors then clash   one against the other.

Vlah Alija   reaches out his white hand,
catches the lance   with his own mighty hand,
as he begins   to speak thus to the ban:
"Strahinić Ban,   good-for-nothing bastard,
what did you think,   O you puny Christian?
I'm not an old   Šumadija woman
for you to chase,   run in all directions.   610
No, I am strong,   the strong Vlah Alija,
who does not fear   the sultan nor vizier.
All the soldiers   in the sultan's army,
to me they all,   all seem to resemble
the tiny ants   crawling in the green grass.
And you, you fool,   you want to fight a duel!"
Having said this,   he heaves his battle-lance;
he tries to kill   the ban with the first blow.

Yet God protects   well that Strahinić Ban.
He has a horse   well seasoned in battle.   620
Just as the lance   whistles on that mountain,
his falcon horse   drops down low on his knees.
The battle-lance   whistles over his head,
its sharpened tip   strikes on a nearby rock,
and the lance splits   into three equal parts,
down to the hilt   and down to the right hand.

When they have smashed   their sharp battle-lances,
they then reach down   and swing feathered maces.
When he strikes forth,   the strong Vlah Alija,
when he strikes forth   at that Strahinić Ban,   630
he pushes him   right out of his saddle
all the way up   toward his horse's ears.

God protects well   that brave Strahinić Ban.
He has a horse   well seasoned in battle,
like no other   possessed by Serb today,
not any Serb,   nor Turkish warrior.
And that fine horse   shakes his head and body
and he throws back   his sire in his saddle.
Strahinić Ban,   when he strikes with his mace
that evil beast,   that strong Vlah Alija,   640

he can't move him   out of his saddle seat.
All the four legs   of his raven black horse
sink in the ground   all the way to his knees.

Then the warriors   break their feathered maces,
they break them up   and scatter their feathers.
Then they draw forth   their razor-sharp sabers,
to seek to end   their fierce duel like heroes.
You should have seen   that brave Strahinić Ban!
He had, they say,   a saber on his belt,
a saber forged   by two skillful swordsmiths,   650
by two swordsmiths   and four apprentices,
from one Sunday   to another Sunday.
They smelted it   from steel into saber,
into a sharp,   battle-worthy saber.
The Turk strikes out;   the ban parries the blow,
with his saber   strikes the other saber,
and he cuts it,   the Turk's, into two halves.
The ban sees that   and begins rejoicing.
He deftly moves,   one side to the other,
hopes to cut off   strong Vlah Alija's head,   660
or at the least   to wound him on his arms.

Warriors then clash   one against the other.
The Turk stops him   from cutting off his head,
and he stops him   wounding him in his arms.
He saves himself   with just half a saber.
He holds the half   closely beside his neck,
and keeps his neck   covered and protected.
He chips away   at the ban's swift saber,
he chips away,   one bit, then another.
And so they hack   their sabers to pieces,   670
hew them away   right to their very hilts,
then throw away   broken bits of sabers,
and they dismount   from their battle-horses;
each reaches out   for the other's white throat.

And so it goes,   these two dragons fighting,
in a clearing   there on Goleč Mountain.
They carry on   that summer day till noon,

until the Turk   is covered with white foam,
foam just as white   as pristine mountain snow,
and Strahin's foam   is both white and bloody,   680
his tunic there   all bloody on his chest,
and his two boots   are also full of blood.

And when the ban   had enough of struggle,
the ban speaks out,   his words all in anguish:
"O my own wife,   may God smite and kill you!
Why do you look   on our woe on this mount?
Take a fragment   of a broken saber,
and strike, my love,   either me or the Turk.
Choose, my dear love,   as your heart commands you."

But then the Turk   speaks out in his anger: 690
"My darling slave,   wife of Strahinić Ban,
do not strike me,   strike that Strahinić Ban.
You'll never be   so dear to him again,
for he will sure   reproach you forever;
he'll reproach you   each morn and each evening
that you have spent   time with me in my tent.
You'll be my love   always and forever.
I will take you   to Jedrene city,
I will order   thirty servants for you,
to wait on you   hand and foot, my dear love.   700
I will feed you   with honey and sugar.
I will deck you   all with golden ducats,
from top of head   down unto the green grass.
So strike you now   at the Ban Strahinić!"

It is easy   for man to fool woman.
She jumps lightly,   as if she's lost her mind.
She quickly finds   broken bit of saber,
she wraps it up   in an embroidered scarf,
for she would not   injure her own white hand.
And she follows   this way now and that way,   710
guarding the head   of Turk Vlah Alija.
And then she strikes   at her former master,
her own husband,   the proud Strahinić Ban,
right on the head,   on the turban feather,

and the turban,   all wound around the head.
She cuts in half   the gold turban feather;
she cuts straight through   his own white-wound turban,
makes a slight cut   there on the hero's head.
The blood begins   to run down the ban's face,
and to threaten   to blind both of his eyes.   720

Strahinić Ban   is startled by all this,
that he would die   a foolish, useless death.
But then a thought   occurs to Strahin Ban.
He cries out loud   from his white throat he cries
to his greyhound,   the yellow Karaman,
the same greyhound   that he had taught to hunt.
The ban cries out   and then cries out again.
The greyhound jumps   and runs to his master
and sinks his teeth   into the ban's wife's flesh.

But all women   are known for various fears,   730
they fear a hound,   any kind of a hound.
She throws away   the saber on the grass,
lets out a shriek   that could be heard afar,
she then takes hold   of the yellow hound's ears,
and they begin   to fight there on the mount.
And the Turk's eyes   almost burst from his head;
he is o'ercome,   stricken by great sadness,
to watch his dear,   what's happening to her.

But the ban's strength   comes back to him again,
the second wind   to a great warrior's heart.   740
So he begins   to swing back and forward,
until the Turk   is toppled off his feet.
Strahinić Ban   is so wild with anger,
he does not need   any of his weapons,
but he goes straight   for the throat of the Turk,
seizes that throat,   he bites it with his teeth,
and he kills him   as a wolf kills a lamb.
The ban stands up,   he shouts out from his throat,
he now commands   his yellow-coated hound,
that his greyhound   release Strahinić's wife.   750

His wife now starts   to run down the mountain,
for she wishes   to run off to the Turks.
Strahinić Ban,   however, won't let her.
So he seizes   her right arm quite firmly,
and he leads her   to his gray battle-horse,
and he mounts her   on the back of his horse,
placing his love   there behind his saddle,
and rides away,   by the most rapid route.
He rides away   now this way, now that way.
Thus he escapes   all that Turkish army,   760
and brings her forth   to Kruševac's plain,
to Kruševac,   the home of his in-laws.

When the old man,   old Jug Bogdan sees him,
and when the nine   Jugovićes meet him,
they spread their arms,   embracing each other,
and each inquires   about the other's health.
When the old man,   old Jug Bogdan, sees him,
the wounded ban,   with cut turban feather,
the tears flow down   his ancient, noble face:
"May the good Lord   save our glorious kingdom   770
if any man   among the sultan's Turks,
if any man   is such a brave warrior
that he can wound   my valiant son-in-law,
the likes of whom   cannot be found afar."
Brothers-in-law   are much frightened by this.

Strahinić Ban   then begins his story:
"Oh, do not fear,   my old father-in-law,
and do not fear,   my dear brothers-in-law.
There is no man   in the sultan's army
who can outfight,   can inflict wounds on me.   780
Let me tell you   who has so wounded me,
and by whose hands   I have come by these wounds.
I was fighting   a duel with a Turk
O Jug Bogdan,   my old father-in-law,
my true love then   struck these wounds upon me,
my faithful wife,   and your dearest daughter.
She sought to aid   not me but the damn Turk."

Jug then flared up   like a burning fire,
and he cried out   to all nine of his sons: 790
"O my dear sons,   draw out your nine daggers,
cut to pieces   this vile bitch, your sister."

The mighty sons   then obey their father
and fling themselves   on their beloved sister.
But Strahinić   steps forth to prevent it.
He speaks these words   to his brothers-in-law:
"Jugovićes,   my nine brothers-in-law,
why do you now   put shame upon yourselves?
For whom do you   draw out your nine daggers?
Since you, brothers,   are such fearless warriors,   800
where were your knives,   where were your sharp sabers,
when you were asked   to go to Kosovo,
to show your hearts   in battle with the Turks
and to help me   the time I needed you?
I won't let you   harm your own dear sister.
I could kill her   without your eager help,
but then I would   have killed all my in-laws.
And I would have   no one with whom to drink.
And so it is   I forgive my true love."

Few warriors,   for there are very few,
are fine as this,   this ban, Strahinić Ban.   810

3 The Battle of Kosovo

---

*A*FTER THE BATTLE of Marica in 1371, the Turkish armies inexorably advanced across the Balkan peninsula. In 1375 Murad I (who had succeeded his father, Orkhan, as sultan in 1362) took Niš, the crossroads of the Balkans and the birthplace of Constantine. As long as the Turks held Niš the Turkish presence in the Balkans was assured. Thus finally a recognition of the need for a united action on the part of the Christian princes seemed dimly to dawn in the minds of the jealous and independent south Slav lords. Lazar was able to join forces with Tvrtko of Bosnia to oppose the Turks at Toplica in 1387 with success. When Murad turned his attention to the Serbs, the Christian nobles had finally united under Lazar at Kruševac.[1]

For some reason—and the reason remains unclear—the Christian princes seem to have decided to engage the Turks and then to draw them toward the western mountains of Zeta, there to fall upon them, destroy their army, and thus begin the reconquest of the valley of the Vardar and hopefully of Bulgaria. According to this plan, we are told, Prince Lazar, the leader of the Christian lords, was to engage the Turks near Prizren and then retreat, leading the Turks into a trap laid by the armies of the Bosnians, Croats, and Wallachians. For everyone had joined together by now, save the Balšas of Zeta, who still refused to fight.

Whether or not this is true, in a meeting before the battle Lazar and the assembled lords decided instead to make their stand on *Kosovo polje*

---

1. See D. H. Low, trans., *The Ballads of Marko Kraljević* (Cambridge: Cambridge University Press, 1922; reprint, New York: Greenwood, 1968), "Introduction II," xxii–xxv.

(Kosovo field, a wide expanse of flat land north of Priština), or "the Field of the Blackbirds."

What followed is known to every Serb. On Saint Vitus's Day, June 28, 1389 (or by the Old Calendar, June 15), after a great feast the night before and a celebration of mass by the Christian forces, the Turks were engaged on Kosovo field. Only Vuk Branković failed in his commitment (or perhaps he was loyal to the original plan). Because Branković left the field when the others remained, he is seen in the Serbian epics, probably without justification, as the great traitor at Kosovo.[2]

Even though Sultan Murad died there, killed by the heroic Miloš Obilić (or so the singers tell us), and even though the first reports of the battle as far away as Paris proclaimed a Christian victory, Lazar was captured and beheaded, and his army devastated. The combined Christian armies had failed to halt the Turkish advance. Niš was not to be recaptured, a wasted Macedonia remained in Turkish hands, and almost all the Balkans fell beneath the shadow of the Turks for nearly five hundred years.

In the eighteenth century a Dubrovnik poet, Jozo Betondić (1709–1764), transcribed from an unknown singer a *bugarštica* song that described in epic terms the events of the Battle of Kosovo. This poem of some two hundred fifty lines, called today in English the "Song of the Battle of Kosovo," is the first known recorded poem recounting the events and motifs that would reappear in the later, less literary and allusive but more dramatic songs in *deseterci* that concerned themselves with the same events.[3]

Less than a century later, in the Leipzig edition of *Srpske narodne*

---

2. The actual events, indeed, even the outcome of the battle itself on St. Vitus's Day, are today historically uncertain (see Koljević, 153–58); but the treason of Vuk Branković, who left the field of Kosovo, is almost universally accepted by the singers. He seems nevertheless to have been unfairly maligned. For, whether it is the case, as Subotić has conjectured, that Vuk is accused of betrayal as a result of a confusion of names (see *Ballads* 85–86) or, as Kostelski argues (*The Yugoslavs* (New York: Philosophical Library, 1952), 343–44, because of his loyalty to the Bosnian King Tvrtko, it is agreed by historians that Vuk remained loyal to the Christian cause, perhaps longer than Lazar's own family, the Hrebeljanovićes.

Master of the Kosovo and ruler of Priština, Vuk Branković was, indeed, Lazar's son-in-law, married to his daughter, Mara. He continued to struggle against the Turks after Kosovo, but he also became the enemy of Stefan Lazarević, Lazar's successor, whose suzerainty he refused to acknowledge. After the death of Tvrtko, he was forced to accept the authority of the sultan in 1392, three years after Stefan Lazarević did so. Records indicate that he was given the freedom of the city of Venice in 1394 and that he was later imprisoned in Bulgaria. See Subotić, *Ballads* 84–87.

3. So it is translated by Pennington and Levi; see 1–7. See also Koljević, 159–67.

pjesme, Vuk would present a set of fragments of songs concerning the day of the battle, which he remembered from his childhood when they were told (or sung) to him by his father. All of them recount scenes and contain elements also to be found in the *bugarštica*. But Vuk had also collected from several of his singers eight other songs, all still widely known among the Serbs.[4] In all eight of these songs are to be found the same elements first found in Betondić's *bugarštica*, elements Vuk remembered from his father's singing. In one song we hear of Stefan Musić's preparation for battle (he is "Stjepan Busić" in the *bugarštica*), in another Milica pleads for the sparing of one of her brothers, in a third we hear of the exchange of toasts in the Serbian camp on the eve of the battle, and of Lazar's curse upon those who fail to be present at the battle. We learn of Lazar's accusation of Miloš Obilić at the high table, a prophecy that is refuted only later in Miloš's heroic death, and we are told of the treason of Vuk Branković (which, along with Lazar's deliberate choice of a heavenly kingdom over an earthly one, is offered, contradictorily, as the reason for the defeat of the Christian forces). As well there are recurrent images; notably that of the cross as Christian symbol, repeatedly associated with the Serbian cause.

These songs describing events before, during, or immediately after the battle of Kosovo seem somehow clearly central to the heroic songs. Although they are sometimes curiously disparate and contradictory, they are almost ritually reenacted, and they remain among the most distinguished, and certainly the best known of the songs, both to south Slavs and to foreign audiences. For it is in these songs (curiously, relatively few of them are extant) as they confront their most exalted and perhaps their most difficult subject, that the genre arrives at its apogee.

Along with his remembered fragments we have included in this collection four of the Kosovo songs—"Tsar Lazar and Tsaritsa Milica," "The Fall of the Serbian Empire," "The Death of the Mother of the Jugovićes," and "The Kosovo Maiden."

---

4. These eight songs—*Carica Milica i Zmaj od Jastrepca* (Tsaritsa Milica and the Dragon from Jastrebac), ii, 43; *Car Lazar i carica Milica* (Tsar Lazar and Tsaritsa Milica), ii, 45; *Propast carstva srpskoga* (The Fall of the Serbian Empire), ii, 46; *Musić Stefan* (Stefan Musić), ii, 47; *Smrt majke Jugovića* (The Death of the Mother of the Jugovićes), ii, 48; *Carica Milica i Vladeta vojvoda* (Tsaritsa Milica and Vladeta the Voivode), ii, 49; *Kosovka djevojka* (The Kosovo Girl), ii, 51; and *Obretenije glave kneza Lazara* (The Prayer of Prince Lazar), ii, 53—all deal with the immediate events leading up to or just after the battle. See *Srpske narodne pjesme*, ii, *Sadržaj* (Table of Contents).

Fragments of Various Kosovo Songs[5]

I was born and brought up in a house where sometimes my grandfather and uncle, sometimes various men from Hercegovina (who would come almost every year to spend the winter with us) would sing and recite songs the whole winter through. I knew from childhood God's plenty of songs; I understood them well, as the people understand them, and they were dear to me as to all the others.[6]

Thus Vuk described his childhood in his Serbian village of Tršić in western Serbia, where his family—Serbs from Hercegovina fleeing the Turks after their reconquest of Serbia in the middle of the eighteenth century—had settled. Even Vuk's father, Stefan, "a serious and God-fearing man [who] gave little attention to songs," "remembered almost against his will from his own father Joksim and his brother Toma, who not only knew a lot of songs and liked singing and reciting them but also composed songs themselves."[7]

Fragments or "pieces" of his father's songs—certainly among Vuk's first encounters with the oral poetry of his people—would be recovered from his own memory for inclusion as a set among the "heroic songs" of his second volume. These fragments are evidence of the nature of the impact of the songs on the consciousness of a sensitive Serbian youth, where they seem not only to have survived as the enactment and concretization of a shared history but also to have served a contemporary use as *exempla*, not only as rationalization but also as a guide to conduct for a colonized people.

The five fragments provide in turn a political rationalization for the battle, a demand for loyalty in the form of a curse imposed on the disloyal, an analogy for the Serbian defeat implicit in the comparison of the final banquet to the Last Supper, evidence of the overwhelming superiority of the Turkish forces as explanation for the defeat, and finally a celebration of moments of heroism in the failed Serbian struggle. These moments of memory, by turns exculpatory and proscriptive, provide evidence of the nature of the significance of the cycle to at least one youthful Serbian imagination, a significance that would perhaps later guide Vuk

---

5. "*Komadi od različnijeh Kosovskijeh pjesama*," II, 222, #50.

6. Duncan Wilson, in his *Life and Times of Vuk Stefanović Karadžić*, 23ff., quotes thus from "information scattered among the introductions and notes to the various collections of Serb songs which he published between 1814 and 1845."

7. Wilson, ibid.

in his decision to offer a great part of his own life to the preservation of the cycle of songs from which it was rendered.

Fragments of Various Kosovo Songs

I

On Kosovo   Tsar Murad descended.
As he arrived,   he wrote a brief letter,
and he sent it   to Kruševac city,
to none other   than the Serb knez, Lazar:
"O you Lazar,   you leader of the Serbs!
It's never been,   and it never will be,
that there can be   one kingdom and two rulers;
one poor *raja*   paying taxes two times.
We cannot both   rule over one kingdom,
but you send me   the keys and the taxes,   10
the golden keys   of all towns and cities,
and the taxes   for the last seven years.
If you don't wish   to send these things to me,
then let us come   to Kosovo's flat field,
with our sabers   to divide the kingdom."

When Knez Lazar   received this brief letter,
he kept reading,   and shedding grieving tears.

II

If but one man   were present there to hear
how Knez Lazar   uttered his bitter curse:
"He who does not   come to Kosovo field,   20
may nothing grow   from the toil of his hands,
nor may there grow   the white wheat in his field,
nor on the hills   the vine in the vineyard!"

III

Serb Knez Lazar   celebrates *slavu*[8]
in Kruševac,   a well secluded town.

---

8. Here *slava* is used to indicate simply a celebration, and not the saint's day of the family, the usual meaning among Serbs. The term *knez* is a royal title, albeit a lord enfeoffed to a tsar, or emperor.

At the table   he seats all the nobles,
all great nobles   and their younger kinfolk.
On the right side   sits the old Jug Bogdan
and next to him   the nine Jugovićes.
On the left side   there sits Vuk Branković   30
and all other   nobles by age and rank:
first duke Miloš,   the proud standard-bearer,
and next to him   the two Serbian dukes:
one of these two   duke Ivan Kosančić,
and the other   Duke Milan Toplica.

The tsar picks up   the golden cup of wine,
and he speaks out   to all Serbian nobles:
"For whom should I   drink this cup of wine now?
If I drink it   first to our oldest lord,
I should drink first   to old Jug Bogdan's health.   40
If I drink it   by rank of lordliness,
I should drink first   to our Vuk Branković.
If I drink it   to the most graceful knight,
I should drink first   to nine brothers-in-law,
brothers-in-law,   the nine Jugovićes.
If I drink it   to manly handsomeness,
I should drink first   to Ivan Kosančić.
If I drink it   to the tallest of you,
I should drink first   to Milan Toplica.
If I drink it   to courage and bravery,   50
I should drink first   to Miloš Obilić.
So I will drink   now to none other's health
but to the health   of Miloš Obilić:
your health, Miloš,   both faithful and a traitor,
at first faithful,   afterwards a traitor!
On the morrow   you will forsake me there,
change to the side   of Murad, tsar of Turks.
To your good health!   I drink my toast to you!
Drink up the wine,   this cup in your honor."

Miloš jumps up,   stands on his nimble feet,   60
and he bows deep   all the way to the ground:
"Thank you, my lord,   glorious Knez Lazar!

Thank you, my lord,   for the toast and the cup,
for your own toast   and all your grace to me;
but there's no thanks   for the words you have said.
For may my faith   strike me down if I lie,
I have never   been unfaithful to you,
I've never been,   nor will I ever be.
For tomorrow   I plan to give my life
for Christian faith   there on Kosovo field.   70
The real traitor   is sitting by your knee,
close by your side,   drinking the cool red wine.
May you be damned,   traitor Vuk Branković!
Tomorrow is   a bright Saint Vitus Day.
We shall then see   there on Kosovo field
who is faithful   and who is the traitor.
And with God's help   and my great faith in Him,
I will then go   to Kosovo tomorrow,
and I will kill   the Turkish tsar, Murad,
and I will stand   with my foot on his throat.   80
If God grant me   and my good fortune too
that I return   alive to Kruševac,
I will take hold   of damned Vuk Branković,
I will tie him   onto my fighting spear,
as a woman   ties yarn onto distaff;
then I'll take him   out on Kosovo field."

           IV
"My sworn brother,   O Ivan Kosančić,
have you searched out   the Turkish force by now?
Are there many,   in their army of men?
Can we put up   a fight against the Turks?   90
Can we beat them   and gain a victory?"

To him answers   Duke Ivan Kosančić:
"O my brother,   my Miloš Obilić,
I have searched out   the Turkish force by now.
There are many   in their army of men.
If all of us,   we all would turn to salt,
we could not salt   the supper of the Turks.
It's already   more than fifteen days now

that I have walked   through all the Turkish horde,   100
I could not see   the end nor know its size:
from marble stone   to the dry maple grove,
from dry maple,   brother, to Sazlija,
to Sazlija,   the arch of the stone bridge,
from the stone bridge   to the town of Zvečan,
and from Zvečan,   brother, up to Čečan,
and from Čečan   to the mountain top,
all is covered   by the Turkish army:
horse after horse,   brave man after brave man,
battle lances   look like a black mountain,   110
and their banners   look as though they were clouds,
and their white tents   glitter like fields of snow.
If the quick rain   were to fall from heaven,
it could not drop   on the earth anywhere,
but on horses   and on brave warriors!
Murad has pounced   on the Mazgit meadow
and has taken   the Lab and Sitnica."

Again Miloš   asks his brother Ivan:
"Tell me, Ivan,   O my dear sworn brother,
where is the tent   of mighty Tsar Murad?   120
I have promised   to our good knez, Lazar
that I will kill   the Turkish tsar, Murad,
that I will stand   with my foot on his throat."

To this answers   Duke Ivan Kosančić:
"You are a fool,   O my dear sworn brother!
There at the tent   of great Sultan Murad,
there in the midst   of the mighty Turk camp,
e'en if you had   the wings of a falcon,
and if you fell   straight from the cloudless sky,
mere feathers can't   bear away so much flesh."   130

Then Duke Miloš   begs his brother Ivan:
"O my Ivan,   my dearest sworn brother,
not blood brother   but like a blood brother,
don't tell Lazar   the same way you told me,
For the good prince   will begin to worry

and the army,   all of them, will take fright,
but tell it thus,   to him this better way:
there are many   soldiers in their army,
but we can strike   at them and fight with them,
and we can win   an easy victory,   140
for their army   is not made of fighters
but it is made   of *hodjas* and *hadjis*,[9]
and of tradesmen   and of young merchants too
who haven't fought,   who've never seen battle;
they have just come   to earn a piece of bread.
And even what   there is of such an army,
many soldiers   have fallen badly ill,
are greatly ill   of serious dysentery,
and good horses   have also fallen ill
with a sickness   by the name of glanders."   150

      V

"Who was that man,   that brave man, mighty hero,
who with one blow   of his razor saber,
his sharp saber   and with his strong right arm,
cut and severed   twenty heads just like that?"

"That hero was   Banović Strahinja."

"Who was that man,   that brave man, mighty hero,
who with his lance   speared two by two the soldiers
and then threw them   into the Sitnica?"

"That hero was   Srdja Zlopogledja."

"Who was that man   that brave man, mighty hero,   160
On a good horse,   a stately sorrel horse,
With a banner   of the cross in his arm,
Who drove the Turks   into small frightened groups
And who pushed them   into the Sitnica?"

"That great hero   was Boško Jugović."

---

9. Pilgrims, religious men (those who have made the hegira or *haj* to Mecca), not fighters.

Tsar Lazar and Tsaritsa Milica[10]

"Tsar Lazar and Tsaritsa Milica" is a Kosovo narrative that seems curiously modern, a tale of war from a familial orientation centered around the concern that one of the Jugović brothers of Lazar's wife Milica survive the battle so that she would have him "to swear by" but also, of course, to provide her protection. It was sung (or recited) to Vuk in 1815 by Tešan Podrugović, a fighter in the Serbian insurrection, and as such it clearly identifies the Serbian as the Christian cause, the Turks as a depersonalized enemy.

It is in the nightmarish and highly selective imagery of the poem that it discloses a profoundly symbolic and primitive imagination. The recurring image of the crosses on the Serbian flag are significant not only to the Christian but the pagan imagination, for long before their conversion the cross was a mystic sign for the Serbian tribes and recurred on their artifacts. Thus their cross-bearing banner signifies differently for the different Jugovic brothers here, yet provides each with a motive for his commitment to battle.[11]

Yet the images frozen in the mind of Milica—whose will comes to dominate the poem and who brings her husband to suspend his curse on those of his cohorts who fail to come to the battle—are those that animate it.[12] The images of Goluban's warhorse called Swan (*labud* is a recurring attribute for the beautiful white horse in Serbian poetry) "spattered all in blood"; the severed hand borne by its wounded rider; the broken lances of both sides; these somehow compel our imagination. All of these are images found in the traditionally represented conversation between Milica and the ravens, but here they are realized only after the lady has lost consciousness. And there is a curiously ironic symmetry in Podrugović's conclusion, when Milica hears Goluban (from whom Lazar's curse had been lifted) close the poem with a curse of his own upon the descendants of the traditionally perfidious Vuk Branković. It is in such symbolically original use of traditional images, and in such shaping of the traditional closure, that one can recognize the genius of the singer.

---

10. "*Car Lazar i carica Milica,*" II, 209, #45

11. See Koljević, 162–64, and Pennington and Levi, 8.

12. Koljević has pointed out that "The first part of the poem seems to be in the masculine epic idiom of action and the choice of the 'honorable cross.' But the brothers' determination to fight and their refusal to stay with Milica is presented partly as the drama of her mind" (169).

Tsar Lazar and Tsaritsa Milica

The tsar, Lazar,   sits down to his dinner,
and beside him   Tsaritsa Milica.
His tsaritsa,   Milica speaks to him:
"O Tsar Lazar,   O Serbia's golden crown,
tomorrow you   will go to Kosovo.
You take with you   your servants and your dukes,
but here at home   you leave me with no one,
O Tsar Lazar,   not one among the men
to take to you   a letter from me here
to Kosovo,   to return with your letter.   10
You take with you   nine of my dear brothers,
all nine brothers,   the nine Jugovićes.
Leave here with me   at least one of the brothers,
just one brother   to swear by for his sister."

The Serbian prince,   Lazar answers to her:
"My dear lady,   Tsaritsa Milica,
which of the nine,   your brothers, do you wish
for me to leave   here at this our white court?"

"Leave here with me   dear Boško Jugović."

The Serbian prince,   Lazar then says to her: 20
"My dear lady,   Tsaritsa Milica,
when tomorrow   the new white day arrives,
the day arrives   and the sun warms the earth,
and the tall gates   of the city open,
and you walk out   out to the city's gates,
all of the men   will ride by in their ranks,
all the horsemen   under their war-banners.
They will be led   by Boško Jugović.
He will carry   the banner with a cross.
You can tell him   that with my full blessing   30
he can give up   the flag to whom he wishes,
so that he may   stay with you at our court."

On the morrow   when the dawn has broken
the city's gates   are both now opened wide,

she walks out there,   Tsaritsa Milica.
And she stands there,   right at the city's gate.
And there they come,   riders in regiments,
all the horsemen   under their war banners,
and they were led   by Boško Jugović,
on a chestnut   caparisoned in gold.   40
Flags of the Cross   now cover all of him,
O my brother,   him and his chestnut horse.
On his banner   there's a golden apple,
from the apple   protrude golden crosses,
from the crosses   dangle golden tassels,
tapping gently   on Boško's broad shoulders.

Toward him steps   Tsaritsa Milica.
And she seizes   the chestnut horse's rein,
she embraces   her brother round his neck,
and she whispers   to him in a low voice: 50
"O my brother,   O Boško Jugović,
our tsar, Lazar,   has granted you to me;
you're not to go   to fight at Kosovo.
He has also   given you his blessing,
you can present   the flag to whom you wish,
just so you stay   with me in Kruševac
so I can have   a brother to swear by."

But to her then   speaks Boško Jugović:
"Go, my sister,   back to the white tower,
for I would not   turn back from the battle,   60
nor would I loose   the banner from my hands,
for if the tsar   had gi'n me Kruševac,
yet all my men   would then say about me:
'Look at Boško,   the coward Jugović!
He did not dare   to go to Kosovo
to shed his blood   in honor of the Cross
and give his life   for the faith of Christians.'"
And then he rode   his horse on to the gate.

And now there comes   the dear old Jug Bogdan[13]
and behind him   seven Jugovićes.   70
Milica stopped   all seven of brothers,
not one of them   would even turn his head.

Sometime later,   a very little time,
comes a brother,   Vojin Jugović, too.
He leads with him   all the tsar's spare horses,
they're all bedecked,   caparisoned in gold.
And she seizes   his mount, the great bay horse,
embraces him,   her brother, round his neck,
and she begins   also to speak with him:
"O my brother,   my Vojin Jugović,   80
our tsar, Lazar,   has granted you to me;
he has also   given you his blessing;
to whom you wish,   you're to give the horses,
just so you stay   with me in Kruševac,
and I can have   a brother to swear by."
But her brother,   Vojin Jugović, says:
"Go, my sister,   back to the white tower,
for I would not   turn back from the battle.
I would not give   up the tsar's spare horses
e'en if I knew   that I would be killed there.   90
O my sister,   I'll go to Kosovo
to shed my blood   in honor of the Cross
and with brothers   to die for our good Faith."
And then he rides   his horse on out the gate.
When she sees that,   Tsaritsa Milica,
she falls down there   onto the hard cold stone;
as she falls down,   she loses consciousness.

---

13. Jug Bogdan, the father of the nine Jugovićes and of Milica, Lazar's wife, according to the Kosovo songs, appears frequently in the cycle. However, since it is known that the historical Milica was the daughter of Prince Vratko, a distant relative of Dušan (it was through his marriage to her that Lazar could claim the throne), it is highly likely that Jug Bogdan is, as we have said, entirely fictitious. Some surmise, however, that Jug Bogdan may have been another feudal lord, one Juga, who ruled from Leskovac, or a territory around that city. Juga is mentioned in records of 1395 as a vassal of Stefan Lazarević (Lazar's son and successor). See Z. Kostelski, *The Yugoslavs: The History of the Yugoslavs and Their States to the Creation of Yugoslavia* (New York: Philosophical Library, 1952), 340–41.

But then there comes   our glorious tsar, Lazar.
When he sees her,   dear Lady Milica,
the tears flow forth,   run down on his white cheeks.   100
He looks quickly   to the left and the right,
and then he calls   his servant Goluban:
"O Goluban,   O my faithful servant,
please now dismount   from your good horse, the Swan,
take the lady   in your two faithful arms,
and carry her   to our slender tower.
God forgives you,   and now with my blessing,
you will not go   to Kosovo to fight,
but remain here   in Kruševac's white court."

When he hears that,   the servant Goluban,   110
he lets the tears   trickle down his white face.
And he dismounts   from his good horse, the Swan,
takes the lady   in his two faithful arms,
and carries her   to the slender tower.
He did not heed,   nor listen to his heart
that he not go   to Kosovo to fight;
so he returns   to his good horse, the Swan,
and he mounts him   and goes to Kosovo.

On the morrow,   when the dawn has broken,
there come flying   the two pitch-black ravens   120
from Kosovo,   that wide and level field,
and they drop down   on the slender tower,
on the tower   of glorious Lazar.
One is cawing,   the other is speaking:
"This the tower   of famous Prince Lazar?
Or is no one   alive in the tower?"
No person there   in the tower hears it,
except for her,   Tsaritsa Milica.

Then she comes out   before the white tower
and she then asks   the two pitch-black ravens: 130
"For our Lord's sake,   you two pitch-black ravens,
whence have you come   on this very morning?
And could it be   you flew from Kosovo?
Have you seen there   those two mighty armies?

Have the armies   engaged one another?
And who, pray tell,   won the fierce battle?"

The two ravens   then answer unto her:
"For our Lord's sake,   Tsaritsa Milica,
yes, this morning   we flew from Kosovo.
We did see there   those two mighty armies.   140
The armies met   each other yesterday.
Both of the tsars   were killed in the battle.
Of the Turkish   only a few survived,
but of the Serbs,   whoever's left alive
is now wounded   and bleeding heavily."

As the ravens   finish in their reply,
there then appears   the servant Milutin.
He bears with him   his right hand in his left,
and upon him   are seventeen sharp wounds,
and his horse, Swan,   is splattered all in blood.   150
To him then speaks   Tsaritsa Milica:
"What has happened,   my servant Milutin?
Did you betray   your tsar at Kosovo?"

Then Milutin,   the servant, speaks to her:
"Help me, lady,   to dismount from my horse,
wash my body   in the coldest water,
give me red wine   to drink and quench my thirst.
For I've suffered   many grievous wounds."
And the lady   then helps him to dismount,
she washes him   in the coldest water,   160
and she gives him   the cool red wine to drink.

When the servant   regains some of his strength,
he is questioned   by Lady Milica:
"What, my servant,   happened at Kosovo?
Where did he die,   the glorious Prince Lazar?
Where did he die,   the good old Jug Bogdan?
Where did they die,   the nine Jugovićes?
Where did he die,   the noble Duke Miloš?
Where did he die,   our dear Vuk Branković?
Where did he die,   Banović Strahinja?"   170

Then the servant   begins to tell his tale:
"All of them died,   lady, at Kosovo.
Where also died   the glorious Prince Lazar,
there are many   high war-lances broken,
broken Turkish,   broken Serbian lances,
more Serbian   than the Turkish lances,
defending there,   my lady, their good lord,
their kindly lord,   the glorious Prince Lazar.
And Jug Bogdan,   lady, he lost his life
right at the start,   in the first skirmishes.   180
There perished, too,   the eight Jugovićes,
for a brother   will not betray a brother
as long as one   of them is still alive.
But there remained   still Boško Jugović.
His cross-banner   still waved o'er Kosovo.
And there he was,   still chasing Turks in droves,
as a falcon   chases the flocks of doves.
And where the blood   was deep up to one's knees,
there died also   Banović Strahinja.
And Duke Miloš,   O lady, he was killed   190
by Sitnica,   the cold water river,
where many Turks   did perish with him too.
Duke Miloš slew   the Turkish tsar, Murad,
all together   twelve thousand Turkish men.
May the good Lord   bless the one who bore him!
For he remains   in memory for the Serbs,
to be told now   and again, forever,
as long as man   and Kosovo exist.

"You ask about   the damned Vuk Branković.
May she be cursed,   the mother that bore him!   200
Also be cursed   all of his clan and race!
He did betray   his tsar at Kosovo
and took with him   his twelve thousand soldiers,
O my lady,   all evil men at arms."

The Fall of the Serbian Empire[14]

"The Fall of the Serbian Empire," which Vuk recorded from a blind woman singer in the Srem, reiterates a motif of the Old Church Slavic texts, a motif perhaps first employed by Jefimija in her "Prayer for Prince Lazar." For Lazar's choice of a heavenly kingdom over an earthly triumph as a explanation for the Serbian defeat on Kosovo field is not original to this song; indeed, it seems so familiar that it is almost casually contradicted in the song's closing lines. The recurrent accounts of Lazar's choice in Serbian literature suggest it as an emblem of the Serbian people's undeviating and indeed almost characterizing loyalty to their Orthodox Christian faith. Lazar's choice seems to enforce the peculiarly obsessional quality of the Kosovo songs, a quality that, given the awarenesses of more recent historical findings, seems to have led the singers away from historical accuracy.[15]

The Fall of the Serbian Empire

From that high town,   holy Jerusalem,
there comes flying   a gray bird, a falcon,
and in his beak   a small bird, a swallow.
Yet this gray bird   is not just a falcon;
it is our saint,   the holy Saint Elijah.
And the swallow   is not just a swallow,
but a message   from the Holy Virgin.[16]
The falcon flies   to Kosovo's flat field.
The message falls   in the lap of the tsar;
for Tsar Lazar   is the message destined: 10
"O Tsar Lazar,   prince of righteous lineage,
which of the two   kingdoms will you embrace?
Would you rather   choose a heavenly kingdom,
or have instead   an earthly kingdom here?
If, here and now,   you choose the earthly kingdom,
saddle horses,   tighten the saddles' girths,

14. *"Propast carstva Srpskoga,"* II, 214, #46.
15. See Koljević, 153–58.
16. Elijah, whose attribute is the raven, did not, by tradition, die, but ascended into heaven, thus transcending death.

let all the knights   put on their mighty swords,
and launch you then   assault against the Turks.
Then their army,   all the Turks, shall perish.

"But if, instead,   you choose the heavenly kingdom,   20
then you must build   a church at Kosovo.
Do not build it   upon a marble base,
but on pure silk   and costly scarlet cloth,
and give your host   orders to Holy Mass.[17]
For every man,   all soldiers, will perish,
and you, their prince,   will perish with your host."

When Tsar Lazar   has heard the whole message,
Lazar is vexed;   he ponders, he thinks much:
"O my dear lord,   what shall I ever do?
And of the two,   which kingdom should I choose?   30
Shall I now choose   the promised heavenly kingdom,
or shall I choose   an earthly kingdom here?
If I do choose,   I embrace the latter,
if I do choose   the earthly kingdom here,
then what I choose   is but a transient kingdom;
the eternal one   is that promised in heaven."

Lazar chooses   the heavenly kingdom;
he refuses   the earthly kingdom here.
So he has built   the church of Kosovo.
He does not build   upon a marble base,   40
but on pure silk   and costly scarlet cloth.[18]
He calls to him,   the Serbian patriarch;
beside him stand   twelve great Serbian bishops.
The whole army   comes to take communion.

No sooner have   the orders been given
than the Turks come   and assault Kosovo.

---

17. The service of Holy Communion to soldiers on the eve of battle was a convention of the Byzantine and thus, presumably, of the Serbian army. See Koljević, 161–62. Lazar built no church at or near Kosovo, although he did build Ravanica, some ten miles west of Ćuprija, near his court at Kruševac. But Ravanica (or Ravna, as it was then known) had been begun in 1376, thirteen years before the battle.

18. Scarlet was the royal color of the Rascian kings.

Old Jug Bogdan   bids his great host go forth
with his nine sons,   all nine Jugovićes,
his nine proud sons,   proud like nine gray falcons.
Each commands there   a host of nine thousand;   50
Old Jug Bogdan,   he has twelve thousand men.
All meet the Turks   and fight them with their swords;
they strike and slay   seven Turkish pashas.
When with the eighth   they begin to battle,
the old leader,   the brave Jug Bogdan, falls;
with him his sons,   all nine Jugovićes,
his nine proud sons,   proud like nine gray falcons,
and with them fall   the whole of their brave hosts.

Now others come,   Mrnjavčevićes three:
Ban Uglješa   and Voivode Gojko,   60
a third man, too,   the brave king Vukašin.
Each one leads forth   a host of thirty thousand.
They meet the Turks   and fight them with their swords;
they strike and slay   eight Turkish pashas there.
When with the ninth   they begin to battle,
two gray falcons,   Mrnjavčevićes, fall;
Ban Uglješa,   Voivode Gojko die.
King Vukašin   is most sorely wounded;
the Turks trample   upon him with their horses.
With these three fall   the whole of their brave host.   70

Archduke Stefan   then bids his host go forth,[19]
and his army,   numerous and mighty,
a great army,   sixty thousand in all.
They meet the Turks   and fight them with their swords;
they strike and slay   nine Turkish pashas there.
When with the tenth   they begin to battle,
but Stefan falls,   Archduke Stefan himself,
and with him falls   the whole of his brave host.

Prince Lazar, then,   bids his great host go forth.
The Serbian host   is numerous and mighty,   80

19. Stefan Musić, another of the heroes in the Kosovo songs, comes late to the battle (as we are told in "Stefan Musić"), but not too late to die there.

some seventy   and seven thousand men,
and they scatter   the Turks at Kosovo.
They leave the Turks   no time to look behind;
there is no chance   for Turks to stand and fight.

Prince Lazar then,   would overwhelm the Turks,
But may God's curse   be on Vuk Branković!
for he betrays   his prince and his wife's father,
and Lazar's host   is overwhelmed by Turks.
Now Lazar falls,   the Serbian Prince Lazar,
and with him falls   the whole of his brave host,   90
his seventy   and seven thousand men.

All this is done   with good grace and honor,
before the eyes   of God the Lord Almighty.

Assisted by Arash Bormanshinov

 # The Death of the Mother of the Jugovićes[20]

Many of the songs of the Kosovo cycle, and possibly the most honored of them, concern events after the battle and describe the realization of what has occurred there from the point of view of a female survivor. In so doing, in attending to the tragic history as it was seen by bystanders, the songs dramatize the symbolization of historical events. As Koljević has so aptly put it, "Instead of telling a story these songs enact a tragic drama of the mind, and this gives rise to their epic idiom in which tokens and symbols work out their ominous forebodings."

The nine brothers called the "Jugovićes" in the songs—the sons of Jug Bogdan—were often seen as the last generation of the Nemanjić dynasty; as such they were of great concern to the singers, for their death without issue meant to them the end of the house of Nemanja. Thus it is that before the Battle of Kosovo, according to "Tsar Lazar and Tsaritsa Milica," Milica calls upon one of them, Boško, to stay behind with her, and Lazar, who has cursed all who do not fight, exempts Boško from his curse. But Boško, of course, refuses and goes to the battlefield to die. Thus the Nemanjić line comes to its end.

20. "*Smrt majke Jugovića*," II, 220, #48.

"The Death of the Mother of the Jugovićes" was sent to Vuk from Croatia by an anonymous collector. Thus it was published in his second volume with the headnote, *iz Hrvatske* ("from Croatia").

The Death of the Mother of the Jugovićes
from Croatia

My God, my God,   what a wondrous marvel,
when the army   gathers at Kosovo!
In that army   are nine Jugovićes,
and a tenth one,   the old man, Jug Bogdan.
The nine's mother[21]   prays long to her dear God
that He give her   the eyes of an eagle
and the wide wings   of the white-feathered swan,
that she might fly   o'er Kosovo's flat field,
and might see there   the nine Jugovićes,
and a tenth one,   the old man, Jug Bogdan.   10

That which she asks,   God grants her readily:
God gives to her   the eyes of an eagle
and the wide wings   of the white-feathered swan,
and so she flies   o'er Kosovo's flat field.
There she finds them,   nine Jugovićes, dead,
as well the tenth,   the old man, Jug Bogdan.
There above them   stand their nine war-lances.
On the lances   are perched nine gray falcons.
Round the lances   are nine fine battle steeds,
and beside them   are nine ferocious hounds.   20
The nine fine steeds   thereon begin to neigh,
the nine fierce hounds   thereon begin to bay,[22]
nine gray falcons   thereon begin to shriek,
but even then   the mother's heart is firm;
her heart won't break,   she sheds no tears at all.
She leads away   the nine fine battle steeds,
and calls away   the nine ferocious hounds,

21. Like her husband and her nine sons, the unnamed mother of the Jugovićes is very likely not historical.

22. The text states that there are nine lions (*devet lava*); this seems a metaphoric description for hounds.

and bears away   the nine gray-winged falcons,
and she returns   to her high white palace.

Then from afar   her daughters-in-law see her,   30
and so toward her   they come ever closer.
The nine widows   thereon begin to wail,
the nine orphans   thereon begin to cry,
and nine fine steeds   thereon begin to neigh,
and nine fierce hounds   thereon begin to bay,
nine gray falcons   thereon begin to shriek,
but even then   the mother's heart is firm;
her heart won't break;   she sheds no tears at all.

When the night falls,   and the dark midnight comes,
Damjan's young horse,   the dapple-gray horse, neighs.   40
Damjan's mother   questions his faithful wife:
"My dear daughter,   and my Damjan's dear wife,
wherefore neighs so   Damjan's dapple-gray horse?
Is Damjan's horse   hungry now for white wheat?
Or does he thirst   for Zvečan's cold water?"[23]

Damjan's wife then   makes this answer to her:
"O my mother,   O Damjan's dear mother,
he does not neigh   because he wants white wheat,
nor does he thirst   for Zvečan's cold water,
for his master,   our Damjan, has taught him   50
to eat fine oats,   tiny oats, till midnight,
and then go forth   on roads after midnight.
The horse now mourns   his dear lord and master,
for he did not   bring him home on his back."
But even then,   the mother's heart is firm;
her heart won't break,   she sheds no tears at all.

On the next morn,   when the sun has risen,
there fly to her   a pair of black ravens,
wings all bloodied,   all up to their shoulders,

23. Damjan is the youngest of the Jugović brothers, according to the songs. His dapple-gray horse, Zelenko, is well known to all Serbian children. The water is from the cistern of Zvečan fortress, an ancient Nemanjić fortification above the Ibar River near Kosovska Mitrovica.

and a white foam   flowing from their beaks.   60
One carries here   a warrior's severed hand;
a wedding ring,   gilded, is on that hand.[24]
He drops the hand   into the mother's lap.

She takes that hand,   the mother of the nine,
she turns it round,   then she turns it over,
and then she speaks   to Damjan's widowed wife:
"My dear daughter,   and my Damjan's dear wife,
can you now tell   just whose hand this might be?"

Damjan's wife then   makes this answer to her:
"O my mother,   O Damjan's dear mother,   70
this is the hand   of our beloved Damjan,
for, my mother,   I recognize this ring.
This very ring   was with me when we wed."

She takes the hand,   the mother of Damjan,
she turns it round,   then she turns it over,
and to the hand   she softly speaks these words:
"O you dear hand,   my precious green apple,[25]
where did you grow,   and where were you plucked off?
On this my lap,   you, Damjan's hand, grew up;
you were plucked off   on Kosovo's flat field."   80

The mother's heart   then is swollen with grief,
as her heart swells   and at the last it breaks
for her nine sons,   the nine Jugovićes,
and for the tenth,   the old man, Jug Bogdan.

 ## The Kosovo Maiden[26]

"The Kosovo Maiden" sharply contrasts with "The Death of the Mother of the Jugovićes." That poem describes the end of the old order as per-

24. Koljević tells us that, in fact, "the most beautiful Serbian rings at the end of the fourteenth century were made not of gold but of silver gilt." See Koljević, 171.

25. *Zelena jabuko* ("green, or unripe, apple"), a term of endearment appropriate to youth, is also used here in an internal rhyme: "*moja ruko, zelena jabuko!*"

26. "*Kosovka djevojka*," II, 231, #51.

ceived by an aristocratic member of its establishment; its protagonist's sense of moral order is sustained, even as she confronts the horror of realization that is the poem's climax. In "The Kosovo Maiden," in which the perceiving character is presented as an innocent peasant girl, one has the sense of a moral and natural order inverted by the battle's horrors.

"The Kosovo Maiden" was first written down from the singing of an old blind woman in the Srem. It opens with the description of a beautiful Sunday morning after the battle and sets this description against detailed representations of the horrors of the battlefield. The poem also sets these horrors against accounts of beneficent acts that resonate with recognitions of the time-honored traditions of the Serbian domestic arts and hospitality.

It is again Koljević who suggested that "the astounding accuracy of historical detail" in this song "may be the result of a memorization of particular formulas . . . characteristic of women singers."[27] Whether or not this is true, one cannot fail to be struck by the force of the poem's final figure, which, in all its loveliness, communicates the horror of an almost unnatural isolation, an isolation that was to be the fate of so many of the Serbs, particularly the women, in the years to follow.

The Kosovo Maiden

She wakes early,   the Kosovo maiden;
rises early,   on a Sunday morning,
on a Sunday,   before a warm, bright sun.
Both her white sleeves   there upon her fair arms,
both her white sleeves   are rolled to her elbows,
and on her back   she carries her white bread.
And in her hands   are two golden vessels;
the one of them   is filled with cold water,
and the other   is filled with rosy wine.
And she sets out   for Kosovo's flat plain.

The maiden walks   over all the war field,   10
o'er the war field   of the prince of honor.
She turns over   every bloody warrior,
and when she finds   a warrior still alive,

---

27. See Koljević, 168, also 171–72.

she washes him   with the cooling water,
she offers him   a cup of rosy wine,
and she feeds him   with her well-baked bread.

She encounters,   as her fate has willed it,
a young hero,   brave Pavle Orlović,[28]
guidon bearer,   a youth who served Lazar,
and she finds him   still alive and conscious.   20
But his right arm   is cut off completely,
and his left leg   is severed at the knee,
and his brave chest   is crushed in and broken.
His bloody lungs   are horrible to see.

She bears him off,   away from his pooled blood,
and she bathes him   with the cooling water,
she offers him   the cup of rosy wine,
and she feeds him   with her well-baked white bread.

When the warrior   regains sufficient strength,
he speaks to her,   young Pavle Orlović: 30
"O my sister,   O Kosovo maiden,
What misfortune   so great has come to you,
that now you turn   all these bleeding warriors?
Whom do you seek,   maiden, on the war field?
Your own brother,   or paternal nephew?
Do you search out   your old, revered father?"

Then she answers,   the Kosovo maiden:
"O my brother,   O dear, unknown warrior,
I do not seek   any of my kindred,
neither brother,   nor paternal nephew,   40
nor do I seek   my old, revered father.
You may recall,   O dear, unknown warrior,
when for three weeks   a group of thirty monks
said holy Mass   for Prince Lazar's army
at the fine church   there at Samodreža.
The whole army   of Serbs did purge their sins.
The last to come   were three mighty voivodes:

28. Pavle Orlović seems to be entirely fictitious.

the first of them,   the voivode, Miloš,
and the second,   brave Ivan Kosančić   50
the third of them,   young Milan Toplica.[29]

"That day I came   to the church door by chance,
and past me strode   the mighty voivode, Miloš,
in all this world   a most handsome warrior.
He dragged his sword   along the cobblestones.
His silken hat   was fur-lined, feather-dressed;
he also wore   a richly colored coat;
around his neck   he wore a silk kerchief.
He glanced about,   and he caught sight of me;
he loosed his coat,   his richly colored coat,   60
he took it off   and offered it to me:
'Take this, young girl,   my richly colored coat;
you should keep me   in remembrance by it,
for with my name   is my coat embroidered.
I'm on my way   to death, you lovely girl,
to Lazar's camp,   that holy prince of ours.
Pray to our God   for me, you lovely girl,
that I return   from this great war unharmed,
and that you, too,   shall find happy fortune.
Then I shall wed   you to my dear Milan,   70
Milan, in God   and by oath, my brother,
who swore to be   my brother by our God,
the Almighty,   and by St. John the Blest.
When you are wed,   I'll serve as his best man!'

"After him strode   brave Ivan Kosančić,
in all this world   a most handsome warrior.
He dragged his sword   along the cobblestones.

---

29. Miloš here is Miloš Obilić (or Kobilić, or Kobilović), historically a lesser Serbian noble, but in the songs elevated in rank. Miloš, as we have seen, was accused of treason on the eve of the battle, but proved himself by entering the camp of the sultan by ruse and killing him. Ivan Kosančić, another of the Serbian nobles, is mentioned in the songs as a spy for the Serbs, who returns to Miloš and, visibly shaken, reports the magnitude of the Turkish army. Milan Toplica was, presumably, a young noble of the valley that Lazar and his army occupied after the fall of Niš to the Turks. The three—the *pobratimi*, or sworn brothers—are mentioned together frequently in the songs. The swearing of brotherhood is an honored ritual in Serbian custom. The traditional oath on the occasion was "by God and by St. John."

His silken hat   was fur-lined, feather-dressed;
he also wore   a richly colored coat;
around his neck   he wore a silk kerchief,   80
and on his hand   a gilded wedding ring.
He glanced about,   and he caught sight of me;
from his own hand   he took his gilded ring.
He took it off   and offered it to me:
'Take this, young girl,   my gilded wedding ring;
you should keep me   in remembrance by it,
for with my name   the ring is graven deep.
I'm on my way   to death, you lovely girl,
to Lazar's camp,   that holy prince of ours.
Pray to our God   for me, you lovely girl,   90
that I return   from this great war unharmed,
and that you, too,   shall find happy fortune.
Then I shall wed   you to my dear Milan,
Milan, in God,   and by oath my brother,
who swore to be   my brother by our God,
by God Himself,   and by St. John the Blest.
When you are wed,   I'll be the first witness!'[30]

"After him strode   young Milan Toplica,
in all this world   a most handsome warrior.
He dragged his sword   along the cobblestones.   100
His silken hat   was fur-lined, feather-dressed;
he also wore   a richly colored coat;
around his neck   he wore a silk kerchief,
and on his arm   a gold embroidered shawl.
He glanced about,   and he caught sight of me,
and off his arm   he took his golden shawl.
He took it off,   and offered it to me:
'Take this, young girl,   my gold embroidered shawl;
you should keep me   in remembrance by it,
for with my name   is the shawl embroidered.   110
I'm on my way   to death, you lovely girl,
to Lazar's camp,   that holy prince of ours.

30. The nearest, but not exact, equivalent of the *kum* at a Serbian wedding is the "best man,"
or first witness.

Pray to our God   for me, you lovely girl,
that I return   from this great war unharmed,
and that you, too,   shall find happy fortune.
Then I shall wed   you as my faithful bride.'
And off they went,   the three most brave voivodes.
It's them I seek   on the war field today."

Then again speaks   young Pavle Orlović:
"O my sister,   O Kosovo maiden,   120
do you see, there,   those battle spears, my girl,
there, where the pile   is highest and most dense?
So—it is there   where the great warriors bled;
blood was as high   as stirrups on a horse,
up to the strap   of stirrup, where they mount,
up to the waist,   the silken belt of soldiers.
There all three fell;   they died there, together.
Now you go home,   home to your white-walled house,
lest the blood stain   your skirt's hem and your sleeves."

As the girl hears   these strange and awful words,   130
she sheds hot tears   down her mournful white face.
She leaves for home,   for her own white-walled house,
and as she leaves   she wails from her white throat:
"O woe is me,   girl of wretched fortune!
Were I to touch,   just touch, a green pine tree,
even that pine,   that green tree would wither."

Assisted by Arash Bormanshinov

4 Marko Kraljević

*A*FTER THE DEATH of Prince Lazar on Kosovo field, the fate of the Serbian kingdom, and of the Serbs, fell into the hands of his extraordinary wife, Milica. Milica competed for hegemony in the Balkans with, among others, Vuk Branković. On the Serbian lands she ruled as regent for her son, Stefan Lazarević, until 1395, when Lazarević came of age. Then Milica retired to a monastery, and the dynasty was able to continue for around seventy years after the battle of Kosovo.

But the entry of the Turks onto the European continent generated many social and cultural changes in the area, especially the migration north and west, first of scholars and intellectuals—which some scholars have identified as the beginning of the Renaissance in Europe—then of broader segments of the general population. Stefan Lazarević proved to be a gentle and a rather literary and humane man, too forgiving to make a strong leader. His loyalty to the sultan cost him much of his kingdom at the hands of Hungarian crusaders. The Brankovićes controlled Old Serbia, so Lazarević now ruled from Belgrade, not Rascia; he had lost much in population as well as land.[1]

Lazarević recovered some of his land to the south of Belgrade and ruled until 1427, leaving his throne to his old rival, Djordje Branković. During his reign Lazarević's court had been a haven for Christian scholars. But the Christian nobles one by one had capitulated to the sultan—"Leaf by leaf they were swallowed like an artichoke," as one historian put

1. See Koljević, 153–58.

it.[2] So Djordje Branković ceded Belgrade to the Hungarians and established his fortress at Smederevo. Salonika fell in 1430 and the newly aggressive Murad II laid siege to and captured Smederevo in 1439. Novo Brdo, an important mining and economic center, remained a center of Christian culture for two more years, but it too fell to the Turks in 1441.

Djordje Branković remained neutral in the Hungarian crusades against the Turks. Hunyadi and the Hungarians were at first successful, defeating the Turks at Varna in 1444, but in a second crusade the Christian forces were defeated, ironically once again on Kosovo field, in 1448.[3] Mohammed II succeeded Murad in 1451 and, as "the Conqueror," entered Constantinople in 1453. So, although Djordje's son Lazar (whose sister Olivera had been the wife of Murad and the mother of Mohammed) technically succeeded him, it was Mohammed who was Djordje's real successor. The Turks completed their conquest of Bosnia in 1466, and of Albania in 1467—in spite of the valiant resistance of George Castriota (known as "Skenderbeg" in the songs)—so that by then all the lands south of the Danube, except Belgrade, the Dalmatian coast under Venetian protection, and Zeta (Montenegro, where the valiant Crnojevićes offered resistance and held the Turks at bay with relative effectiveness), were in Turkish hands. Belgrade fell to Suleiman the Magnificent in 1521, and many of its citizens were forcibly repopulated in Belgrat, outside the walls of what was now Istanbul. Now the Balkans were indeed a Turkish *pashalik.*[4]

So it is no surprise that the years of the Turkish occupation saw the population of the Balkans diminish. Many, especially the Serbian townspeople, left their homes to cross over into the Hungarian lands of what is today Croatia or into the Srem or Baranja, Bačka, and the Banat (today the Vojvodina), lands granted to Serbian noble families by Hungarian kings. In 1583 a Roman Catholic prelate complained that Serbs made up half the population of Catholic Hungary; whether or not it was true, certainly these lands offered a refuge to Orthodox Serbs during the Turkish occupation. But in and around the Balkan mountains, south of the Sava

2. See Temperley, *History of Serbia*, 104. Other historical surveys of the period that have been useful here are Jelavich, *History of the Balkans*, and Jireček, *Istorija Srba.*

3. After the battle Janos Hunyadi, the leader of the Christian forces, was held captive for a time by Djordje Branković, thus providing further evidence for the treacherous actions of the Brankovićes.

4. For administrative purposes Serbia was divided into four, with pashas at Belgrade, Vidin, Niš, and Leskovac. See Clissold, ed., *Short History of Yugoslavia*, 106, and Edwards, *Yugoslavia*, 169–70.

and the Danube, the populace that remained were mostly peasants who worked the land of the *spahis,* either Turks or, more often, converted Slavs or Albanians, who provided cavalry for the sultan. The Serbs who remained continued to live in their *zadrugas,* or extended family communities, always near to their sacred mountains, accepting Turkish authority but not their religion, which the Turks in their turn did not attempt to impose on them. For the Turks were content to reduce them to a simple *raja,* or "herd," an infidel but obedient peasantry with diminished rights and almost no judicial standing.[5]

There were many responses on the part of the singers to this situation. But the best known, and certainly the most ethically complex, of the heroic songs sung during the time of the Turks were those setting forth the life and exploits of a fourteenth-century prince of Prilep in what is today Macedonia, Marko Kraljević. Marko Kraljević, or "Marko the Prince," occupied an anomalous place in late medieval Balkan history, and it is perhaps that anomaly that has generated the special qualities of his heroism and the unique devotion to him as a central figure in the oral poetry. For Prince Marko (or *Kral Marko,* "King Marko," as he is known in Macedonia) it was a place that satisfied a psychological need for a defeated people. For Marko was conceived by the singers as a disempowered hero, who nevertheless achieves his ends by great personal strength and cunning, and by whatever other means are at hand.

Historically Prince Marko (Marko Kraljević) was the son of Vukašin Mrnjavčević (whom we have already seen presented by the singers as a dwarfish monster), the elder of the two noble brothers who refused to accept the authority of Uroš IV after the death of Stefan Dušan in 1355. Vukašin declared himself king at Prilep. As we have also seen, his and his brother Uglješa's rebellion was important in the factionalization of the Balkan Christian nobles, which led to their defeat at the battle of Marica in 1371. Marko succeeded his father at Prilep after the latter's death at Marica in 1371, and in 1385, a few years before the battle of Kosovo, he became vassal lord to Sultan Murad II. But Marko, and his people, remained Christian and apparently relatively independent. Indeed, his kingdom

---

5. Indeed, at least in the early years of the Turkish domination the Serbian peasant may well have enjoyed greater religious tolerance than he would have under the more aggressive Roman Catholic Hungarians. One song tells how Janos Hunyadi answered Djordje Branković, who had asked what faith would be imposed if Serbia accepted Hungarian liberation, with a word, "the Latin"; when the same question was asked of the sultan, he said, "I will leave the people to bow in the mosque or to cross themselves in church as they will." See Clissold, 105.

was sufficiently autonomous for him to mint his own silver currency, which bore a Christian inscription. For some reason Marko seems not to have fought on the side of the Turks at Kosovo, but he died in their service in Wallachia at the battle of Rovine in 1394.

It is of his death there that the first extant account of him arises; in 1427 it was recorded by Konstantin Filozof that on the eve of the battle of Rovine he told his best friend, "[I] pray God to give His help to the Christians, even if I am the first to be killed in this war." Thus, in the first record we have of him, the anomalous nature of Marko's situation as Christian knight and Turkish vassal was recognized.

That anomaly was being confronted and rendered even more complex in Dalmatia a hundred years later. In 1547, in a report of the city of Split to the Venetian senate, there is mention of a blind soldier singing of Marko in the streets and being joined by his audience. A few years later Marko appears in a *bugarštica*, as a brigand and fratricide, quarrelling with his brother, the gentle Andrija, over the division of booty, losing his temper, and killing him. Apparently there was an effort to rehabilitate Marko, for, in the eighteenth century, songs tell how Marko revenges his brother Andrija's death at the hands of the Turks by killing his murderers. And throughout the century, in the decasyllabic songs of Dalmatia and Slavonia, the story of Prince Marko continued to grow in moral complexity. The Marko of the songs took on qualities of superhuman strength and endurance, but at the same time he came to be presented as a trickster, who gains his ends by ruse, not through sheer power. And at the same time Marko was shown to be defiant of his overlords, the Turks. So this mighty man of Macedonia, this successor in his region's mythology to the Thracian horseman and to Saint George himself, became at the same time recognizably—and comically—a peasant hero.

The Serbian singers who sang to Vuk of Marko presented a similarly anomalous character. Now provided a magical sword and a magnificent and highly intelligent horse (Šarac, that dappled horse, takes on a character of his own), and endowed with a strength sufficient to squeeze water from wood dried nine years, Marko is still superman and confidence man, noble knight and scoundrel, ready to die for honor and to kill for fun, the protector of the oppressed, but hotheaded and a heavy drinker, a noble who does peasant's work and has a peasant's interests and cunning. With these singers—or singer, for Vuk heard most of the Marko songs from Tešan Podrugović—all these contradictions are described with a rich narrational irony, a sense of the comic that at the same time reflects a recognition of how Marko's situation as hero and buffoon was relevant to all the Christian peoples of the Balkans.[6]

 ## Marko Kraljević Recognizes His Father's Saber[7]

Among the songs sung to Vuk by Tešan Podrugović, "Prince Marko Recognizes His Father's Saber" has some elements of historicity. For Marko's father Vukašin was killed in battle at Marica in 1371, and the song is certainly real enough, both psychologically and politically. For this song—which opens in a recitation of entirely conventional elements: the redemptive woman, the linen cloth as her instrument of redemption, the sanctity of the sworn filial (or in this case sisterly) relationship—devolves into an account of almost gratuitous cruelty associated with absolute power: a man is killed only because the killer desires a "steel sword."

But this cruelty generates a "sisterly" curse, which comes to pass with Marko Kraljević as God's instrument. And Marko thus remains, like Achilles, sulking in his tent, until he insultingly confronts the sultan himself, only to have his wrath bought off by the frightened leader with a hundred ducats. Certainly Marko's vindication here is a bit debased, but perhaps—as is so often the case in Podrugović's Marko songs—given his situation, it is as complete as one might expect.[8]

Marko Kraljević Recognizes His Father's Saber

A Turkish girl   rose early in the morn,
well before dawn,   before the shiny light,
to wash linen   in Marica's river.
Before the sun   the water was most clear;
after sunrise   it became quite murky,
began to flow   murkily and bloody,
for it carried   dead horses and fur caps.
Before the noon   it bore wounded warriors,
and thus it brought   one such wounded hero.

---

6. For the above account we are much indebted to Koljević, 52–58, 177–81.
7. "*Marko Kraljević poznaje očinu sablju*," II, 245, #57.
8. See Koljević, 187–89.

The river flow   caught him in its whirlpool,   10
twisted him round,   there in the Marica.

Then the warrior   saw her by the water,
and he began   to call her his sister.
"Sister in God,   O beautiful maiden,
throw me an end   of the cloth you're washing,
and pull me out   of Marica's river.
Then I'll leave you   in peace and in honor."[9]

The Turkish girl   with God's name took his word,
threw him an end   of the cloth she's washing,
and pulled him out   of Marica River.   20
The warrior bore   seventeen grievous wounds.
He wore strange clothes   most strange-looking clothing,
and on his hip   a keen, well-forged saber,
on the saber   a triple-headed hilt,
and on each head   three shining precious stones
of a value   of three of tsar's cities.

The warrior spoke   to the Turkish maiden:
"O my sister,   O you Turkish maiden,
who is present   in your stately white home?"
The Turkish girl   then answered the warrior: 30
"I have at home   my own aged mother,
and a brother,   my own Mustaf Aga."

The wounded man   then talked to her again:
"O my sister,   O you Turkish maiden,
go and tell him,   brother Mustaf Aga
to receive me,   in your stately white home.
I have with me   three large belts of treasure,
with three hundred   ducats in each of them.
I will give you   one belt as a present,
the other one   to your Mustaf Aga,   40
and the third belt   I will keep for myself,
thus to take care   of all my grievous wounds.

---

9. A frequent event in the songs is the salvation of a warrior by a Serbian girl by use of a piece of linen; but here the girl is Turkish.

If with God's will   I do survive my wounds,
I will leave you   in peace and in honor,
both you and yours,   your good brother Mustaf."

The Turkish girl   went to her whitewashed home,
told her brother,   the good Mustaf Aga:
"O my brother,   O good Mustaf Aga,
I have just seen   a much wounded hero
by the river,   the cool, swift Marica.   50
He has with him   three large belts of treasure,
with three hundred   ducats in each of them.
He will give me   one belt as a present,
and another   to you, brother Mustaf,
and the third belt   he will keep for himself,
thus to take care   of all his grievous wounds.
Do not, brother,   fall into temptation
to slay him there,   that much-wounded hero,
but bring him here   to our white home instead."

And so the Turk   went to the Marica.   60
When he saw him,   that much-wounded hero,
he then looked down   and saw his well-forged saber;
he drew it forth   and he cut off his head.
He then took off   all his lovely clothing
and left quickly   for his whitewashed manor.
His dear sister   came out front to meet him,
but when she saw   that which he had just done,
she spoke to him,   brother Mustaf Aga:
"Why, O brother,   may God pay you in kind,
why did you slay   my good brother in God?   70
What did tempt you   to such an evil deed?
What was it for?   All for a steel saber?
O may God grant   that it cut your head off!"
When she'd said this,   she ran to the tower.

A short time passed   since she had spoken thus.
The Turkish tsar   ordered in a letter
Mustaf Aga   should go to the army.
And Mujo went   to the great tsar's army.
There on his belt   he wore the forged saber.

When he arrived   in the tsar's great army,   80
the great and small   watched the well-forged saber,
but no one could   draw it from its scabbard.
The saber passed   around from hand to hand,
until it came   to Marko Kraljević.
Then the saber   unsheathed all by itself.

But when Marko   looked close at the saber,
he saw on it   three clear Christian letters:
one was the mark   of old Novak the smith,
the second that   of the king, Vukašin,
the third the mark   of Marko Kraljević.   90
Marko then asked   the Turk, Mustaf Aga:
"So help you God,   you young Turkish soldier,
where did you find   this sharp, well-forged saber?
Did you buy it   for a sum of money?
Did you win it   in a glorious battle?
Did your father   leave it in legacy,
or did your wife   bring it upon marriage,
bring it to you   as a part of dowry?"

Mustaf Aga,   the Turk, answered him thus:
"So help me God,   you infidel Marko,   100
since you ask me,   I'll tell you honestly."
And he told him   just the way it happened.

Then he answered,   did Marko Kraljević:
"Why, O you Turk,   may great God be your judge,
why did you not   help him to heal his wounds?
I would have now   given you aga's wealth
through our master,   the honorable tsar."

Mustaf Aga   answers him in these words:
"Don't be a fool,   you infidel Marko;
if you could gain   all those aga's treasures,   110
then you'd take them,   all of them for yourself.
So return it,   that sharp well-forged saber."
At that Marko   of Prilep swung the sword,
and he cut off   the head of Mustafa.

The men there sped   to tell it to the tsar,
who sent for him,   Marko, through his servants.
As they hurried,   one by one, to Marko,
they called Marko,   but he did not answer.
He just sat there   drinking the cool red wine.
When at long last   he was annoyed enough,   120
he turned his coat   of sheepskin inside out,
he took with him   his heavy six-spiked mace,
and he went forth,   straight to the tsar's own tent.

He was angry,   our Marko Kraljević.
So he sat down   in his boots on the prayer rug
and he looked there   from the side at the tsar,
with bloody tears   running out of his eyes.[10]
When the tsar saw   Marko's frightful anger
and before him   his heavy six-spiked mace,
he moved away,   but Marko moved closer,   130
and thus he pushed   the tsar to the white wall.

Then the tsar put   his hand in his pocket,
and he took out   a hundred gold ducats,
and he gave them   to Marko Kraljević:
"Here, Marko, go   and drink your fill of wine!
Who has made you   so frightfully angry?"
"Do not ask me,   O my foster-father![11]
I've recognized   my father's saber now,
and if great God   had placed it in your hands,
I would have been   just as angry with you."   140
And he got up   and went to his own tent.

 ## Prince Marko's Plowing[12]

"Prince Marko's Plowing" was recorded on at least two occasions. The earlier version was written down around 1720 by an unknown German

---

10. Marko's disrespect for Islamic custom is indicated by his inappropriate dress, his failure to remove his boots on entering the sultan's tent, and his position—not vis à vis but "at the side" of his collocator.

11. Vukašin was enfeoffed to the sultan, thus, ironically, under his protection.

12. "*Oranje Marka Kraljevića,*" II, 313, #73.

gentleman in his collection of Slavic soldiers' songs sung in the Austrian camps in Slavonia. This manuscript, which lay unnoted for two hundred years in archives, was discovered in 1913 in Erlangen University Library; it tells of Marko's agreeing, then refusing, to plow, and of his subsequent tricking, killing, and robbing of an Arab traveler. Vuk's was the later version; it was recorded from an anonymous singer. Vuk's is less violent and is well the superior version.[13]

In the song Marko's mother is identified as Jevrosima. She appeared in "The Wedding of King Vukašin" as *dilber Jevrosima,* or "the beautiful Jevrosima," and marries Vukašin at the end of the poem. Now, in the Marko poems, she is much older, and is as wise as she was once beautiful. But this queen-mother's concerns in "Prince Marko's Ploughing" are those of a peasant—with the burdens of difficult laundry and the sufficiency of the food supply—most realistic and unheroic. Indeed, here Marko's devotion to his mother (it is unwavering throughout the songs) consists in his accepting (in his own way) her wise advice to give up heroics for commitment to agricultural tasks. This is advice that the later *guslars* could very well understand.

Prince Marko's Plowing

Bold Prince Marko   sits and drinks the red wine
with his mother,   dear old Jevrosima.[14]
And as these two   finish off the bottle,
the old mother   starts to talk to Marko:
"O my dear son,   my own son, Prince Marko,
stop this fighting,   this incessant warfare,
for no good comes   out of all this evil,
and your mother   is now very tired
of the washing   of blood from your clothing.
So take the plow   and a team of oxen.   10
Do some plowing;   plow the fields and valleys.

---

13. See Koljević, 81, 87.

14. Jevrosima, Marko's aged mother, was represented in "The Wedding of King Vukašin" as the sister of "Duke Momčilo," a historically ambiguous Hercegovinan noble (or high outlaw) whom Vukašin killed in ambush/battle out of lust for Momčilo's traitorous wife, Vidosava, who was subsequently discovered and killed. Historically, however, Momčilo seems to have died in battle with the Turks in 1361, and Vukašin did not marry his sister. See Koljević, 127–28, and Low, *Ballads of Marko Kraljević,* 1–9.

Sow some white corn;   we could use some produce
which would nourish   both you and your mother."

Now Prince Marko   does his mother's bidding.
He takes a plow   and a team of oxen,
but he doesn't   plow the fields and valleys;
rather, he plows   right down the tsar's highway.

Down that road come   the Turks' janissaries;
they have with them   three large bags of booty.
And they call out   to that bold Prince Marko: 20
"Hold it, Marko,   don't plow up the road here!"

"You Turks hold it!   You stay off the furrows!"[15]

"Hold it, Marko,   don't plow up the road here!"

"You Turks, hold it!   You stay off the furrows!"

Now when Marko   gets fed up with this talk,
he picks right up   his plow and his oxen,
and he kills them,   the Turks' janissaries.
Then he seizes   the three bags of booty,
and he takes them   to his dear old mother:
"Look here what I   plowed up for you today!"   30

Assisted by Dragana McFadden

 Marko Drinks Wine at Ramadan[16]

At the end of the seventeenth century, years after Suleiman the Magnificent had passed from the scene and during the crisis of domestic and imperial administration after the revolt of the janissaries, which led to the decline of the empire, repressive prohibitions were issued from the Divine

---

13. According to Turkish law, any *raja*, or Christian subject, meeting a Muslim (a Turk) on a road must stop, dismount, and do the Muslim's bidding. On the other hand, no *spahi* (Turkish landlord) was permitted to interfere in the peasant's use of his fields—other, of course, than to collect rents and crop shares due him. Thus, by law and custom, the road was the Turk's, the fields the Serb's. See Temperley, *History of Serbia*, 115–22, and von Ranke, *History of Servia*, 38–53.

16. "*Marko pije uz ramazan vino*," II, 307, #71.

Porte against the *raja*. Among them were prohibitions against the wearing of brightly colored (and thus expensively dyed) clothing and against the drinking of alcohol during Ramadan, the forty days of fasting in the Islamic calendar. The idea of dancing with Turkish girls probably rarely even occurred to the Christian peasantry.[17]

But what certainly did occur to the Christian peasants was the possibility of defiance—especially if the defiance bore no consequence. Certainly such would be difficult for a real person, but not for an imaginary hero. And as the Germans had their Till Eulenspeigel, so the South Slavs had their Marko Kraljević. In this song, sung to Vuk by an anonymous singer, Marko serves an important function of the hero of folk poetry; he defies authority, in this case the sultan's decrees, and gets away with it. Whether the sultan here—anachronistically, Suleiman—is wise enough to temper justice with mercy and generosity (for the true peasant always believes that justice resides on high), or whether his motive is pure fear is left for the hearer (or reader) to judge.

Vuk wrote down "Marko Drinks Wine at Ramadan" from an anonymous singer.

Marko Drinks Wine at Ramadan

Tsar Suleiman	sends sternly forth a law:
no wine at all	be drunk at Ramadan,
that no *dolmans*[18]	of green cloth should be worn,[19]
that no sabers,	too well-wrought, be carried,
that no dancing	with Turk girls be allowed.
Marko dances	a *kolo*[20] with the Turk girls,
Marko girdles	his well-wrought sharp saber,
Marko puts on	a *dolman* of green cloth,
Marko drinks wine	freely at Ramadan,
and he forces	the *hodjas* and *hadjis*
to drink wine there	all together with him.

The Turks hurry	to complain to the tsar:
"Tsar Suleiman,	our father and mother,

10

---

17. See Koljević, 189–91, and Pennington and Levi, 61.
18. The *dolman* is a long, embroidered belt, much prized by nobles of the time.
19. Green was a color associated with high rank and thus forbidden to the *raja*.
20. The *kolo* is a round dance with a quick step, known throughout the Balkans.

did you not send   your stern legal decree:
no wine at all   be drunk at Ramadan,
that no dolmans   of green cloth should be worn,
that no sabers,   too well-wrought, be carried,
that no dancing   with Turk girls be allowed.
Marko dances   *kolo* with Turkish girls,
Marko girdles   his well-wrought sharp saber,   20
Marko puts on   a dolman of green cloth,
Marko drinks wine   freely at Ramadan.
It's not enough   to drink wine by himself,
but he forces   the *hodjas* and *hadjis*
to sit with him   and drink the red wine too.

When Suleiman   understands their complaints,
he now sends forth   most quickly two heralds:
"Go right away,   O you two young heralds,
and tell the prince,   Prince Marko Kraljević,
that the sultan   summons him for a talk."   30

The two heralds,   two young lads, then set forth.
When they come up   to Marko Kraljević,
they see Marko   drinking wine in his tent.
In front of him   stands a cup of twelve *okes*.[21]
The two heralds   begin to speak to him:
"Do you hear us,   O Marko Kraljević!
The tsar summons   you to him for a talk,
for you to go   to him for a *divan*."[22]
Marko's anger   grows to great dimensions.
so he seizes   his cup full of red wine,   40
and then with it   he strikes the tsar's heralds.
The huge cup breaks,   but so do the two heads;
both wine and blood   spill and intermingle.

Marko then goes   to the tsar for a talk.
There he sits down   there by the tsar's right knee.
His sable cap   he pulls over his eyes,

21. A Turkish measure of liquid, similar to a liter.
22. Here the term *divan* is used to describe not the sultan's court in the physical sense, but a meeting for a conversation at that court, or as a verb, *divaniti*, "to converse."

His mace he draws　　yet closer to himself,
his sharp saber　　he places on his lap.[23]

Tsar Suleiman　　begins to speak with him:
"My foster son,　　O Marko Kraljević,　　　　　　　　50
did I not send　　forth my own stern decree:
no wine at all　　be drunk at Ramadan,
that no *dolmans*　　of green cloth shall be worn,
that no sabers,　　too well-wrought, be carried,
that no dancing　　with Turk girls be allowed.
Some good people　　tell me of offenders,
and they accuse　　you, Marko, of those sins:
that you do dance　　a *kolo* with Turk girls,
that you girdle　　your waist with a saber,
that you put on　　a *dolman* of green cloth,　　　　60
that you drink wine　　freely at Ramadan.
You even force　　the *hodjas* and *hadjis*
to sit with you　　and drink the red wine too.
And why do you　　pull your cap o'er your eyes?
And why do you　　draw your mace close to you?
And why do you　　hold your saber with you?"

Then Prince Marko　　answers the sultan thus:
"Foster father,　　O dear Tsar Suleiman!
If I do drink　　red wine at Ramadan,
if I do drink,　　my faith so permits me;　　　　　70
if I do force　　the *hodjas* and *hadjis,*
it is because　　my honor won't allow
to drink alone　　while they only watch me;
for why would they　　then come to the tavern?
If I do wear　　the *dolman* of green cloth,
I'm a warrior,　　and it looks well on me.
If I girdle　　my well-wrought sharp saber,
I have bought it　　with my own good money.
If I do dance　　a *kolo* with Turk girls,
my dear sultan,　　I am not married yet;　　　　　80

23. Thus Marko violates Ottoman custom by not waiting to be assigned a seat, by failing to uncover, and by bearing arms to a meeting with a superior.

you too, my tsar,   have been a bachelor.
If I do pull   my cap over my eyes,
my brow burns hot   when I talk to the tsar.
If I do draw   my mace closer to me,
and if I place   my saber on my knee,
I am afraid   there might be a quarrel.
If a quarrel   should indeed break out here,
woe be to him   who's closest to Marko!"

The sultan looks   in all four directions
to find someone   that's closer to Marko,   90
but there's no one   anywhere near Marko,
and the closest,   himself, Tsar Suleiman.
The tsar moves off,   but Marko moves closer,
till he presses   the tsar to the white wall.
The tsar reaches   down into his pocket,
and he pulls out   a hundred gold ducats.
He gives money   to Marko Kraljević:
"Here, Marko, go,   and drink your fill of wine."

 ## A Maiden Outwits Marko[24]

A song deeply invested in the wedding customs of the South Slavs, "A Maiden Outwits Marko" presents a situation fraught with danger and concluded in comedy. For in this song Prince Marko is the victim of a woman's intelligence. His potential for rage and violence is dissipated—struggles among nobles almost always resulted in tragedy for peasants—and thus disaster is prevented, and peasant wile triumphs over noble power. Thus the singer—perhaps it was Živana—has once again manipulated the Marko material to her purposes.

Vuk got this song from a blind woman *guslar* from Grgurevac. It was first published in the second volume of his 1845 edition of *Srpske narodne pjesme.*

24. "*Djevojka nadmudrila Marka,*" II, 177, #41.

A Maiden Outwits Marko

A poor maiden has truly a bad time;
for if she dines, she will have no supper.
If she's lucky to eat lunch and supper,
she has nothing left to buy her clothing.
Then good fortune smiles on her after all;
Prince Marko did ask her to marry him,
so did also the valiant Duke Janko;
the third, Pavle Ustupčić,[25] gave a ring.

All three suitors, set forth for a wedding.
Each takes with him a thousand wedding guests. 10
They all go straight to the maiden's dwelling.
Marko rides first, behind him rides Janko.
Behind Janko rides Pavle Ustupčić.

After a while, Marko Kraljević turns,
and he then speaks to his good friend Janko:
"Where're you off to, my dearest friend, Janko?
Why have you brought so many wedding guests
and put to strain so many good horses?
The lovely bride, she is not meant for you;
rather for me, for Marko Kraljević." 20
Janko's silent and utters not a word.

Janko then turns to Pavle Ustupčić
and speaks quietly, quietly in a few words:
"Where're you off to, my dearest friend, Pavle?
Why have you brought so many wedding guests
and put to strain so many good horses?
The lovely bride is neither yours nor mine
but for our friend, our Marko Kraljević?"
Pavle's silent and utters not a word,
He just rides on before the wedding guests. 30

As they arrive at the maiden's white court,
the bride's mother sees them from a distance.
She then walks out before them cheerfully,

25. A little-known nobleman.

dancing sprightly   a quick and courtly *kolo.*
She leads inside   the guests in groups of three:
first she leads in   the three grooms' own *kums,*
and next to them   she seats the senior guests,[26]
and next to them   the proud suitors themselves.
She then welcomes   all other wedding guests:
"All you guests here,   well-adorned wedding guests,   40
please be seated,   all good and faithful friends."

After a time,   when the guests had rested,
then there rises   our Marko Kraljević.
He unsheathes   his Damascene saber
and places it   there right on his strong knees.
And he now turns   to his faithful Janko
and speaks to him   in a calm, friendly voice:
"Listen to me,   my dear friend, Duke Janko,
and you also,   my Pavle Ustupčić;
let us all place   our three golden apples   50
and these three rings,   golden, on this table.
Have them bring out   the beautiful maiden.
Let her decide   whose apple she might choose:
either apple   or the golden ring here.
And whose ever   apple or ring she takes,
will determine   to whom belongs the girl."

Marko's wise words   are heeded right away.
They then bring forth   their three golden apples,
and they place them   with rings on the table.
The lovely girl   is then brought before them.   60
At that moment   speaks Marko Kraljević:
"Do you hear me,   O beautiful maiden?
Yours is the choice   of a golden apple,
golden apple   or a golden ring now."

When the maiden   understands Marko's words,
though she is poor,   she is very clever,
and she speaks thus   to Marko Kraljević:

---

26. Again the translation is incomplete, for *stari svat* includes the suggestion of the "second witness" as well as the "senior guest" (in age) at a wedding.

"My *kum* in God,   dear Marko Kraljević,
you, the best man,   o valiant Duke Janko,
and all you guests,   well-adorned wedding guests,   70
brothers in God,   our good and faithful friends.
Golden apple   is a game for children,
and golden rings   are the signs for warriors;
I'll give my hand   to Pavle Ustupčić."

After Marko   understands the girl's word,
he shouts out loud   just like a forest beast.
He strikes his hand   down on his mighty knee,
and then he speaks   to the poor maid sharply:
"Bitch of a girl,   you pretty poor maiden,
someone must have   taught you how to do this.   80
You must tell me   who's given you advice."

The poor maiden   calmly answers to him:
"My dearest *kum,*   dear Marko Kraljević,
it's your saber   that's given me advice."

Marko then smiles   at the pretty poor girl,
and he speaks thus   to her in a calm voice:
"It's your good luck,   you beautiful maiden,
that you didn't   reach for the gold apple,
neither apple   nor the golden ring there.
For otherwise,   so help me God and Faith,   90
I'd have cut off   both of your slender arms,
and your fair head   would not stand on your shoulders,
nor on that head   a green wedding garland."

 # Marko Kraljević and Alil Aga[27]

"Marko Kraljević and Alil Aga" is one of the more delightfully comic of
the Marko Kraljević songs. It not only humorously exploits the opposition
of Christian and Islamic, of Slavic and Turkish custom and stereotype, curiously anachronistic chivalric references in the corrupt world of late Ot-

27. "*Marko Kraljević i Alil-aga,*" II, 257, #61.

toman hegemony, but at its end it also celebrates order, the resolution of differences, as Marko and his Turkish antagonist become *pobratimi*, or blood brothers, and unite to enforce the power and order of the sultan.

The song was sung to Vuk by Živana, a blind woman singer—also the singer of two other of the Marko songs—in Zemun, now a part of Belgrade, probably in late 1820. Živana was widely traveled, having been as far away as Bulgaria, and these travels may be the source of her rich awareness of cultural difference. But Živana's knowledge seems to be historical as well. Bey Kostadin, and possibly Alil Aga, as well as Marko's wife, Jelica, are all historical characters, although the latter two are commonly used names. Historically, Bey Kostadin was indeed Marko's feudal neighbor to the east; Alil Aga may have been the *vizier* at the time of the battle of Kosovo.[28] But none of this explains the reconciliatory ending, which makes the song one of the finest of the cycle.

Marko Kraljević and Alil Aga

Two sworn-brothers   rode their horses slowly
through the city,   Tsarigrad[29] or Stamboul.
One of the two   was Marko Kraljević,
and the other   was the Bey Kostadin.
Marko began   to speak to his brother:
"My sworn-brother,   my dear Bey Kostadin,
I am going   through Tsarigrad city.
I might well meet   an ill-disposed hero.
He might bid me   to meet him in contest.
So I'll pretend   to be seriously ill;   10
dysentery's   a really bad sickness."
And so Marko   pretended to be ill.
He was not sick;   he was very crafty.
He bent himself   over on good Šarac,
and with his heart   he pressed on his saddle.
And so he rode   through Tsarigrad city.

But then bad luck   was soon to come his way.
Alil Aga,   the sultan's man, came on

28. Koljević, 199–202, 200.
29. *Carigrad* is the Serbian name for Istanbul.

Alil Aga   with thirty janissaries.
Alil Aga   then spoke thus to Marko: 20
"You there, warrior,   you, Marko Kraljević,
I challenge you   to test of bow and arrow,
and if your God   and luck will be with you
and you should win   that same contest today,
then you shall take   my stately white manor,
and all that is   inside and out of it,
and its lady,   my dear and faithful wife.
But if I win   that same contest today,
I seek neither   your manor nor your wife,
only the right   to hang you by the neck   30
and to possess   your valiant horse, Šarac."

Then Prince Marko   gave him a quick answer:
"Leave me in peace,   you damned, accursed Turk!
I'm in no mood   for bow and arrow shoot,
for I suffer   from a heavy sickness,
for I am ill;   it's called dysentery.
I can hardly   hold myself on horseback,
let alone make   a contest with arrows."

The cruel Turk   would leave him in no peace,
seized the *dolman,*   the right end of Marko's.   40
Marko drew out   a sharp knife from his belt,
and he cut off   the right end of the *dolman.*
"Leave us, you plague,   may the devil take you!"

The cruel Turk   would leave him in no peace,
seized the *dolman,*   the left end of Marko's.
Marko drew out   the sharp knife from his belt,
and he cut off   the left end of the *dolman:*
"Leave us, you plague,   may the devil take you!"

The cruel Turk   would leave him in no peace.
He seized Šarac   firmly by the bridle.   50
With his right hand   he grabbed Šarac's bridle
and with his left   seized Marko by the chest.
Marko flared up   like a living fire.

He stood upright   on his valiant Šarac.
He drew firmly   the reins of his Šarac
so that Šarac   began to dance about
and jump over   the horses and horsemen.

Then Marko called   Bey Kostadin to him:
"My sworn-brother,   my dear Bey Kostadin,
go, my brother,   quickly to my manor,   60
bring me from there   a sharp Tartar arrow,
on that arrow,   called a Tartar arrow,
there are sewn there   nine white falcon feathers.[30]
I am going   with Aga to the *kadi*
there to confirm   our covenant in the court,
that afterwards   there'll be no strife between us."
The bey returned   to Marko's white manor
and Marko went   with Aga to the *kadi*.

As he entered,   sultan's Alil Aga
took off his shoes,   sat beside the *kadi*.   70
From his pocket   he drew forth twelve ducats,
and he placed them   under the *kadi*'s knees.
"O *effendi*,[31]   here are twelve gold ducats.
Do not render   for Marko a true judgment."

Marko clearly   understood their language;
he'd no money,   no ducats, sadly, none.
So he lay down   his mace across his knees.
"Do you hear me,   O *effendi kadi*?
It is better   that you give true judgment,
for you see here   my gilded six-edged mace.   80
If I happen   to smite you with the mace,
no medicine   will do you any good.
You will forget   where your judgment seat is,
and you will not   even see the ducats."

30. Skillful mounted archers, the Tartars, because of the invasions into the Ottoman lands in the late fourteenth and early fifteenth century, were known and feared by the Turks. And there would be, as well, many Tartars—often soldiers—living among them as late as the fifteenth century.

31. *Effendi* is a Turkish honorific.

A true fever   gripped *effendi kadi*
as he looked there   at the gold six-edged mace.
Kadi's hands shook   as he gave true judgment.

As the warriors   departed to the field,
with Aga went   thirty janissaries,
but nobody   followed after Marko,   90
except only   certain Greeks and Bulgars.
When they arrived,   there at the shooting field,
Alil Aga   said these words to Marko:
"Come, golden knight,   let your arrows fly forth.
For you make boast   to be a great fighter,
you did so boast   in the sultan's *divan*
that you can smite   a cruciform eagle,[32]
the proud eagle   that flies faster than clouds."

Then Prince Marko   told him again calmly:
"Well, Turk, I am   a knight of high prowess,   100
but here you are   preferred ahead of me,
for here you are   the ruler and master,
and on this field   you should go before me,
for it is you   that has challenged me now.[33]
Therefore, Turk,   you loose your arrow first."

So the Turk loosed   his first sharp white arrow,
loosed the arrow;   and they measured by ells:[34]
the arrow flew   a hundred and twenty ells.
Then Marko loosed   his first sharp white arrow,
and he sent it   over two hundred ells.   110

The Turk then loosed   his second white arrow,
and he sent it   over three hundred ells.

32. The *orla krstatoga* or "cruciform eagle" here may be simply a reference to the cross shape of a soaring eagle seen from the ground or it may be intended for more complex symbolic values. See Low, *Ballads*, 88 n.

33. According to courtly tradition, the challenger strikes the first blow in a chivalric contest. But here Marko offers another, more ironically practical one, as well, and thus tricks Alil Aga to allow Marko the final arrow. For, as both Marko and Alil Aga must recognize, a Muslim in the Ottoman Empire was always of higher rank than a Christian. See Koljević, 199–200.

34. Ell, an old English unit of length equal to twenty-seven inches or here, an arm's length.

Then Marko loosed   his second white arrow,
and he sped it   over five hundred ells.

The Turk loosed then   his third sharp white arrow,
and he sent it   over six hundred ells.
At that there came   Kostadin to Marko
and he brought him   the sharp Tartar arrow,
that sharp arrow,   called the Tartar arrow;
there are sewn there   nine white falcon feathers.   120
So then Marko   shot the Tartar arrow.
It flew away   out there into the mist,
so that with eyes   no one could follow it,
much less measure   its distance into ells.

And then the Turk   began to weep large tears
and to beseech   Marko in God's own name:
"Brother-in-God,   O Marko Kraljević,
by God most high,   and by your Saint John, too,
and by your fair,   honorable religion,
you do deserve   my manor you have won,   130
and my lady,   my dearest, faithful wife,
but hang me not,   brother, I beseech you."

To Aga's plea   Marko Kraljević said:
"O you Turk, may   the living God smite you!
Call me brother,   but why give me your wife?
I have no need   of your lovely lady,
for among us   it's not like among Turks.
A brother's wife   is to us a sister.
In my own house   I have a faithful wife,
a lady wife,   her name is Jelica.   140
I'd forgive you   everything, my brother,
except that you   have destroyed my *dolman*.
For that reason   give me three loads of gold,
that I may have   my torn *dolman* mended"

The Turk jumped up   beside himself with joy.
Then he embraced,   and he kissed our Marko,
and he took him   to his stately white house.

He honored him　　and feasted for three days,
and he gave him　　as well three loads of gold.
His wife gave him　　a gold-embroidered shirt,　　　150
and with the shirt　　a kerchief silver-wrought.
He gave him too　　three hundred swift horsemen,
to see him off　　to his lordly dwelling.
From that day on　　they spent their days in peace,
guarding the land　　for the noble sultan.
Thus wherever　　a foe attacked the land,
Alil Aga　　and Marko drove him back;
and wherever　　towns were to be captured,
Alil Aga　　and Marko captured them.

 ## Marko Kraljević and Mina of Kostur[35]

"Marko Kraljević and Mina of Kostur" repeats many elements of a *bugarštica* set down near the Bay of Kotor in the early years of the eighteenth century. There are even elements—that of the hero who assumes monkish disguise to recover his kidnapped wife—from a much older song, a German song of Wolfdietrich. But "Marko Kraljević and Mina of Kostur" is intensely comic, as are neither of these predecessors. Vuk's singer, who remains unknown, has manipulated incongruously—perhaps even deliberately—disparate cultural elements as well as allusions to other heroic songs, notably "The Wedding of King Vukašin." He (or she) has filled the tale with repeated references to Marko's notorious taste for wine, so that our hero's exploits against Arab armies are joined to his guile in the great house of Mina of Kostur, and all is concluded in the delightful final line, in which Marko's essential humanity is triumphantly displayed to the hearer.

The chronicles tell us of a "Minha" or Duke Mihailo of Sibinj, but he was hardly a contemporary of Marko. Duke Mihailo of Sibinj was killed by Dmitar Jakšić in 1510. But even an anachronism such as this adds to the song's delight.

There are several versions of this song, but the version offered here, which Vuk wrote down from an anonymous singer, has the greatest amount of comical detail.

---

35. "*Marko Kraljević i Mina od Kostura*," II, 261, 362.

Marko Kraljević and Mina of Kostur

Marko sat down   to dine with his mother,
to eat dry bread   and to drink the red wine.
Then to Marko   there arrived three letters:
one from Stamboul,   from the great white city,
from Bajazet,   he the Turkish sultan.[36]
The second came   to him from far Buda,[37]
From the king there,   from the King of Buda.
The third letter   from the town of Sibinj,[38]
From the duke there,   Janko Sibinjanin.[39]

In the letter   that arrived from Stamboul,   10
the tsar called him   to serve in the army
in Arab lands,   most dangerous places.[40]
In the letter   to him from far Buda,
the king called him   to attend a wedding
as the best man   at the king's own wedding;
the king would wed,   marry a lady queen.
In the letter   from the town of Sibinj,
Janko called him   to be a godfather,
a godfather   to his two infant sons.

Marko then asked   his devoted mother: 20
"Please advise me,   my devoted mother,
where I should go   first for these three summons.
Should I go first   into the tsar's army?
Should I go first   to attend the wedding
as the best man   to the King of Buda?

36. Marko Kraljević was in fact vassal to Bajazet I (1389–1403), who succeeded Murad II, who died at Kosovo, and was defeated by Timor in 1402. Bajazet II (1481–1512) was a militarily aggressive and expansive sultan, seemingly similar to the sultan represented here.

37. Buda, now a part of Budapest.

38. Sibiu, in central Romania.

39. Janko Sibinjanin is, according to D. H. Low, none other than János Hunyadi. See Low, *Ballads*, 91 n.

40. *Arapi* or "Arabia"—here translated as "Arab lands"—is difficult to identify with certainty. Pennington and Levi identify them as Karamania. Vuk in his notes spoke of "Maurus" or "Ethiops" (Mauritius or Ethiopia). Certainly, however, whether in campaigns of conquest or in defense against Timor in 1402, Bayazet's military adventures were known to many Serbs, who served in his armies. See Pennington and Levi, 47, and Low, *Ballads*, 91 n.

Or should I go   to Janko of Sibinj,
to christen there   Janko's two infant sons?"

Marko's mother   answered him in these words:
"O my dear son,   O Marko Kraljević,
to a wedding   one goes out of pleasure;   30
to christening   one goes out of duty;
to the army   one goes because of need.
Go, my dear son,   into the tsar's army;
God will surely   forgive us, my dear son,
although the Turks   will not understand us."

Marko heeded   his dear mother's advice.
He made ready   to go to tsar's army.
He took with him   his servant, Goluban.
Before he left,   he spoke to his mother:
"Listen to me,   my devoted mother.   40
Shut the town gates   early every evening,
and open them   later in the morning,
because, mother,   I have had deep quarrels
with that damned rogue,   that Mina of Kostur,[41]
and I'm afraid,   O devoted mother,
that he may come   to rob our white manor."

So Marko left   to serve the tsar's army
with his faithful,   his servant, Goluban.
When they arrived   at lodging the third night,
Marko sat down   to eat his evening meal.   50
His Goluban   was serving him the wine.
He drank his glass,   did Marko Kraljević,
he drank his glass   and promptly fell asleep.
He dropped his glass   on the dining table;
the glass fell down   but the wine did not spill.

So Goluban   woke up his dear master:
"O my master,   O Marko Kraljević,
you've seen service   in the army before,

---

41. *Kostur,* or Castoria, bordered Marko's state to the southwest. It is presently a northern province of Greece. See Pennington and Levi, 47.

but you've never   fallen asleep like this,
or dropped a glass   of wine out of your hand."   60

Marko woke up   out of his heavy sleep
and then he spoke   to his man, Goluban:
"O Goluban,   good and faithful servant,
I just dozed off   and had a wondrous dream,
a wondrous dream   at a wondrous moment,
where a long patch   of fog was descending
there from Kostur,   that white town of Kostur.
It wound itself   all around Prilep town.
And in that fog   was Mina of Kostur.
He is robbing   our court and white manor,   70
robbing it all,   and setting it on fire.
He's run over   my mother with horses,
and he's captured   my faithful, lovely wife.
He has taken   horses from my stables
and carried off   treasures from my own chests."

Then Goluban   spoke to his master thus:
"Don't be afraid,   O Marko Kraljević.
A good hero   dreams always a good dream:
a dream deceives,   but only God is truth."[42]

When they arrived   there in Stamboul city,   80
the tsar gathered   a mighty force of arms.
They departed   then across the blue sea
to Arab lands,   most dangerous places.
They then conquered   the cities by the sea,
all together,   forty and four of them.
When they came up   below Ikonia,
they then fought there   against the place three years,
laid siege to it   but could not capture it.
Marko mowed down   many Arab warriors,
and he carried   their heads to the sultan,   90
and the sultan   rewarded Marko well.

---

42. Of course, the dream of the fog as well as Goluban's reply here alludes to "The Wedding of King Vukašin."

But these same Turks   did not like what took place;
they spoke to him,   the honorable tsar:
"O our master,   our sultan, Bajazet!
This prince Marko   is not of our heroes,
for he's cutting   the heads of dead soldiers
and bringing them   to you for a reward."

When he heard that,   Marko Kraljević heard,
he entreated   the honorable tsar:
"O my master,   O my foster-father,   100
tomorrow is   my family's *slava;*
it's our *slava,*   the Feast of our Saint George.
Please let me go,   O my foster-father,
to celebrate   St. George's Day, my *slava,*
as tradition   and our customs dictate,
and let me take   my friend, Alil Aga,
that we can drink   our fill of wine in peace."
The tsar would not   refuse such a request,
and so he gave   Prince Marko permission
to celebrate   St George's Day, his *slava,*   110
and he let him   take Alil Aga, too.

Marko then went   into the green forest,
there far away   from the sultan's army.
In the forest   he did pitch his white tent,
sat under it   to drink the dark red wine
with his good friend,   brother-in-God, Alil.
When at daybreak   came the morning sun,
the Arab guards   were not long to notice
that Marko was   no more with the army,
and they shouted,   the guards of the Arabs: 120
"Go attack now,   you fierce Arab soldiers!
There is no more   of that frightful warrior
on that huge horse,   that immense dappled horse."
And so they struck,   the fierce Arab soldiers.
And the sultan   lost thirty thousand men.

Then the sultan   wrote Marko a letter:
"Come here quickly,   my foster-son, Marko,
for I have lost   thirty thousand soldiers!"

Marko sent him   the following reply:
"What do you mean,   quickly, foster-father?   130
I have not had   my fill of dark red wine,
nor have finished   celebrating *slava!*"

At the daybreak   of the second morning,
the Arab guards   began to shout again:
"Go attack now,   you fierce Arab soldiers!
There is no more   of that frightful warrior
on that huge horse,   that immense dappled horse."
And so they struck,   the fierce Arab soldiers.
And the sultan   lost sixty thousand men.

Then the sultan   wrote Marko a letter: 140
"Come here quickly,   my foster-son, Marko,
for I have lost   sixty thousand soldiers!"

Marko sent him   the following reply:
"Wait a little,   my dear foster-father,
I have not yet   celebrated enough
with my in-laws   and with my many friends."

At the daybreak   of the third bright morning,
the Arab guards   began to shout again:
"Go attack now,   you fierce Arab soldiers!
There is no more   of that frightful warrior   150
on that huge horse,   that immense dappled horse."
And so they struck,   the fierce Arab soldiers.
And the sultan   lost a hundred thousand.

Then the sultan   wrote Marko a letter:
"Come here quickly,   my foster-son, Marko,
come here quickly,   my foster-son in God,
for the Arabs   have overturned my tent!"
At that Marko   mounted his horse, Šarac,
and he returned   to the sultan's army.

The next morning,   when the day had broken   160
and the armies,   two huge armies battled,
the Arab guards   spotted Marko quickly
and shouted at   the top of their voices:

"Go back quickly,   you fierce Arab soldiers!
For that warrior,   the frightful one's returned
on that huge horse,   that immense dappled horse!"
Then Marko rode   into the Arab hordes,
split their army   into three even parts.
One part Marko   chopped up with his saber;
the second part   he trampled with Šarac;   170
and the third part   chased before the sultan.
Marko himself   received many deep wounds:
seventy wounds   he suffered in that fight,
seventy wounds   from those Arab soldiers.

So Marko fell   across the sultan's lap.
The lord, sultan   then asked Marko softly:
"My foster-son,   O Marko Kraljević,
are these the wounds   of death you have received?
My son Marko,   can you overcome them?
Should I send now   for doctors and ointments?"   180

Marko answered,   Prince Marko Kraljević:
"O my master,   my dear foster-father,
The wounds received   are not the wounds of death.
And I feel now   I can overcome them."

The tsar reached down   into his deep pockets
and gave Marko   a thousand gold ducats,
to go and seek   healing for his deep wounds.
He sent with him   two faithful servants, too,
to take great care   that Marko did not die.
But Marko sought   no doctors nor ointments.   190
Instead he went   from one inn to another,
seeking where he   can find a better wine.

Just when Marko   had had his fill of wine,
and when his wounds   had just begun to heal,
a small letter   found its way to Marko,
and it told him   his manor had been robbed,
not only robbed   but set all to burning;
and his mother   run over by horses,
and that his wife   has been taken captive.

Then came laments   from Marko Kraljević,   200
at the tsar's knee,   his dear foster-father's:
"O my master,   my dear foster-father,
my white manor   has been robbed and plundered,
my faithful wife   has been taken captive,
my old mother   run over by horses,
and my treasures   taken from my own chests.
All this was done   by Mina of Kostur."

The tsar sultan   then consoled our Marko:
"Do not worry,   my foster-son, Marko.
If your manor   has been burned and ruined,   210
I will make it   even more beautiful
here next to mine,   and looking just like mine.
If your treasures   have been taken away,
I will make you   aga, tax-collector,[43]
so you'll collect   more treasure than you had.
If your dear wife   has been taken captive,
I will find you   a better wife to wed."

An answer came   from Marko Kraljević:
"Thank you kindly,   my dear foster-father!
If you set out   to build me a new court,   220
my poor people   will be cursing at me:
'Look at that whore,   that Marko Kraljević!
His old manor   has been burned and ruined,
may his new one   be forever empty!'
If you make me   aga, tax-collector,
then I cannot   collect any taxes
without hurting   my impoverished people,
or else they'll be   cursing me again:
'Look at that whore,   that Marko Kraljević!
His old treasure   has been taken away;   230
may the new chests   stay forever empty!'
And why should you   marry me to another
when my true wife   and love is still alive?
But just give me   three hundred janissaries,

43. Taxes were collected on a franchise basis in the Ottoman Empire. The process generated widespread dissatisfaction and corruption throughout the Balkan lands.

have forged for them   many sharp scimitars,
and give to them   many light hoes also.
I will then go   away to Kostur town
and there attempt   to win back my dear wife."

The tsar gave him   three hundred janissaries,
had forged for them   many sharp scimitars,   240
and gave to them   many light hoes also.
Marko advised   his janissaries thus:
"O my brothers,   three hundred janissaries,
you must go now   away to Kostur town.
When you come there   to that white town, Kostur,
the sight of you   will make the Greeks happy:
'Aren't we lucky,   here come the field workers!
for they will work   our vines for little pay.'
But do not work   in vineyards, dear brothers,
but sit outside   that white town of Kostur,   250
drink your red wine   and drink your clear *raki*
till I arrive   at Kostur town also."

So they went there,   three hundred janissaries,
so they went there,   away to Kostur town.
But Prince Marko   went to the Holy Mount.[44]
There he confessed   and took communion,
for he had killed   many in his short life.
Then he put on   the clothing of a monk,
let his black beard   grow down to his own waist,
and on his head   he put a monk's tall hat.[45]   260
Then he mounted   his faithful horse, Šarac,
and he went straight   there to white Kostur town.

When he sought out   that Mina of Kostur,
Mina sat there   drinking the cool red wine,
and Marko's wife   served him that cool red wine.

---

44. Mount Athos, "the Holy Mountain," is the site of Hilandar, the holiest of monasteries of the Serbian Orthodox Church, for it was here that Saint Sava, the church's founder, prayed as a monk.

45. From the beard and tall hat, as well as from the place from which he sets out, it is clear that Marko's disguise is that of an Orthodox monk.

He asked Marko,   Kostur's Mina asked him:
"In dear God's name,   O you unknown black monk,
where did you get   that immense dappled horse?"

Marko answered   in the following way:
"God is my truth,   O Mina of Kostur.   270
I have served there   in the tsar's great army,
in Arab lands,   most dangerous places.
There was with me   there a most foolish man
by the strange name   of Marko Kraljević,
and he was killed,   that foolish man was killed.
I buried him   there where he had been killed
according to   our habits and customs,
and they gave me   his horse as a soul's gift."[46]

When he heard that,   heard Mina of Kostur,
out of great joy   he leaped up to his feet,   280
and he then spoke   to Marko Kraljević:
"Praise be to you,   O you unknown black monk!
Listen to me,   nine long years have gone by
and I've waited   all that time for such news.
For I raided   that Marko's white manor,
I plundered it   and set it on fire too.
His faithful wife   I have taken captive.
but I have not   married her to this day,
for I waited   to hear Marko was dead.
And now you'll be   our priest at the wedding."   290

He took the book,   that Marko Kraljević,
he took the book,   and he married Mina,
and to whom yet,   but to his own dear wife!
They then sat down   to drink the cool red wine,
to drink red wine   and to make all merry.
But then he spoke,   Mina of Kostur spoke:
"Listen, Jela,   you, my heart and my soul,
up to this time   you've called yourself Marko's,
but from now on   you are Mina's lady.

46. The "soul's gift" is the fee paid an Orthodox priest for officiating at a funeral.

Go, my sweetheart,   to the chest in the cave,   300
and bring up here   three bags of gold ducats,
to reward him,   this unknown black monk here."

So Jela went   to the chest in the cave
and she brought up   three bags of gold ducats,
but they were not   Mina's own gold ducats
but the ducats   from Marko's robbed treasure.
And she brought up   a rusted saber too,
and she gave it   to the unknown black monk:
"Take this also,   O you unknown black monk,
in memory   of Marko Kraljević."   310

Marko then took   the saber she gave him,
took the saber   and looked it up and down,
and then he spoke   to Mina of Kostur:
"O my master,   O Mina of Kostur,
would it be right,   on this your wedding day
for me to dance   the strange dance of a monk?"[47]

Mina answered   in the following words:
"It is quite right,   O you unknown black monk.
It is quite right,   and why should not it be?"
Marko jumped up   on his two nimble feet;   320
he whirled smartly   two and three times around.
The whole building   was trembling and shaking.
He then quickly   drew the rusted saber,
and waved with it   from the right to the left.
Then he cut off   the head of Mina there.

He then shouted   at the top of his voice:
"Come, attack now,   O my dear laborers!
There is no more   Mina of Kostur here."
There then rushed in   three hundred janissaries
to the manor   of Mina of Kostur.   330
They then plundered   his white stately manor.
They seized his house,   then set it on fire.

---

47. Marko now seems to be disguised as a dervish, an Islamic monk whose strange mesmeric dance was known throughout the Ottoman Empire, or at least he is mistaken for one by Mina.

Marko then took his faithful wife away,
and he gathered Mina's untold treasure,
and they all went to the white town, Prilep,
singing with joy and with merrymaking.

 ## Marko Kraljević and the Twelve Arabs[48]

"Marko Kraljević and the Twelve Arabs" is the second of two songs that Vuk recorded from the blind Živana in Zemun, probably in 1820 during his first and unsuccessful effort to gain the support of Miloš Obrenović in Belgrade. The song, which first appeared in his third collection, is an example of the extraordinary care with which the singers represented the humanity and generosity of Marko, and the recognition that those characteristics are never pure.

Unlike the song that precedes it, here "Arab lands" presumably refers only to Turkish territory, for Marko's return to Prilep seems immediate. Yet the concern of this female singer for the fate of women in that land was a very real one.

Marko Kraljević and the Twelve Arabs

He pitched a tent, Prince Marko Kraljević,
in Arab lands, bitter and desolate.
Under the tent he sat down to drink wine.
He had no time to drink even one glass
when a slave girl, frightened, rushed suddenly
into the tent of Marko Kraljević,
and right away she entreated to him:
"Brother-in-God, O Marko Kraljević,
my blood brother in God and in Saint John!
Please protect me from Arabs on this day. 10
Into the hands of three have I fallen,
and, on this day, in the hands of the fourth.
All of them are of twelve Arab brothers.
They don't treat me like any other slave,

48. "*Marko Kraljević i 12 Arapa,*" II, 268, #63.

but they beat me   with a long three-branched whip,
and they force me   to kiss them on their face.
I can hardly   look at any of them,
much less myself   to bestow them kisses."

Marko took her   by her two trembling hands,
he sat her down   right next to his right knee.   20
He covered her   with his shining mantle,
and in her hand   he placed a glass of wine:
"Here, poor maiden,   drink a glass of red wine.
Today the sun   is shining down on you,
since you have come   to me here in my tent."

Scarcely had she,   the maiden, seized the glass
and raised the glass   to her lips to drink wine,
when suddenly   twelve Arabs barged inside
on their coursers,   twelve fine Arab horses.
and they began   to call Marko a whore: 30
"You dirty whore,   you Marko Kraljević!
Have you become   the second tsar on earth
that you kidnap   a slave girl from Arabs?"

But Prince Marko   only laughed at the twelve:
"Get out of here,   you young Arab children,
don't make my soul   sin because of you."
But the twelve Moors   then became more angry,
and each of them,   raging, drew his saber.
They overturned   the tent on Marko's head;
they cut the ropes   of Marko's silken tent,   40
and the tent fell   on the falcon, Marko,
and on his flag,   battle-flag with a cross,
and on Šarac,   Marko's stout, faithful steed.

When he saw this,   when Prince Marko saw this,
when he then saw   his silken tent o'erturned,
his wrath blazed up   like a living fire.
He jumped quickly   upon his nimble feet,
and he mounted   his stout, faithful Šarac,
and behind him   he placed his sworn sister.
He girdled her   three times with his girdle   50

and the fourth time with his own saber belt.
Then he pulled out his sharp, well-forged saber
and made a run at twelve raging Arabs.
He cut them up, not at their tender throats,
but he sliced them at their silken girdle.
From one Arab two fell to the firm ground;
out of twelve Moors he made twice as many;
out of twelve Moors he made four and twenty.
Then he set out across the level field,
like a bright star across the serene sky,   60
straight to his court in the town of Prilep,
went straight ahead to his stately white court.

Once there he called his mother, Jevrosima:
"Jevrosima, my dearest, old mother,
my dear mother, and my sweet nourishment,
here is, mother, my sworn-sister in God.
Feed her, mother, as you have nourished me.
Give her to wed like your own sweet daughter,
so that we'll gain new and friendly in-laws."

Jevrosima gave her a daughter's care   70
and nourished her, and gave her in marriage
there in Rudnik, a white town quite nearby,
in the good house of the Dizdarićes,
a house with nine loving, caring brothers.
And so Marko gained many new in-laws.
He visited often his sworn sister,
as a sister born by his own mother,
and he often drank his fill of wine there.

 ## Marko Kraljević and Musa the Robber[49]

"Marko Kraljević and Musa the Robber," one of the most popular of the Marko songs, draws its comedy from the diversity of its sources. In it

49. "*Marko Kraljević i Musa kesedžija,*" II, 26, #67. Kesedžija is a pejorative term for a highway robber, a "bag-snatcher."

Prince Marko takes on the identity of another Marko, a Serbian knight from Dalmatia who was remembered for spending much time in Turkish prisons after being captured by the Turks while in the service of a Romanian lord. While in prison Marko's bones rot after the fashion of a story about "Akir the Wise," a detail taken from a Serbian medieval text. But the food Marko eats, the "honey and sugar" he was fed as an aristocratic youth, suggests the table of a wealthy bey of the late eighteenth century. Musa, Marko's opponent in the song, has the name of a son of Sultan Bajazid II, 1446–1512; he was killed in battle. But this Musa is identified as "Musa the Albanian"; he plunders Turkish caravans—events of the eighteenth and nineteenth centuries. And, like Vergil's Erul in Canto 8 of the *Aeneid,* Musa has three hearts.

Even the *vila,* who once again assists Marko, is ambiguously moral—apparently a cross between a *bela* (white) *vila* and a *crna* (black) *vila.* And the sultan, who originally had Marko imprisoned, must release him so that he can serve as his champion. Such skillful and ironically playful mixing of diverse and contradictory elements was the *forte* of Tešan Podrugović, who recited the song to Vuk during Easter 1815 at Sremski Karlovci.[50]

Marko Kraljević and Musa the Robber

He drinks red wine,   Musa the Albanian,
there in Stamboul,   in a white, smoke-filled inn.
And when Musa   has become quite tipsy,
he then begins   to talk as drunk men do:
"There have been now   nine long, eventful years
that I have served   the great tsar in Stamboul,
and I have earned   neither a horse nor arms,
nor a *dolman,*   neither new nor used one.
But, so help me,   my firm faith in great God,
I'll turn outlaw   on the flat coastal plain,   10
I will shut down   every coastal ferry,
and I will block   every road on the coast,
I will build, too,   a tower on the coast,
around the tower   I'll place large iron hooks,
on which I'll hang   the tsar's *hodjas* and *hadjis.*"

---

50. See Koljević, 196–98, and Pennington and Levi, 54.

All the lad says,   the Turk, while he was drunk,
he carries out   when he has sobered up:
He turns outlaw   in the flat coastal plain,
he then shuts down   every coastal ferry,
and he shuts down   every road on the coast.   20
As the treasures   of the sultan pass by,
as many as   three hundred loads a year,
Musa takes it,   all by and for himself.
He builds himself   a tower on the coast,
around the tower   he places iron hooks,
and he hangs there   the tsar's *hodjas* and *hadjis*.

When the complaints   finally reach the tsar,
he dispatches   the vizier, Ćuprilić
and with him too   the three thousand soldiers.
When they arrive   in the flat coastal plain,   30
Musa meets them   by the shore of the sea,
and he captures   the vizier, Ćuprilić;
he then ties up   his hands behind his back,
and he sends him   to the tsar in Stamboul.

The tsar begins   to search out his best fighters
and promises   great treasures to the one
who will kill him,   Musa Kesedžija.
But of all those   who go forth on that plain,
none to Stamboul   returns alive again.
The tsar begins   to have greater worries,   40
but Ćuprilić,   the *hodja*, says to him:
"O my master,   O great tsar of Stamboul,
if he were here,   that Marko Kraljević,
he would have killed   Musa Kesedžija."

The tsar gives him   an angry, desperate look,
and he begins   to shed sharp, angry tears.
"Leave me alone,   you *hodja*, Ćuprilić!
Why do you speak   of Marko Kraljević?
Even his bones   must have rotted away,
for it has been   more than three long years now   50
that I've placed him   in the deepest dungeon,
and I have not   opened it since that time."

Then Ćuprilijć,   the *hodja*, tells him this:
"O my master,   your grace is unsurpassed.
What would you give   to that one good person
who can show you   Marko alive and well?"

The sultan then   responds to that question:
"I would make him   a vizier in Bosnia,
to be vizier   for nine unbroken years,
without asking   then one dinar from him."   60

The *hodja* then   leaps to his nimble feet,
opens the door   of the frightful dungeon,
and he leads out   that Marko Kraljević;
he leads him out   before the mighty tsar.
Marko's long hair   reaches down to the ground;
one strand swept back,   the other covers him;
his nails so long   that he could plough with them.
The damp stone walls   have nearly caused his death;
he has turned dark   like a dark gray stone.

The tsar then speaks   to Marko Kraljević: 70
"Are you, I pray,   still alive, dear Marko?"
"I am, O tsar,   but not by very much."
And then the tsar   begins to tell to Marko
of all the harm   Musa had done to him.
And then the tsar   asks Marko Kraljević:
"Can you muster   enough strength in yourself
to take yourself   to that flat coastal plain
and to kill there   Musa Kesedžija?
I will give you   as much gold as you ask."

Marko answers   the tsar with these calm words: 80
"Oh, in God's name,   my tsar and my sultan,
the damp stone walls   have almost caused my death.
I can hardly   see straight with my own eyes
yet let alone   wage a fight with Musa.
But you place me   somewhere in a tavern,
bring on to me   much of wine and *raki*,
and a plenty   of thick slabs of mutton,
and a plenty   of white bread that's twice-baked.

Let me sit there   for several long days,
and I'll tell you   when I'm ready to fight."   90

The tsar summons   three young, skillful barbers;
one is washing,   one is shaving Marko,
and the third one   clips his long fingernails.
The tsar leaves him   in a brand new tavern,
has brought to him   much of wine and *raki,*
and a plenty   of thick slabs of mutton,
and a plenty   of white bread that's twice-baked.
Marko sits there   the full length of three months,
till he regains   some of his life and strength.

The great tsar then   asks Marko Kraljević: 100
"Can you muster   enough strength in yourself?
I am fed up   with complaints of the poor
against Musa,   that damned robber, Musa."
Marko answers   the tsar then with these words:
"Please bring me here   some dry branch of dogwood,
wood well seasoned,   nine years in the attic,
for me to see   whether I am ready."

They bring him then   the dry dogwood branches.
Marko squeezes   the wood in his right hand.
The wood splinters   in two or three pieces,   110
but not a drop   of moisture drips from it.
"Well, my great tsar,   the time has not come yet."

Another month   passes on in waiting,
and Marko feels   he has become stronger
and fit enough   to fight Musa in duel.
He asks again   for a branch of dogwood.
They bring Marko   the dry dogwood branches.
When he squeezes   the wood, in his right hand,
the wood splinters   in two or three pieces,
and two droplets   of moisture drip from it.   120
Marko declares   to the great tsar firmly:
"The time has come,   O tsar, for the duel."

Marko then goes   to Novak the blacksmith:
"O my Novak,   you blacksmith, forge a sword

the likes of which   you've never forged before!"
He gives him there   thirty shiny ducats,
and then he goes   to a brand new tavern.
Three to four days   he spends drinking cool wine.
He returns then   to Novak the blacksmith:
"Have you, Novak,   forged me the sword I asked?"   130
Novak brings out   a sword he had just forged.
Marko then speaks   to Novak the blacksmith:
"Is it, tell me,   a good one, O Novak?"
Novak tells him   in a quiet, sure voice:
"Here is the sword,   and here is the anvil;
see for yourself   whether the sword is good."

Marko then swings   the sword in his right hand
and he strikes there   the anvil, does Marko,
and as he hits,   the anvil splits in two.
Then he inquires   of Novak, the blacksmith: 140
"In great God's name,   O Novak, you blacksmith,
have you ever   forged a sword that's better?"
Novak, the smith,   answers him right away:
"In great God's name,   O Marko Kraljević,
I have forged one,   better sword than this one,
a better sword   for a better hero:
When that Musa   turned outlaw on the coast,
ah, what a sword   I did forge for that man!
When he struck it,   that sword on the anvil,
the whole anvil   shattered into pieces."   150

Anger flares up   in Marko Kraljević,
and he speaks thus   to Novak, the blacksmith:
"Give me your hand,   O Novak, you blacksmith,
so that I can   pay you for my sword now."
Novak the fool,   as if a snake bit him,
makes an error   and holds out his right hand.
Marko then swings   at it with his sword
and he cuts off   the arm at the shoulder.
"Now you cannot,   O Novak, you blacksmith,
forge a better   or a less good weapon.   160
But I'll give you   one hundred ducats here,

to feed yourself   for the rest of your life."
He gives him then   one hundred good ducats,
and then he mounts   battle-ready Šarac,
and rides out straight   to the flat coastal plain.
There he wanders,   asking about Musa.

One bright morning   Marko gets up early
in the deep gorge   near the town, Kačanik,[51]
and there he is,   Musa Kesedžija!
He sits calmly,   his legs crossed on his horse,   170
and throws his mace   high up into the clouds
and catches it   with his own strong white hands.
When they ride up   close to one another,
Marko speaks to   Musa Kesedžija:
"Out of my way,   Musa, you damned robber,
out of my way   or bow down before me."

To that Musa,   the Albanian, answers:
"Pass by, Marko,   don't start any quarrel.
Either pass by,   or come and have a drink,
but I am not   moving out of the way,   180
e'en if a queen   has given birth to you
in a castle   on a deep soft mattress,
and has wrapped you   in a pure silk clothing,
and has sewn up   your clothes with golden threads,
and has fed you   with honey and sugar.
For I was born   to a mean Albanian,
beside the sheep   on a cold, barren rock;
she wrapped me up   all in coarse, black clothing,
and covered me   with blackberry offshoots,
and fed me there   with cold oatmeal porridge.   190
It was she who   bade me make a firm oath
never to turn   aside for any man."

When he hears that,   stern Marko of Prilep,
he then lets loose   his long, sharp battle lance
over the ears   of his mighty Šarac,

---

51. *Kačanička klisura*, a picturesque gorge near the town of Kačanik, about forty miles north-west of Skopje, on the road from Priština to Skopje.

aimed at the chest   of Musa, the brave one.
Musa fends it   with his own mace smartly.
He flings the lance   backward over his head,
and he draws then   his own long battle lance
and throws it straight   at Marko Kraljević.   200
Marko fends it   with his own mace deftly
and he breaks it   into three sharp pieces.
Both heroes then   draw their fine-forged sabers,
and they fight on,   attacking each other.
He wields his sword,   Marko the Prince wields it.
The brave Musa   fends it with his mace
and he breaks it   into three sharp pieces.
Then he quickly   draws his own sharp saber
and strikes away   at Marko Kraljević.
Marko uses   his own mace skillfully;   210
he knocks away   the blade from its own hilt.

They then take up   their sharply spiked maces,
and they begin   to strike at each other.
They break away   the spikes off their maces
and they throw them   down into the green grass.

They then jump down   from their splendid horses,
seize each other   by their own strong-boned arms,
and they begin   wrestling on the green grass.
Thus one warrior   tries to best the other,
that brave Musa   and Marko Kraljević.   220
Neither Musa   can vanquish strong Marko,
nor can Marko   vanquish the strong Musa.
So they fight on   a summer day till noon.
Musa's covered   all over with white foam,
and Marko, too,   with foam white and bloody.

At last he speaks,   Musa Kesedžija:
"Strike, then, Marko,   or let me take a swing."
He tries to strike,   does Marko Kraljević,
but he cannot   do Musa any harm.
He takes his turn,   Musa Kesedžija;
he brings Marko   down to the soft green grass   230
and he sits down   on his valiant chest.

Then Prince Marko   begins to moan aloud:
"Oh where are you,   *vila*, sister in God?
Where are you now,   may you be dead for good?
Was it false oath   that you swore to me then
always to help   in my grave hour of need
and whenever   I get into trouble?"
The *vila* speaks   from up high in the clouds:
"Why, O brother,   O Marko Kraljević,   240
didn't I say,   dear, didn't I warn you,
never to start   quarrel on a Sunday?
It is not fair   for us two to fight one.
Where are they now,   the vipers you're hiding?"[52]

Musa looks up   at the cloudy mountain,
whence that *vila*   seems to have been speaking.
Marko draws out   the knives he was hiding
and splits open   Musa Kesedžija
from the belly   right up to his white throat.
The dead Musa   lies heavy on Marko,   250
so that Marko   can barely free himself.
But when Marko   has turned Musa over,
he notices   three hearts in brave Musa,
three sets of ribs   one over the other.
One of his hearts   has become quite tired,
but another   dances, prances wildly,
and on the third   is a serpent, sleeping.

When the serpent   wakes up from its slumber,
the dead Musa   jumps up from the ground.
Then the serpent   speaks this way to Marko: 260
"Give thanks to God,   O Marko Kraljević,
that I did not   wake out of my deep sleep
while my Musa   was still alive and well.
You would have seen   three hundred more troubles."

When he sees that,   Prince Marko Kraljević,
large tears begin   to roll down his white face:

---

52. Thus the *vila*, while complaining about the unfairness of two-on-one, offers Marko tactical advice, for the "vipers" of which she speaks are a code for Marko's hidden daggers.

"Woe be to me,   in the name of dear God,
for I have killed   a foe better than I."
And he cuts off   the dead head of Musa,
he throws it there   into Šarac's feed bag,   270
and he rides off   for white Stamboul city.
There he throws down   the head before the tsar;
out of sheer fright   the tsar jumps to his feet.

Then to the tsar   speaks Marko Kraljević:
"Don't be afraid,   O, my tsar and master!
How would you have   met Musa still alive,
since you're trembling   before his dead head here?"

The tsar gives him   three large loads of treasure.
Marko goes then   to his white Prilep town.
Musa remains   on top of Kačanik.   280

 ## Marko Kraljević and the *Vila*[53]

Tešan Podrugović had once been a *hajduk,* and he had the zest for violence, the honesty, the wry humor, and the "scowl" (which Vuk noted) to make him the perfect teller of Marko's exploits. The poem that follows, "Marko Kraljević and the *Vila*," is almost certainly one of those recited by Podrugović in Sremski Karlovci in 1815.[54]

Podrugović's version of the song is outrageous—comic and violent—as are many of the Marko songs. There are at least two other versions. As in other songs, Marko's ambiguous relationship with the *vila* is apparent. It is again unclear whether she is of the "black" or "white" variety. In some of the songs she proves to be Marko's ally, even in one, his "blood sister." And it is, of course, also a bit bizarre to find that Miloš Obilić, who proved himself loyal to the death at Kosovo, would be Marko's blood brother. But so it often was thus with Podrugović.

---

53. "*Marko Kraljević i vila,*" II, 158, #38.
54. See Wilson, 108 and n.

Marko Kraljević and the *Vila*

Pobratimi,   brothers by oath, ride forth
over the rocks   of high Miroč Mountain.[55]
The one brother   is the bold Prince Marko,
and the other,   his brother, Duke Miloš.[56]
They ride abreast,   on their two fine horses;
they ride abreast,   bear chivalric lances.
Their white faces   they join there in kissing
out of the love   they hold as sworn brothers.
Then Prince Marko   falls asleep on Šarac.

When he wakens,   he says to his brother,   10
"O my brother,   my brother, Duke Miloš,
a heavy sleep   just now fell upon me;
sing to me now,   and talk to me a bit."

Then Duke Miloš   answers to Prince Marko:
"Ah, Prince Marko,   dear and true sworn brother,
I'd sing to you,   but I drank too much wine
all last evening,   up there with the *vila,*
on the mountain   there with Ravijojla,[57]
and she told me,   she gave me fair warning,
if she hears me,   if she hears me singing,   20
she will shoot me,   she will let me have it,
in the throat, here,   and in my throbbing heart."

Now Prince Marko   answers in this fashion:
"Ah, sing, brother;   do not fear the *vila,*
for I'm with you,   I, the mighty Marko,
and here's Šarac,   a most clairvoyant horse,
and here's my mace,   golden, with its six spikes!"

55. A mountain in northeastern Serbia, on the south bank of the Danube near the present Romanian border.

56. Miloš Obilić, who was, of course, not likely the historical Marko's *pobratim,* or brother by mutual oath, an extremely binding form of sworn loyalty between two men, and by extension, between a man and a woman.

57. A popular name for a *vila.*

So then Miloš   begins with his singing.
First he sings him   a truly lovely song
of our people   who are great and ancient,   30
how each of them   ruled over a kingdom
in a pure place,   in Macedonia,
how each did build   himself a holy church.
The song pleases   Prince Marko immensely.
He leans forward   on his saddle's pommel.

Marko dreams on   while Miloš is singing,
but the *vila,*   Ravijojla, hears him.
Now she begins   to sing songs to Miloš.
Miloš sings too,   then the *vila* answers.
Miloš sings well;   his fine voice is better   40
than the *vila*'s;   he has the better voice.[58]
Ravijojla   then becomes quite angry,
and she runs up   onto Miroč Mountain.
she draws her bow   and lets fly two arrows,
and one hits him,   poor Miloš, in his throat,
and the other   right in his hero's heart.

Then says Miloš,   "God! O Holy Mother!
O my Marko,   by God my sworn brother!
O my brother,   the *vila* has got me!
I told you so,   didn't I tell you, brother,   50
that I shouldn't   sing near Miroč Mountain?"

Marko wakes up   from his blissful slumber,
and he jumps down   from his great piebald horse.
Then he tightens   Šarac's girth quite firmly;
he embraces   and kisses dear Šarac.
"O my Šarac,   my dear horse, my right hand,
if you catch her,   *vila* Ravijojla,
I will shoe you   with shoes of pure silver,
of pure silver   and of bright, shining gold!

58. Vuk's note here is translated: "They must have had a singing contest before this, and the *vila* must have forbidden him to sing because his voice was better than hers." See *Srpske narodne pjesme,* 2: 159 n. 31), and Noyes and Bacon, eds. and trans., *Heroic Ballads of Servia,* 121 n.

I'll cover you   in silk cloth to your knees,   60
and from your knees,   right down to your pasterns!
I'll braid your mane   with threads of purest gold
and adorn it   with tiny, shiny pearls!
But if you fail,   if you don't find the *vila*,
I'll gouge your eyes,   I'll tear them from your head!
I'll break your legs,   I'll smash them one by one!
And I'll leave you   behind, to live like that,
to drag yourself   from fir tree to fir tree,
just as I would   without my sworn brother!"

Then he mounts him,   sits on Šarac's shoulders,   70
and so they ride   across Miroč Mountain.
While the *vila*   flies over the mount's crests,
Šarac gallops   through the mountain's middle,
but he cannot   see nor hear the *vila*.
When he at last   sees the accursed *vila*,
Šarac jumps up   to a height of three spears;
he jumps forward,   a good four spears forward.
And thus quickly   Šarac finds the *vila*.

Now the *vila*   finds herself in trouble;
she flies straight up,   well above the white clouds.   80
But then Marko   brings out his spiked war mace,
and he clubs her,   strikes her with abandon,
hits the *vila*   between her white shoulders,
and he pulls her   all the way to the earth.

Then he begins   to club her once again,
he spins her 'round,   spins her from right to left;
he is using   his mace with six gold spikes.
"Why, O *vila*,   may God rightly kill you,
why did you shoot   Miloš, my sworn brother?
You'd better get   some herbs for that hero,   90
if you would like   to keep your head for long!"

Then the *vila*   in God's name calls him brother:
"In God's own eyes   you're my brother, Marko,
and I beg you,   by God and by Saint John,

let me free now!   I'll go to the mountain,
there I'll gather   herbs of Miroč Mountain
to cure Miloš,   to heal the hero's wounds."

Marko's mercy   is in the name of God.
Though in his heart   he is sad for Miloš,
he lets her go   on up to the mountain,   100
and she gathers   herbs of Miroč Mountain.
She gathers herbs,   and she speaks to Marko:
"I am coming,   O my sworn brother!"

Now she's gathered   enough herbs on Miroč,
so she takes them   and heals the hero's wounds.
This makes Miloš's   voice even lovelier,
it's lovelier   than it has ever been,
heals Miloš's heart,   now stronger than ever,
now it's truly   healthier than before.

Now the *vila*   goes back up the mountain,   110
and Marko goes   with his true sworn brother,
and they ride on,   on to Poreč County;
they cross water   at the river, Timok,
near Bregovo,   a large, pleasant village.[59]
Then they ride on,   on to Vidin County.[60]
But the *vila*   tells the other *vilas*:
"O now hear me,   you, my sister *vilas*,
don't you dare shoot   heroes in the mountains;
you'll hear the voice   of that bold Prince Marko!
You'll meet that horse,   the clairvoyant Šarac!   120
You'll feel that mace,   that mace with six gold spikes!
How I've suffered   from this violent hero,
really suffered,   barely escaped alive!"

Assisted by Dragana McFadden

---

59. They have ridden south through the valley of the Poreč River and crossed the Timok River, a southern tributary of the Danube that flows north near the northern part of the present Serbian-Bulgarian border.
    60. Now they have turned eastward, for Vidin is a city in the northwest corner of present-day Bulgaria.

The Death of Marko Kraljević[61]

Perhaps the greatest of the songs of Marko Kraljević is that which tells of his death. It is only then that Marko comes truly to know himself and to recognize the world around him for what it is. But, paradoxically, it is also in this song that the hearer recognizes the virtue of Marko's very boldness, especially when it is contrasted with the overcautiousness of a subject people who are afraid to disturb Marko's body until it has lain dead for a week. And even though the song tells of Marko's death, it never loses its sense of the comic, surely the best defense of all against all oppression.

"The Death of Marko Kraljević" is deeply rooted in its mythologies and folk tradition. One meets here the executioner God and sees Marko gain knowledge of both the time of his death and of his own true nature in gazing on the reflection of his own image. One notes also an emphasis upon the duty of burial, which seems to supersede mere tradition or even the will of a particular noble. Indeed, as Koljević puts it, "most of the 'facts' in the poem reflect—in slightly comic light—much older legends and some of the customs of pagan times."[62]

Certainly much of the distinction of the song is due to its singer, not Tešan Podrugović but Filip Višnjić, perhaps the greatest of all the *guslari* who sang to Vuk, but a singer not usually associated with the Marko cycle. It was at Šišatovac monastery in 1815, while visiting its archimandrite, Lukijan Mušicki, that Vuk first encountered Višnjić and heard the following song.

The Death of Marko Kraljević

He rode early,   our Marko Kraljević,
on Sunday morn,   before the bright sunshine,
by the sea shore,   toward Urvina Mountain.[63]
When our Marko   was upon the mountain,
his horse, Šarac,   there began to stumble,

---

61. "*Smrt Marku Kraljevića*," II, 314, #74.

62. See Koljević (to whom we are indebted for much of this discussion), 209–11, 210 and n. Koljević cites S. Matić, ed., *Pjesme junačke najstarije*, vol. 2 of *Srpske narodne pjesme*, by Vuk Stefanović Karadžić (Belgrade: Prosveta, 1953), 747–50, for a further discussion of primitive elements in the song.

63. Historically, Marko Kraljević met his death while fighting on the side of the Turks in the Romanian village of Rovine in 1394. The transposition of "Rovine" to "Urvine," the symbolic al-

to stumble there,   and to shed salty tears.
Our Prince Marko   was troubled by these things,
so he uttered   these words to his Šarac:
"What's the trouble,   Šaro, my good fellow?
You've been with me   a hundred sixty years;   10
in all that time   we have been together,
in all that time   your foot has never failed,
but now, today,   you begin to stumble,
to stumble here,   and to shed salty tears!
In God's own name,   this is no good omen;
one of us will   surely lose his head now,
either your head   will be lost, or my head!"

Just as Marko   spoke these very words,
so the *vila* cried   from Mount Urvina,
and she called out   to Marko Kraljević: 20
"My sworn brother,   my Marko Kraljević,
would you, brother,   know why your horse stumbles?
For his master   Šarac's heart is heavy,
for soon you two   must part from each other."

But now Marko   gave the *vila* answer:
"You, white *vila,*   may your voice be silenced![64]
How can you say   I would part with Šarac!
I with Šarac   have seen fields and cities,
we two traveled   the world from east to west.
I know no horse   finer than my Šarac,   30
nor any knight   who has overcome us.
I would never,   never part with Šarac,
not while my head   stands here on my shoulders!"

But the *vila,*   the white *vila,* answered:
"My sworn brother,   my Marko Kraljević,
truly no one   can take Šarac from you,
and you never   can meet your death, Marko,
from a warrior,   nor from any weapon,

___

teration from village to mountain, and the relocation of the place to a seaside site are testaments
to the singer's symbolic imagination.

64. Marko's curse is only playful, his outrage only mocking disbelief.

whether war spear   or a mace of battle,
so you need not   fear any man on earth.   40
Yet you shall die;   you'll feel death's pain, Marko,
from our old God,   the executioner.
But if you won't   believe these words I speak,
when you arrive   upon the mountaintop,
look about you,   look to your right, your left,
you will see there   two tall, slender fir trees
that stand taller   than other forest trees,
that are dressed out,   covered in their greenness.
Just between them   stands a well of water.
Ride your Šarac   up to that very place,   50
dismount from him,   tie him to a fir tree,
then bend downwards,   o'er the well of water;
you will see there,   mirrored, your very face.
Then shall you know   the time of your own death."

Marko followed   the good *vila*'s advice.
When he arrived   upon the mountaintop,
he looked round him,   looked to his right, his left,
and he saw there   two tall, slender fir trees
which stood taller   than other forest trees
and were leafed out,   covered in their greenness.   60

He rode Šarac   up to that very place;
he dismounted,   tied him to a fir tree;
he bent downwards   o'er the well of water,
and he saw there,   mirrored, his very face.
And when Marko   saw his face mirrored there,
he, moreover,   knew the time of his death.

Marko shed tears,   and he uttered these words:
"False world power,   O my lovely flower,[65]
you are lovely,   and yet life is so short,
oh, it's so short,   mine but three hundred years!   70
Now the hour   comes when I must leave you."

65. This line, *Laživ sv'jete, moj lijepi cv'jete!*, depending as it does on the rhyme of *sv'jete* (world) and *cv'jete* (flower), loses much of its beauty in translation.

Then Prince Marko   drew forth his trusty sword,
drew his own sword   out from his golden sash,
and then he went   to where his Šarac stood.
With his own sword   he cut off Šarac's head,
so he'd never   fall into Turkish hands,
so he'd never   be a slave unto them,
so he'd not bear   their copper water pots.
And when Marko   had thus killed his Šarac,
he gave his horse   a splendid burial,   80
better than that   which he gave Andrija.[66]

He took his sword,   broke it in four pieces,
and thus the Turks   could never seize on it
and never boast   of taking it from Marko,
for it for them   would be prize from Marko,
and so Christians   wouldn't revile Marko.

After Marko   had broken his own sword,
he broke his spear   into seven pieces,
and he hurled them   up into the fir tree.
And then Marko   took his ridged battle mace,   90
Marko took it   in his own good right hand,
and he cast it   from Urvina Mountain,
all the way out   into the great, gray sea.
Of this weapon   our Marko said these words:
"When that mace there   shall come forth from the sea,
there shall appear   one who is my equal!"

Now when Marko   had destroyed his weapons,
then from his sash   he brought forth an inkhorn,
from his pocket   he took writing paper,
and then Marko   wrote down this last letter: 100
"Whosoever   comes up Mount Urvina,
to the cold well   here between the fir trees,
who finds the corpse   of Marko Kraljević,
then he will know   that Prince Marko is dead,
and he will find   by him three belts of gold.

---

66. Marko's brother Andrija, according to some of the songs, was killed by Marko in a fit of rage. Marko, repentant, then had him magnificently buried.

The gold is pure,   all in yellow ducats.
One of the belts   is for him who finds me,
so he'll give me   a proper burial.
The second belt   is to adorn churches,
and the third belt   for the blind and crippled,   110
so that the blind   can go forth in the world
and sing their songs   in Marko's memory."[67]

Now when Marko   had finished his letter,
he placed it there   upon the fir tree's branch,
so from the road   it could be clearly seen;
his gold inkhorn   he dropped into the well.
His own green coat   he took from his shoulders
and spread it out   on grass beneath the fir.
He crossed himself   and sat down on his coat,
he drew his hood   over his very eyes,   120
and he lay down   never to rise again.

Beside the well   lay the dead Prince Marko
day after day;   he lay there a full week.
Whosoever   happened to pass that way
and there to see   our Marko Kraljević
thought that surely   Prince Marko was sleeping,
and as he passed   left much space between them,
for fear he'd wake   this Marko Kraljević.

Where good luck is   there's bad luck to be found;
where bad luck is   there is good luck also.   130
So it was then   surely the best of luck
that brought Vaso,   of the Holy Mountain,
the *iguman*   of the white church Vilindar,
with his deacon,   Isaias, beside him.[68]
Now when Vaso,   *iguman*, saw Marko,
with his right hand   he signaled his deacon:
"Softly, my son,   make sure you don't wake him,

67. Filip Višnjić himself, of course, was a blind singer, so perhaps the line may be a bit of special pleading.

68. Vaso is not historical, but "Vilindar," a folk expression for Hilandar, is the holiest of Serbian monasteries, located on Mount Athos. An *iguman* is an Orthodox prior, or the superior, in a monastery.

for after sleep   Marko's in a bad mood;
he might well put   an end to both of us!"

But as he looked   to see how Marko slept,   140
he noticed there   the letter above him;
he took it down,   then he read the letter.
The letter said   that Prince Marko was dead,
and thereupon   the monk stepped from his horse
and with his hand   he touched the brave Marko.
But our Marko   was dead for a long time,
and so Vaso,   *iguman*, wept sad tears,
for he was grieved,   he deeply felt the loss.

From Marko's sash   he took three belts of gold,
and he tied them   all around his own waist.   150
Then that Vaso   considered carefully
where to take him,   to bury Prince Marko.
He considered,   and then he decided.
On his own horse   he placed dead Prince Marko,
and he bore him   down along the seashore.
With the dead prince   he sat down in a boat,
sailed directly   to the Holy Mountain.
Then he took him   before Vilindar's church,
and he bore him   into the church itself.
Over Marko   he read a proper mass,   160
and on this earth   Prince Marko's final prayer.
In the center   of Vilindar's great church,
there, the old man   buried our Prince Marko.
But he left there   no sign to mark his grave,
so none would know   where Marko lies buried,
and so no foe   could take revenge on him.[69]

69. There are many versions of Marko's burial. Perhaps a better known account is set forth by Temperley: "There is some real evidence for showing that he died in battle in the year 1394. Before the battle, in which he was compelled to fight on the Turkish side, he is said to have remarked to a friend, 'I pray God that He may aid the Christian and that I may be among the first to fall.' He had his wish, and died while the Christian shouts of victory were ringing in his ears. This slender historical foundation is the origin of that beautiful legend that he rests sleeping in a cave near his own castle of Prilep, and will once more come to the aid of the Serbs when the day comes that the Turk is to be driven from the land. So deeply is this legend written in Serbian hearts, that thousands of soldiers saw Marko leading them to victory on his famous dappled horse when they drove the Turks from Prilep in 1912" (98).

5   Under the Turks

T HE ORTHODOX CHRISTIANS who remained on the lands south of the Danube and the Sava were an oppressed people, the object of economic and human exploitation. The *raja* were subjected by their Turkish masters to the "blood tax." Each year male children were taken, supposedly as young as the age of eight, were converted to Islam, enrolled for service in the "new army" or *janissary,* the sultan's elite infantry (where they could be called upon to discipline their own fathers), and forbidden to marry. Later, especially in the seventeenth and eighteenth centuries, girls were also taken from Serbian villages to fill the sultan's *harem.*

Except for certain annoying regulations, however, the *raja* were left to live their lives in relative peace. For the fighting seemed to be at an end; the sultans who succeeded Mohammed II, Bayazid II and Selim I, seemed uninterested in further conquest in Europe. Suleiman II, the "Magnificent" (1520–1566) did return to the conquest of the Hungarian lands, and during his reign much local government in the Serbian lands was left in the hands of elected village representatives, called *ober-knez,* usually Orthodox Christians.

Only the Bosnian Serbs were converted. For the most part the South Slavs remained loyal to their church, which had suffered greatly. The patriarchs at Peć[1] had long struggled with those of Greece for autonomy. So when the Turks had come to Serbia, the Greeks again had seen their

---

1. A town in western Kosovo, near the Montenegrin border, during the Turkish occupation the official seat of the Serbian Orthodox Church.

chance, and the patriarchate at Peć was subordinated to the Ohrid arch-diocese, where Greek bishops had long held sway. Now almost exclusive-ly Phanariots, these Greek bishops, accommodated the Turks and were hostile to Slavic texts and rituals, and they would come to be an increas-ingly unpleasant presence in the Balkans.

In 1557 through the intercession of Mehmed Pasha Sokolović, a re-markable grand vizier of Serbian origins who had risen to power through the janissaries, the autonomy of the patriarchate at Peć was restored. Soko-lović's brother became Patriarch Macarius there, and Peć would become again a great center of Serbian Orthodox consciousness and conscience. But a hundred years of Phanariots had exacted their toll. Churches had been damaged and ancient frescoes defaced. Monasteries—often the only schools available to the children of the peasants but taxed by the Turks—had been abandoned. Many of their texts that survived were lost or burned by the Phanariots. The few monks who remained were often illit-erate, reduced to subsistence farming. What had once been a great monas-tic system for the transmission of learning had now been devastated.

The new patriarchate did much to repair the damage. Printing presses were introduced to generate and disseminate Slavic texts; the first Cyrillic press, established at Obod in Montenegro in 1493, was destroyed by the Turks, but others appeared at Gračanica and even in Belgrade. Church leaders like Patriarch Pajsije (c. 1550–1647) traveled from monastery to monastery, collected and preserved old manuscripts, and encouraged the work of copying them.

The churchmen provided secular leadership as well. Jovan II, another patriarch, provoked the insurrection of St. Sava of 1593, an uprising of Serbs that was not finally crushed until 1609, after the Austrians, to whose invading armies the Serbs looked for aid, made peace with the Turks. Yet, as the seventeenth century wore on, and the Sublime Porte's control over its Balkan peoples—and over its own rebellious janissaries—declined, corruption of local officials and the cruelty of the janissaries (no longer trusted in Istanbul and now assigned to more remote posts) increased. But Turkish armies in Europe—first at St. Gothard in 1664, later at the very gates of Vienna (the high water mark of Turkish conquest in Europe) in 1683, then at Buda in 1686, began to be defeated. Vienna was saved; Turk-ish control of Hungary was loosened by 1688. Even Belgrade, the Turks' major fortress on the Danube, fell to an Austrian army and the Turks were driven from the lands north of the Sava River. And the patriarch at Peć, Arsenije III Čarnojević, again emerged as secular leader of the Serbs.

After the fall of Belgrade the Austrian army continued south, defeated the Turks on Kosovo field, and even took Skopje itself. And as they passed they ignited the fires of Serbian revolt. The Austrians even offered a king, one Djordje Branković, allegedly a descendant of his namesake. But then Jesuits were seen in Serbia, and Arsenije became convinced that the Austrians, like the Hungarians, intended a Latin rite for the Serbs. When the Austrians reached Peć they were coolly received, and the Serbs' zeal for revolt faded. Now without the rebellious Serbs and far from Vienna, the Austrians were increasingly vulnerable to the Turkish army. The Turks turned the tide of battle, drove the Austrians north, and recaptured Belgrade, leaving the Serbs vulnerable to Turkish reprisals.

Leopold I offered the Serbs refuge in the recently regained lands of southern Hungary and promised religious freedom and the right to elect their own governor, or *vojvoda* (hence the name "Vojvodina"), and it was Arsenije who in 1690 led thirty thousand families north from Old Serbia to the flatlands north of the Sava, and across the Danube to the Srem and Bačka, and to the Banat, deeper in Hungary. By the Treaty of Karlovci of 1699 Serbia remained under Turkish control, although the Austrians retained Slavonia. Albanians and Turks now settled in the empty lands of Old Serbia, and Peć turned its attention to Montenegro. Sremski Karlovci, the see of a new Serbian metropolitan, would become the center of Serbian culture for the new century. Not too long afterward, with new activity in Montenegro, Vuk's family would become refugees, north to Bosnia.

The songs describing the years after the battle of Kosovo thus reflect a depopulated land and a diminished culture, much altered from that of the aesthetically refined and tradition-oriented values implicit—although not clearly comprehended by the singers—in the Kosovo songs. The post-Kosovo Serbia set forth in the songs is a world of materialist values, of warriors in conflict with one another over questions of property, not honor. Yet the moral norms of the songs about earlier times remain, if only as a standard to judge the conduct of the combatants.

Radul Bey and the Bulgarian King Šišman[2]

"Radul Bey and the Bulgarian King Šišman," which Vuk heard from a Bosnian merchant, is set in the eastern Balkans in the late fourteenth cen-

2. "*Radul-beg i Bugarski kralj Šišman*," II, 318, #75.

tury. Šišman was historically a contemporary of Marko Kraljević and a Christian monarch whose kingdom centered around Trnovo in what is today central Bulgaria. Šišman remained for a time relatively autonomous, albeit surrounded by Turks. Although his name is Romanian, and he is based in Bucharest, Radul Bey was obviously a Moslem convert and a vassal of the sultan. His brother, Duke Mirčeta, is apparently Christian. Thus the song reflects the religious and feudal divisions that followed on the death of Dušan and fragmented the Balkans after the battle of Kosovo.

"Radul Bey and the Bulgarian King Šišman" celebrates as well the reconstitution and survival of a family divided by such strife, a reconstitution symbolized by the reconciliation of two brothers that is brought about—as is usual in the songs—by the intelligence of a good wife. For this reconciliation, and the attendant alliance of representatives of various Balkan peoples, saves them all and brings victory and wealth. Such is the lesson of the song but, unfortunately, such is not the lesson of history.

Another version of "Radul Bey and the Bulgarian King Šišman" appeared in the Erlangen manuscript. However, the version Vuk collected that follows here is the version usually preferred.

Radul Bey and the Bulgarian King Šišman

May our dear God   be praised for everything!
Two fierce serpents   quarrelled with each other,
Two fierce serpents,   two close, loving brothers:
Bey Radul Bey   began the quarrelling
with Mirčeta,   his one and only brother,
but about what?   Really about nothing—
about dry land,   Karavlaška's bare land,
Karavlaška   and Karabogdanska.
Mirčeta sought   primacy o'er the land,
Bey Radul Bey   would not grant it to him.   10
Instead he seized   the Duke Mirčeta,
imprisoned him   in his darkest dungeon,
and threw the keys   in the Danube River.

He threw the keys   in the Danube River,
and then forgot   about his own brother.

God and fortune   were on Mirčeta's side.
Bey Radul Bey   had a most kindly wife,
who had pity   on her brother-in-law.
At night she had   divers and fishers dive
and they retrieved   the keys of the dungeon.   20
She visited   her brother-in-law there
and she brought him   a set of new, clean clothes,
and she fed him   white bread and other goods,
and she gave him   the good chilled wine to drink.
And so it was   three full years quickly passed.

When the fourth year   began to run its course,
a letter came   written by King Šišman
from Trnovo,   the land of the Bulgars.
The letter came   to the bey, Radul Bey:
"Greetings to you,   my dear bey, Radul Bey.   30
A son is born   in our family here,
and I ask you,   in the name of our God,
and of our saint,   our Saint John the Baptist,
to visit us   in our Trnovo town,
and to our son   serve as his godfather,
so that we can   be friends forever, bey."

Bey Radul Bey   received the white letter.
After he'd read   and studied that letter,
great tears began   to run down from his eyes.
But then again,   Radul Bey considered   40
that it could be   the king might play a trick
and do him in   by misusing his trust.
Radul Bey called   his wife, Andjelija,
and he began   to speak with her in earnest:
"Listen to me,   my faithful wife and love,
for I've received   an important letter
from King Šišman,   the king of the Bulgars.
The king names me   as his son's godfather,
but this could be   a ruse and deceit,
for this same king   could mean to deceive me   50
and to kill me   by his word of honor,
and to capture   all my lands and cities

and take you, dear,   take you as his own love.
What's your advice,   my faithful wife and love?"

His wife and love   spoke clearly and wisely:
"O my master,   my lord, bey, Radul Bey!
Are we women   to give advice to men?
What good advice   can I give to you, bey,
when best advice   is deep in the dungeon,
your own brother   and my brother-in-law,   60
Duke Mirčeta,   O my lord and master?
He will give you   the best advice there is."

Then Radul Bey   answered her angrily:
"Hold your tongue there,   my love, may God smite you!
that you mention   my brother Mirčeta.
Even his bones   have turned to dust by now."

When she heard that,   Radul Bey's faithful wife,
she went quickly   to the dark dungeon's gate,
and she led forth   the good Duke Mirčeta.
She then took him   to that white court of theirs,   70
and she summoned   a skillful young barber,
to shave the duke,   the weak Duke Mirčeta.
She then gave him   clothing fit to his rank,
and went with him   straight to the bey's quarters.

When Radul Bey   saw the Duke Mirčeta,
he leapt quickly   to his feet before him,
spread his arms wide,   he kissed him on the face,
he asked the duke   about his present health:
"O my brother,   are you still alive?"
Duke Mirčeta   answered him quite calmly: 80
"Yes, my brother,   but I'm not a strong man.
The dungeon's rot   all but killed me, brother.
I can just keep   my poor soul in my body."

Then Radul Bey   began to talk sadly
about the text   of King Šišman's letter.
"Listen to me,   my brother, Mirčeta,
advise me now,   and teach me what to do:

should I depart   now for Trnovo town
along with three   hundred Ugričićes?"[3]

Duke Mirčeta   then answered him calmly: 90
"O my brother,   you good bey, Radul Bey,
why do you need   three hundred Ugričićes
only to make   three hundred sad widows?
But where are our   own old faithful servants?
Is Radosav   the Serb still living, pray?
and is Djuro,   the drunkard, still with him?
Is Manojlo,   your Greek servant, still here?"

Then Radul Bey   answered him quite promptly:
"Yes, God be praised,   they are all still alive.
Still Manojlo,   the Greek, serves us at home.   100
and with him still   is Djuro, the drunkard.
Only Rado,   the Serb, is gone from us.
He is, they say,   off in far Vidin town."

Duke Mirčeta   then spoke to him again:
"Write a letter   to Radosav the Serb,
tell him to wait   there at Bosut River.
Then take with you   your two faithful servants,
and set you forth   to old Trnovo town.
Don't be afraid   of King Šišman, brother.
If he wants you   to drink red wine with him,   110
the drunk Djuro   will drink red wine for you.
If they begin   to speak Greek among them,
then Manojlo,   a Greek, will speak for you.
As well, if there   is fighting to be done,
then Radosav,   a Serb, will fight for you."

When Radul Bey   heard all of this advice,
he sent notice   to Radosav the Serb
to wait for him   there at Bosut River.
Then the bey took   with him his faithful servants.
Just as he came   to the cold, swift river,   120

3. The Ugričićes were a family of noblemen, warriors from Hungary well known in their time.

awaiting him   was Radosav the Serb.
There they warmly   kissed each other's faces,
and Rado kissed   his hand and his coat's end.
Then they travelled   to old Trnovo town.

They were met there   by the king most warmly.
He then ordered   their horses to stable
and escorted   the bey to his quarters.
Then all sat down   at a readied table,
and they drank wine   all for a whole long week.
With King Šišman   were twelve trusted courtiers,   130
and with the bey   his three faithful servants.
That Radul Bey   often looked about him,
often observed   the rooms of the white court
to see whether   they'll now bring forth the boy.

And then, behold,   there arose King Šišman;
he lifted up   a huge cup of red wine,
a cup, they say,   that holds twelve full liters,
toasted the bey,   then passed the cup to him.
The bey passed it   to Djuro the drunkard.
Djuro drank it   without any trouble.   140

When he saw that,   the Bulgarian king,
he then began   to speak Greek to his men
about murder,   how to kill Radul Bey
and his servants,   his three faithful servants.
But Manojlo   understood Greek language,
and he shouted   to Radosav the Serb:
"Do you not hear?   We are to be slaughtered!"

When Radosav,   the Serb, heard his loud cry,
he then drew out   his shiny green saber
and he killed there   King Šišman on the spot,   150
there together   with his twelve counselors.
Then they plundered   that old Trnovo town
and they captured   great wealth in that city,
they took with them   many horses, falcons,
and they returned   to Bucharest city.

Woe to brother   who's without another!

The Death of Duke Prijezda[4]

"The Death of Duke Prijezda" came to Vuk as it had been sung by blind Jeca in Zemun. The song is one of two songs that tell the story of the fall of the fortress at Stalać, an important event in the Turkish conquest of Serbia, occurring around 1410. The other, earlier and inferior, version is a chronicle, distanced in its point of view; it is to be found in the Erlangen manuscript. Jeca's version, much less "objective," centers on the experience of the commander of the fortress, a Duke Prijezda. Historically, Prijezda did not command at Stalać but at Novo Brdo, some thirty years later, in 1441, when that rich silver town and cultural center, the last Serbian center to fall, came uncertainly under Turkish control. So both accounts are fusions of two different historical events.

Nevertheless, Jeca's version has, at least, a remarkable thematic unity and emotional power. Again a justification for a Serbian defeat, it combines historical and traditional materials such as the variant on the formulaic opening, the inordinately powerful if not magical sword, and the flying—or at least amazingly mobile—horse. Yet the song resolves itself in its ending, an expansion on that of the Erlangen version, which develops the poignancy of the double suicide. Thus the conclusion, which offers the sultan only the emptiest of victories, gives redemptive purpose to this tragic story of loss.[5]

The Death of Duke Prijezda

Written letters   follow one another.
Where are they from,   to whom are they going?
They're from Mehmed,   mighty Turkish sultan.[6]
They are addressed   to the town of Stalać,[7]
to Prijezda,   the duke of Stalać town:
"O Prijezda,   O duke of Stalać town,
dispatch to me   three of your possessions:
first you send me   your own battle saber,

---

4. "Smrt vojvode Prijezde," II, 357, #75.

5. See Koljević, 89–90. Koljević later calls "The Death of Duke Prijezda" "the greatest example of a tragic feudal drama in the Serbo-Croat oral epic tradition" (319).

6. Mehmed (Mohammed) I, sultan from 1389 to 1421.

7. Stalać fortress was located at the juncture of the Western Morava and Morava rivers, northeast of Kruševac, in eastern Serbia.

the one that cuts   through all wood and through rocks,
through wood and rocks,   and cold iron as well.   10
And the second,   you send me your gray horse,
your own gray horse   that can fly through the air,[8]
clear two fort walls   all in one single leap.
And third, send me   your own dear faithful wife."

Duke Prijezda   sees and reads the letter,
Sees one letter   and then writes another:
"O Tsar Mehmed,   mighty tsar of the Turks,
bring your army   as large as you desire,
below Stalać,   whenever you desire,
attack Stalać   however you desire;   20
I'll not give you   any of the three things.
For I have forged   the saber for myself,
and I have raised   the gray horse for myself,
and I've brought home   my wife to be my own.
I'll not give you   any of the three things."

The tsar, Mehmed,   gathered his large army,
brought his army   and besieged Stalać town.
He buffeted   Stalać for three full years,
he could knock down   not a stick nor a stone.
He could neither   win the town of Stalać,   30
nor would he cease,   and abandon his siege.

So one morning,   a day before Sunday,
the Duke's fair wife   mounted to the ramparts,
on the ramparts   of the small Stalać town.
From there she sees   the Morava River,
the Morava,   murky beneath the walls.
Prijezda's love   then says these words to him:
"O Prijezda,   O my dearest master,
I am afraid,   O my dearest master,
the Turks will dig   tunnels and blow us up."   40
But Prijezda,   the duke, interrupts her:

8. The horse is called *Ždral* (meaning, literally, "crane"), but that word is also used to refer to a gray horse.

"Quiet, my love,   bite your sweet tongue, will you?
How can they dig   underneath Morava?"

Then came Sunday,   the first after that talk.
The noblemen   then all attended church,
and all stood tall   throughout the church service.
When they came out   of the church afterward,
Duke Prijezda   began to talk to them:
"O my dear lords,   my loyal supporters,
the wings with which   I will fly high and wide,   50
now let us dine,   and let us drink red wine,
and then let us   open the city gates;
we shall attack,   make battle with the Turks.
God and fortune   give whate'er they will."

Then Prijezda   summoned his faithful wife:
"My faithful wife,   go down to the cellar,
bring us some wine   and good *raki* to drink."
Jela took with her   two small golden pitchers,
and she went down   to the lower cellar.
But when she came   down to the wine cellar,   60
she saw it full   of mean janissaries
drinking cool wine   from their leather slippers,
to the good health   of Jela, the wife,
and to the soul   of the duke, Prijezda.

When she saw it,   the noble Jela saw,
she dropped quickly   the pitchers to the ground
and she hurried   back to her master's hall:
"Your wine has turned   sour, my good master,
your wine sour,   your *raki* even worse!
For your cellar's   full of janissaries,   70
and they drink wine   from their leather slippers,
they drink red wine,   drink wine to my good health.
But they also   would bury you alive,
in burying you   they now drink to your soul."

Duke Prijezda   jumped to his nimble feet,
opened the gates   before Stalać city,

and they attacked,   made battle with the Turks.
They fought the Turks   in hand-to-hand combat,
till sixty lords   fell on the battlefield.
Sixty lords fell,   all with thousands of Turks.   80

Duke Prijezda   then returned to his fort,
and behind him   he closed the city gates.
He then drew out   his own battle saber
and he cut off   the head of his gray horse:
"O my gray horse,   my dear priceless treasure,
the tsar, sultan,   will never ride on you."
He then destroyed,   broke his battle saber:
"My sharp saber,   my right hand in battles,
the tsar, sultan,   will not hold you in hand."
He then went up   to his dear wife's chambers   90
and took his wife   by her noble white hands:
"O Jelica,   who is a wise lady,
would you rather   that you perish with me
or that you be   the dear wife of a Turk?"

And the lady,   Jelica, shed salt tears:
"I would rather   die with you in honor,
than now to be   the shamed love to a Turk.
I will never   abandon my own faith,
I won't trample   on this our Holy Cross."

Then they took hold   of each other's white hands,   100
and they climbed up,   up to Stalać's ramparts,
and there she spoke,   the lady, Jelica:
"O Prijezda,   O my dearest master!
The Morava   has always nourished us,
let her water,   Morava's, bury us."
And then they leaped   into the Morava.

The tsar, Mehmed,   captured that Stalać town,
but he captured   none of the three treasures.
The Tsar Mehmed   of Turkey cursed in rage:
"O Stalać town,   may God grind you to dust!   110
I brought with me   o'er three thousand soldiers,
but five hundred   only I have left now."

Porča of Avala and Vuk, the Fiery Dragon[9]

One of the most droll and most amusing of the songs of the Turkish occupation, "Porča of Avala and Vuk, the Fiery Dragon" introduces to us one of the folkloric heroes of the Belgrade region, Vuk the Fiery Dragon, a somewhat caricatured (and somewhat comic) version of the Despot Vuk Branković (1471–1485).[10] Vuk Karadžić's singer clearly recognized the comic possibilities of the contest to the death between this fantasized champion of the Belgrade Serbs and the villainous and lustful Porča, who like so many Turks was known to kidnap beautiful Serbian maidens.

The Jakšić brothers, whom we shall meet later, are present here, but only as spectators. Porča and his boastful sidekick, his prophetically named *pobratim*, Alija Djerzelez, whose name is derived from *jelen*, or "deer," are both fictitious, perhaps representatives of the sort of Moslems who oppose Vuk, the Fiery Dragon. Djerzelez, more deer than *pobratim*, at the end runs away to Sarajevo, a city then securely in Turkish hands and thus safer for Moslems. For the singer here seems to laugh away the whole pomposity of armed conflict, a position certainly shared by many of the peasants of the occupied Balkan uplands, or even the Serbs of Belgrade itself.

Porča of Avala and Vuk, the Fiery Dragon

Two sworn-brothers   spent much time drinking wine
on Avala,   a hill above Belgrade.
And one of them   was Avala's Porča,
and the other   Alija Djerzelez.
After they'd drunk,   had their fill of drinking,
and when they'd reached   a state of vulgar boasting,
first there spoke   Avala's friendly Porča:
"My sworn brother,   Alija Djerzelez,
don't you worry,   drink to your heart's desire,

---

9. *"Porča od Avale i Zmajognjeni Vuk,"* II, 415, #93.

10. Vuk Branković, a descendant of the Branković dynasty—and a namesake of the infamous Vuk Branković of the Kosovo era—was a ruler in the borderlands between Hungary and the Turks. He was known as a brave warrior and a great diplomat, receiving favors from both the Hungarians and the Turks. The nickname *Zmajognjeni*, the Fiery Dragon, he may have acquired either because of his bravery or because he had received the Hungarian decoration of the Dragon.

I've a vineyard   near the porch of my house.   10
I have much wine,   plenty in the cellar,
I have much wine   and plenty of good *raki*."

To him answered   Alija Djerzelez:
"It's all for naught,   O my dear sworn-brother;
it's all for naught,   all your wine and *raki*,
for you've no one,   no good young wine-server
who can serve us   the wine and the *raki*.
For it's no fun   without a young wine girl."

Then our Porča   truly became angry,
and he spoke thus   to Alija Djerzelez: 20
"My sworn brother,   just keep drinking your wine,
while I go forth   to stately Belgrade town.
I will bring you   a young wine-serving girl,
either a girl,   or a beautiful bride."

Then he inquired,   Alija Djerzelez:
"When you go forth   to stately Belgrade town,
are you afraid   of anyone but God?
Are you afraid   of the young Jakšićes?"

To him answered   Porča of Avala:
"So help me God,   O my dear sworn brother,   30
I'm not afraid   of anyone, save God,
I do not fear   the two young Jakšićes.
But, my brother,   I am a bit afraid,
I am afraid   of Vuk the Fiery Dragon
from the spacious   flatland of the Srem,
from the village   there of Kupinovo.
Kupinovo   is a long way from here,
and the wide Srem   a spacious, level land,
but I don't wish   to meet Vuk in Belgrade."

Then he shouted,   Porča of Avala: 40
"My good servants,   bring me my white horse here!"
Then while Porča   did prepare his saddle,
his good servants   led out his swift white horse.

Porča leapt up   on his horse's shoulders
and rode straight out   down the field of Vračar.

When he then came   to the calm Sava River,
he rode along   by the Sava River.
And sure enough,   the two young Jakšićes
were drinking wine   in Nebojša tower,
there together   with Vuk, the Fiery Dragon.   50

Vuk, the Dragon,   surveyed the surroundings
and was looking   at the Sava River.
When he saw there   Porča of Avala,
he spoke calmly,   Vuk, the Fiery Dragon:
"Do you see him,   you two young Jakšićes?
Who could it be   by the Sava River?"

After they looked,   the two young Jakšićes,
they recognized   Porča of Avala
And then they spoke   to Vuk, the Fiery Dragon:
"Our sworn brother,   Vuk, the Fiery Dragon,   60
that's that bastard,   Porča of Avala.
No day passes   without his sly visit,
his abduction   of a live prisoner,
or a dead one,   if he can't catch one live."

Thereupon spoke   Vuk, the Fiery Dragon:
"O our dear God,   thank you for everything!
for nine long years   I've been praying to you,
God Almighty,   the only truthful One,
to let me meet   Porča of Avala.
You have answered   all my prayers today."   70
Then he added,   Vuk, the Fiery Dragon:
"Up on your feet,   you two young Jakšićes;
go and find me,   somewhere, a poor maiden,
and put on her   a silk and velvet dress.
Give her also   a small golden pitcher,
and then bring her   there to the Sava's banks,
so she can trick   that Turkish fellow there,
make him waste time,   some time talking to her,

while I ready   myself and my dun horse."
So Vuk hurried   to ready his dun horse.   80

The Jakšićes   made the maiden ready,
and they dressed her;   she could not seem finer,
and they gave her   a small golden pitcher,
and they brought her   there to the Sava's banks.
Just as the maid   arrived at the river,
she there began   to draw river water,
and here he came,   Porča of Avala.
He bid the maid   good-day and God's blessing,
and she returned   his greetings in good grace.
He spoke to her,   Porča of Avala: 90
"In dear God's name,   O you pretty maiden,
draw me water   in your golden pitcher
so I may drink   the cool river water."

The fair maiden   began to talk to him:
"Dismount your horse,   O you valiant stranger,
dismount your horse,   and drink this cool water."

Then to her spoke   Porča of Avala:
"So help me God,   O you pretty maiden,
this horse of mine   has a foolish nature,
once I get off,   he won't let me remount.   100
So please give me   water from the pitcher,
because I thirst,   I am very thirsty."

The girl heeded   his insistent request;
she scooped water   in her golden pitcher
then offered him   water from her pitcher.
But Porča took   no water nor pitcher.
He seized the girl   by her white, slender arm,
and he threw her   behind him on the horse,
tied her firmly   with a strong silken rope,
and galloped off,   down the field of Vračar.   110

Vuk observed all,   Vuk, the Fiery Dragon.
He then quickly   mounted his swift dun horse,
and he galloped   down the field of Vračar.

He overtook   Porča of Avala,
and then he spoke   to the frightened Porča:
"Stop, you bastard,   Porča of Avala,
stop a moment,   so that we can duel."
But when Porča   saw and recognized him,
he threw away   the maiden in the grass,
and he ran fast   down the field of Vračar.   120
Vuk then chased him,   Vuk, the Fiery Dragon.
He pursued him,   but he couldn't catch him.
And thus they rode   up Avala Mountain.

They were seen by   Alija Djerzelez,
who called loudly   to his faithful servants:
"O my servants,   lock up the doors quickly
all the towers   and all the front gates there!
See, here they come,   two fast, valiant warriors,
chase each other,   there in the green forest;
soon they'll be here,   chase one another here!   130
When they can find   none of our doors open,
our brave Porča   then must stand his ground here,
and he will slay   Vuk, the Fiery Dragon."

His good servants   obeyed orders quickly,
and shut up tight,   quickly, all the front doors.
But when the two   warriors reached the tower,
Porča rode fast   around his white tower
and kept shouting: "Open the gates quickly!"
But no one dared   open the gate for him.
And Vuk chased him   three times around the tower,   140
till he caught him,   right by the castle gate,
and there Vuk cut   his cowardly head off.
Then he mounted   his well-groomed, well-fed horse,
and placed the head   of Porča in the feed bag,
and he rode straight   to stately Belgrade town.

All of this saw   Alija Djerzelez
and then he spoke   words of thanks to his God:
"O our dear God,   thank you for everything,
especially   for all the fastened doors

on all the gates   and on all white towers,   150
otherwise, Vuk   would have caused much more pain."
Then Djerzelez   fled to Sarajevo.

 ## The Division of the Jakšićes[11]

"The Division of the Jakšićes" sets forth an event in the lives of two fifteenth-century Serbian lords when property is bequeathed to them and divided between them, in violation of the tradition that feudal estates were never to be divided.[12] The song is given a cosmic setting; the Sun's (the Day Star or Morning Star) and Moon's discussion of the matter serves as its opening and offers to its events a distancing point of judgment. But the events themselves—although turning around words of truth spoken by a hawk—are material enough, and the main actors are historical, Dmitar having killed Duke Mihailo of Sibinj in 1510.[13] And indeed, all of them, including the younger brother Bogdan's wife Andjelija (or "Angel"), seem driven almost entirely by the most mundane of materialist considerations. For, even though horse and hawk bear symbolic and even legal reference, the dispute is clearly a dispute over simple possession—the sort of dispute that characterized so much of the history of the Balkans in the fifteenth century. It is only after possession becomes no longer possible that fraternal love, the highest of the traditional values of the Balkans, comes to be of importance. Thus, especially in its ironic ending, "The Division of the Jakšićes" seems to manipulate its symbolic elements in ways to bring it to the edge of almost subversive political allegory.[14]

Vuk recorded "The Division of the Jakšićes" from his own memory of his father's singing of it. He showed the text to Jakob Grimm and in 1823, on Vuk's journey to Germany, Grimm appended the poem to a letter of introduction of Vuk to Goethe in Weimar. Goethe became very interested, and asked Vuk for more songs and translations. As a young man Goethe had, of course, done a secondhand translation of the *Hasanagini-*

11. *"Dijoba Jakšića,"* II, 442, #98.
12. The two brothers Jakšić belong to a nobleman's family in northeastern Serbia of the fifteenth century. Dmitar and Stefan (Bogdan of the song) participated in many battles against the Turks. Dmitar drowned near Smederevo in 1486.
13. See Koljević, 195.
14. See Koljević, 111–12.

ca for Herder's *Volkslieder* in 1778–1779, but it was "The Division of the Jakšićes" that first interested him in Vuk's collections.[15]

The Division of the Jakšićes

The Moon speaks out   hard words for the Day Star:
"What have you done   with your time, O Day Star?
wasted your time,   where have you wasted time?
wasted your time   there for three long white days?"

Then the Day Star   to the Moon makes answer:
"What have I done?   I have spent all my time
above Belgrade,   above that big white town,
where I looked and   saw a mighty wonder,
how two brothers   shared their father's lands,
Mitar Jakšić   and his brother Bogdan.[16]   10
These two brothers   made a fair agreement;
they divided   in two their father's land.
That Dimitar   took land in Karavlaška,
Karavlaška   and Karabogdanska,[17]
all the Banat,   down to Danube's waters.
And all the Srem,   the plain was for Bogdan;
all of the Srem   and the plains of the Sava,
and Serbia,   southwards to Užice.[18]
Dimitar took   all of lower Belgrade,
and Nebojša,   the fort on the Danube,   20
and Bogdan took   all the upper city
and Ružica   the church in the center.[19]

But on one point,   one small point they quarrelled.
It was nothing,   and yet it was something:
a jet black horse   and a gray falcon too.

15. See Wilson, 177–80, 192.
16. *Mitar* is a traditional south Slavic shortening of *Dimitar* or "Dimitrius."
17. According to Wilson, Wallachia and Moldavia. See Wilson, 364 n.
18. Užice, a town in the southern part of Western Serbia.
19. Thus Dimitar took the city of Belgrade as it exists today south of the juncture of the Sava and the Danube, and Bogdan took Zemun, probably at the beginning of the nineteenth century a fair division.

As the elder,   Dimitar claimed the horse,
the jet black horse,   also the gray falcon;
and neither one   would Bogdan surrender.

Then one morning,   at the light of daybreak,
Mitar mounted   on the great jet black horse,   30
and then he took   also the gray falcon,
and he set out   hunting up in the hills.
But he had called   his wife Andjelija:
"O listen well,   Andjelija, my love,
you must poison   Bogdan, my own brother;
if you refuse,   as I say, to kill him,
don't wait for me,   there in my white castle."

Andjelija,   after she heard his words,
she sat down there,   worried and unhappy,
her thoughts heavy,   she spoke thus to herself: 40
"How sad I am,   in such a dilemma;
if I poison   his very own brother,
our God would think   that this is a great sin,
and a great crime   in the eyes of people;
of all mankind,   high and low, they'll blame me,
say, 'Look at her,   look at that cursed woman,
her who poisoned   her own husband's brother!'
But if I fail,   if I don't poison him,
then I must leave   my noble husband's house."

She thought a bit   and then made up her mind.   50
Then she went down   to a lower chamber,
and she took up   a large holy chalice,
made of pure gold,   made all of beaten gold,
which she had brought   from her own father's house.
She filled it up   with red wine to the rim.
Then she took it   to her husband's brother,
kissed his garment   and then kissed his hand,
and she bowed down   before him to the ground.
"In your honor,   brother of my husband,
I bring to you   this cup full of red wine;   60
will you give me   the black horse and falcon?"

At that moment   he felt sadness for her,
and he gave her   the black horse and falcon.

Meanwhile Mitar,   in the hills all day long
had there hunted,   but he could kill nothing.
And chance led him,   as the evening drew on,
to a green lake   high in the hills he came,
and there he saw   a drake with golden wings.
Then Dimitar   loosed the great gray falcon;
he wished to take   the drake with golden wings.   70
And yet this drake   no way would be taken;
this brave creature   seized the great gray falcon,
and then it broke   the gray falcon's right wing.

When he saw that,   Dimitrije Jakšić,
he straight took off   his lordly apparel,
and he swam out   far into the still lake,
and thus he saved   his wounded gray falcon.
Then he inquired   of his wounded falcon,
"How do you feel,   O my great gray falcon?
How can you bear   the loss of your right wing?"   80
Then the falcon   answered in his shrill voice,
"O I feel now   without my own right wing
as a brother   feels without his brother."

Dimitar then   thought and recalled to mind
that his dear wife   would poison his brother.
So he mounted   upon his jet black horse,
and rode quickly   to Belgrade, white city,
hoping to find   his brother still alive.
When he arrived   at Čekmek, the small bridge,[20]
he spurred him on,   his black horse, to cross it,   90
but then the horse   fell through holes on the bridge,
and the black horse,   falling, broke both forelegs.
When Dimitar   saw his great misfortune,
he then took up   the saddle from the horse,

---

20. The Čekmek bridge, which spanned the Sava, is the passage from Dimitar's land to his brother's.

and he placed it   ashoulder with his mace,
and thus in haste   came to the white city.

When he arrived,   he called out to his wife:
"Andjelija,   o my dear, faithful love,
have you killed him,   poisoned my own brother?"
Andjelija   thus to him made answer: 100
"I've not killed him,   poisoned your own brother,
ah, but rather,   I've made peace between you."

Recast from a translation by Duncan Wilson [21]

 ## The Wife of Hasan Aga [22]

One of the first recorded songs, *Hasanaginica,* or "The Wife of Hasan Aga," was the first of the songs to attract a readership in western Europe. The Italian abbot Alberto Fortis, having read Macpherson's *Ossian* in Cesarotti's Italian translation, began to travel in the Dalmatian islands in search of similar material, although his Serbo-Croatian was far from adequate. He was supplied by Dalmatian friends with a text of "The Song of Miloš Kobilić and Vuk Branković," probably taken from a version by Andrija Kačić Miošić, a Franciscan monk, which he had published in 1771. Three years later, in his book entitled *Viaggio in Dalmazia,* a book devoted to the culture and customs of the people he called the *Morlacchi,* Fortis presented—in the original Serbo-Croatian from a manuscript sent him by friends in Ragusa and in a parallel Italian translation—the *Hasanaginica.*

Fortis's *Viaggio* was fully translated into German by 1776, and it was from this German language text that Goethe made his translation, *Klaggesang von der edlen Frauen des Asan Aga,* which appeared with Herder's own translation of "The Song of Miloš Kobilić and Vuk Branković" in his *Volkslieder.* Jernej Kopitar, Vuk's supporter, showed him Goethe's translation in 1813, two years before Vuk's first modest collection appeared, in *Kleine serbische Grammatik.* And then, of course, there would be others: Walter Scott's (which remained unpublished until the twentieth century), and John Bowring's (based on a popular German version by a disciple of

---

21. See Wilson, 364–66.
22. "*Hasanaginica,*" III, 372, #80.

Goethe, Therese Albertine Luise von Jakob, or "Talvj") of 1827, and Prosper Mérimée's spurious French version of the same year in *La Guzla*.[23]

In his later collections, Vuk was not sure what to do with *Hasanaginica*. For it was neither a *junačka pesma*—a "heroic song," usually sung in accompaniment by a *gusle,* a narrative dealing with dangerous travels, wars, or fighting—nor was it a *ženska pesma*—a lyric song or round dance sung without the *gusle,* often connected with folk custom or belief and treating of more personal subjects. For, although it was conducted in the *deseterac* (but without the *gusle*) and was narrative in form—even built around the story of a wedding journey, as are a number of the heroic songs—its concerns were not with heroism nor with physical action but with domestic and even maternal matters. Vuk did not include the song in the Leipzig edition, but later, along with others he placed the song in a category described simply as "ballads."[24]

It is certainly the case that the *Hasanaginica* is a domestic poem, a poem about maternal love; certainly as such it was dear to the hearts of the Romantic poets of several countries. But this poem has clear historical reference; Pintorović was a historical figure present on the Dalmatian coast in the middle of the seventeenth century during the Candian War between Venice and the Ottomans. And the poem also is concerned with broader themes, themes generated directly by the Turkish occupation of the Balkans. Christian ideas of marriage as sacrament come into conflict here with Islamic permissiveness in divorce. Social rank is important. The heroine, the sister of a bey or a governor, is of more exalted social rank than her husband, an *aga;* thus her absence at his bedside at the beginning of the poem is particularly hurtful to the Moslem husband, albeit appropriate according to Balkan Christian belief, which requires that a wife not be present to observe her husband in moments of weakness. And her second husband, a *kadi,* is of the highest rank of all, thus particularly galling to *Hasan Aga*.[25]

Thus "The Wife of Hasan Aga" can be read not only as a sentimental ballad but as a tragedy of cultural conflict, a tragedy in which neither party is to blame. By such a reading, we may be able to save the poem from its translators.

23. See Low's *Ballads of Marko Kraljević,* ix–xxiii, which provides a succinct and interesting account the history of the translation of the poem. See also Koljević, 4–7.

24. See "Vuk's Introduction to Book I of his 'Leipzig Collection' of Serb 'Popular Songs,' 1824," Wilson, Appendix E, 395–400, 395; and Pennington and Levi, 167.

25. Pennington and Levi make similar observations, on 167–68.

The Wife of Hasan Aga

What shines so white   there in the green forest?
Is it white snow   or a flock of white swans?
If it were snow,   it would have melted now;
If it were swans,   they would have flown away.
It is not snow,   nor is it the white swans;
it is the tent   of Aga Hasan Aga.
He lies there ill   with grievous battle wounds.
Both his mother   and his sister are there,
but not his wife,   for she is too ashamed.

After his wounds   have now begun to heal,   10
he then sends word   to his dear faithful wife:
"Don't wait for me   in my white court again,
not at my court,   nor among my people."
While the lady   listens to the message,
while the poor one   still ponders over it,
trampling horses   are heard out in the court.
The aga's wife   then rushes forth headlong
to throw herself   from the tower's window.

Her two daughters,   maidens, run after her:
"Come back to us,   O our dearest mother!   20
It is not he,   our father, Hasan Aga,
but our uncle,   the bey, Pintorović."

So she comes back,   Hasan Aga's woman,
and throws her arms   around her brother's neck:
"My dear brother,   it is a great disgrace
to send me off,   away from my children."
The silent bey   says not a single word,
but puts his hand   in his silken pocket,
and he draws forth   a writ of annulment,
that which dissolves   marital vows in full,   30
that returns her   with him to her mother.

When the lady   has examined the writ,
on their foreheads   she kisses her two sons,
kisses her girls   both on their rosy cheeks.

But from her boy,   sleeping in the cradle,
she cannot part,   nor tear herself away,
till her brother   takes her by her white hands,
and withdraws her   away from her own son.
Then he seats her   behind him on his horse,
and together   they ride to their white home.   40

With her own kin   she stays but a short time,
not long, indeed,   not even a full week.
For a good wife,   from a good family,
suitors will come   from all lands to woo her.
Most often comes   Kadi of Imotski.[26]
Then the lady   pleads to her own brother:
"In the true name   of our love, my brother,
don't marry me   to any other man,
or my sad heart   will surely break in grief
just at the sight   of my orphaned children."   50
But the proud bey   pays no heed to her pleas,
and he gives her   to Imotski Kadi.

Then the lady   pleads unto her brother
to write for her   a letter on white paper
and to send it   to Imotski Kadi:
"Your bride sends you   her most cordial greetings
and she begs you   kindly in this letter,
when you gather   your great wedding party,
when you set out   then for her white dwelling,
please bring with you   a long veil for the bride,   60
so that, later,   passing the aga's court,
she does not see   her five orphaned children."
When the *kadi*   receives the white letter,
he gathers all   wedding guests together,
gathers his guests,   and set forth for his bride.

The wedding guests   go gaily to the bride
and merrily   they turn homeward with her.
When, returning,   they pass the aga's court,
the two daughters   see her from the window,

26. A *kadi* is a judge. Imotski is a town in Western Hercegovina.

and the two sons   come running out to her.   70
And as they do,   they speak to their mother:
"Come to see us,   O our dearest mother,
so that we may   offer you a dinner."

And when the wife   of Hasan Aga hears,
she speaks to him,   bridesman of the party:
"Brother in God,   bridesman of the party,
stop the horses   beside the aga's court,
for I would give   presents to my orphans."
The horses stop   beside the aga's court.
She gives fine gifts   to all of her children: 80
to her two sons   gives each a gilded knife;
to each daughter   a dress down to the ground;
and to the boy   sleeping in the cradle,
to him she sends   a bundle of fine clothes.

When the noble   Hasan Aga sees this,
he calls sadly   to him his two young sons:
"Come here to me,   my poor orphaned children,
because she has   little pity for you,
your own mother,   with a heart of cold stone."

When she hears that,   wife of Hasan Aga,   90
she then falls down,   her white face struck the earth.
At that instant   she parts from her own soul
all from the grief   of seeing her orphans.

 ## Janko Jurišić[27]

Many of the poems after Kosovo are partly conceived in the world of fantasy, the world of dreams of freedom and memories of heroism that generate anachronisms, that compose wished-for realities out of the remembered or imagined facts of history. Thus it was in part at least the work of the singers to compose as well as to record the past, or even to imagine it as an alternative world for an oppressed people.

"Janko Jurišić," which Vuk heard from a Bosnian merchant and in-

27. "Jurišić Janko," II, 231, #52.

cluded in the 1833 edition of *Srpke narodne pjesme,* is a part of such an undertaking. Almost certainly it was originally conceived in the late seventeenth or early eighteenth century, during the most difficult period of the occupation for Balkan Christians, when many Serbs had been deported to Belgrat. In it the singer places Marko Kraljević on Kosovo field fighting on the Christian side, which as we shall see, certainly could never have happened. And he places Suleiman the Magnificent, who ruled as sultan in the latter half of the seventeenth century and who was generally regarded as the greatest of the Ottomans, on Kosovo field as well. But the facts of history, which are always changing over time, are perhaps not always of paramount importance. Rather, as we have seen in the Marko Kraljević songs, sometimes it is the song itself, and the version of history it provides, that matters.

Janko Jurišić

Someone's crying there in Stamboul city:
is it a snake or the good white *vila*?
It is neither a snake nor white *vila,*
but a hero, that Janko Jurišić.
If he's crying, it is for good reason,
for already three long years have passed
since black darkness swallowed up brave Janko
in the dungeon of a tyrant ruler,
that tyrant tsar by name of Suleiman.
And the darkness has so troubled Janko   10
that he cries out in the morn and evening.
Thus he troubles even the cold stone there,
not to mention the tyrant Suleiman.

Tsar Suleiman makes a sudden visit,
and he arrives at the dungeon's doorway,
and he summons that Janko Jurišić:
"O you bastard, you Janko Jurišić,
what's your trouble, and why so urgently
do you cry out in my famous dungeon?
Are you hungry or tormented by thirst?
Or are you torn by a man's desire,   20
by a desire for your sort of woman?"

He then answers,   brave Janko Jurišić:
"You're of good cheer   to talk like that, O tsar.
I am neither   hungry nor am thirsty,
and I have lost   all desire for woman
from the moment   this dungeon swallowed me.
No, it's darkness   that causes me trouble.
O great sultan,   if you believe in God,
demand treasure   as much as you would like,
but let me out   of this accursed dungeon."   30

Tsar Suleiman   then speaks to poor Janko:
"O you bastard,   you Janko Jurišić,
I do not want   a ducat of money,
but I ask you   to tell me honestly
who were those three   valiant dukes and heroes
that made mincemeat   of my gallant army
when I passed o'er   the field of Kosovo?"

He then answers,   brave Janko Jurišić:
"You're of good cheer   to talk like that, O tsar.   40
Since you have asked,   I'll tell you honestly.
The one hero,   the first among the dukes,
who pursued them,   your Turks, especially,
and who chased them   to Lab and Sitnica,
that was the lad,   brave Marko Kraljević.
And the brave duke   who was behind Marko,
and he who cut   many Turkish heads off,
that was Ognjan,   the young novice, Ognjan,
the dear nephew   of Marko Kraljević.
And the third duke   of whom you inquired,   50
the one who broke   his sharp sword in battle
and who was forced   to kill Turks with his spear
and to throw them   high over his own head
in the rivers,   Lab and Sitnica,
that none other   but Janko Jurišić.
Here he is, tsar,   in your cursed dungeon;
do with him now   whatever you desire."

Tsar Suleiman   then answers Jurišić:
"O you bastard,   you Janko Jurišić,

the one torture   that pleases you the most,   60
with that torture   I'll put an end to you.
Would you rather   swim in the deep blue sea,
or would prefer   to burn live in the fire,
or would prefer   that we tear you apart,
tear you apart   among the horses' tails?"

And then Janko   answers the sultan thus:
"You're of good cheer   to talk like that, O tsar.
No one would like   to be tortured like that,
not if there is   any other manner.
I'm not a fish   to swim in the deep sea;   70
I'm not a tree   to burn up in the fire,
I'm not a whore   to be torn to pieces,
torn to pieces   among the horses' tails.
Rather, instead,   I'm an honest warrior.
Give me, O tsar,   a weakling of a horse,
never ridden,   not in full thirty years,
never ridden,   never used in battle.
And give me, too,   an old, useless saber
never unsheathed   not in full thirty years,
never unsheathed   nor used in a battle,   80
covered over,   all over with brown rust,
all so rusty   no man can unsheathe it,
and let me go   out in a wide, green field
And send out there   two hundred janissaries,
let them cut me   to pieces with their swords,
so I can die   as a proper warrior."

Tsar Suleiman   grants him all his wishes.
First, he gives him   a weakling of a horse
never ridden,   not in full thirty years,
never ridden,   never used in battle.   90
And he gives him   an old, useless saber
never unsheathed,   not for full thirty years,
never unsheathed,   nor used in a battle,
covered over,   all over with brown rust,
all so rusty   no man can unsheathe it.
He lets him go   out in a wide, green field,
and after him   two hundred janissaries.

After Janko   has mounted the weak horse,
he whips him so,   that old and weakling horse,
that the poor horse   runs forth that much faster,   100
runs forth across   a wide, empty, green field,
and two hundred   janissaries follow.
One Turk rides fast,   faster than the others,
so he would be   he who beheads Janko
and thus receive   the tsar's golden ducats.
Thus he o'ertakes   that Janko Jurišić.
When Janko sees   himself in great trouble,
he then invokes   the name of the true God,
and he unsheathes   the saber at his belt;
it is drawn forth   as a new-forged saber.   110
And then he greets   that Turk janissary
with his saber,   and with his strong right arm.
He strikes a blow   at the Turk's silken waist,
and two halves fall   from the horse of that Turk.

As the Turk falls,   brave Janko then dismounts.
Janko dismounts   his tired, weakling horse,
and he then mounts   the white horse of the Turk.
He takes away   the saber from that Turk,
and gives battle   to all remaining Turks.
One half of them   he slays with his saber,   120
the other half   sends running to the tsar.
And he rides off   across the wide green field
to his castle   in good health and good cheer.

6   The Songs of Outlaws

*I*N THE SEVENTEENTH CENTURY, throughout Europe and the British Isles, but notably in the Balkans, there was a marked increase in highway robbery. This activity has been seen—although certainly not universally so—as a product of social conditions, for when other methods for the redistribution of wealth fail, robbery can serve. In the Balkans, even before the Turkish invasion, but particularly at the end of the seventeenth century, there was an extended period of peace, but a period when the land was occupied by idle former soldiers and by exploitive and largely independent janissaries, too dangerous and destabilizing to be kept in Istanbul. Taxation was increased to dangerous levels, the corruption of officials as well as tax collectors became a way of life, and the taking of booty by force became, under various forms, a widespread and significant activity.

Certainly it is not uncommon that social victims—whether they come from a peasantry or a recently urbanized class of former agricultural workers or soldiers unskilled in any productive work save agriculture—be driven to brigandage for survival, and thus it is not atypical in folk songs that brigandage is celebrated or at least justified. Frequently in the Balkans robbery came to be seen as a form of social or political protest, even of nascent nationalism. It was celebrated as such, both on the Dalmatian coast in the *bugarštice* and by the *guslars* in the hills, in the folk songs.

In Montenegro, where much of the Christian population had managed to remain in areas outside of Turkish control, outlawry was hardly to be distinguished from military conflict. Montenegrins continued to fight against Ottoman military units, led campaigns of blood vengeance against their Islamized Slav or Albanian neighbors, and led sorties into Turkish occupied Hercegovina as well. Here the fighters held their own land and lived in their families in periods of peace. Thus Vuk would describe their activities as *vojevanje za slobodu* ("fighting for freedom") and collected songs about them in his fourth volume, where his songs of insurrection were gathered, not in the second volume under "*hajduk* songs."

The situation was similar on the Montenegrin coast, an area with a rich tradition of oral poetry. Here again the struggle was essentially a military one, centered on control of the fortress of Herceg-Novi, which commanded the Bay of Kotor, and the real war was between Turkish and Venetian navies. Here local Slavs served in salaried Venetian units, albeit under Slav commanders (they were known as *sirdars*); certainly booty was not an inconsiderable goal and source of support as well.[1] And their heroics were celebrated in the *bugarštice* of the seventeenth and eighteenth centuries. Further up the coast, in the sixteenth and seventeenth centuries, were to be found the *uskoks,* or pirates in the employ of the Austrians, who raided both Turkish and Venetian shipping and even occasionally conducted inland raids into Turkish territory. But their activity was terminated by treaty and they were exiled from Senj in 1618.

In the uplands of Serbia the situation was much different. Here brigandage was a localized affair. Many individuals were drawn into the activity for more or less justifiable but private reasons, for encounters with the injustice of local Turkish or Slav officials, for love of fighting, in a passion for elegance, or for a simple unwillingness to accept one's lot in life. Here individual outlaws fled to the mountains and joined or formed bands who raided with little discrimination neighbor, traveler, and Turkish official alike. However, as time passed and these brigands became more and more organized, their activities increasingly came to take the form—or at least the appearance—of popular rebellion against political authority; the first Serbian insurrection is the culminating case in point, for by the early nineteenth century *hajduk* bands offered themselves to the leaders of the insurrection as already formed fighting units.

Vuk Karadžić, in his *Srpski rječnik* (Serbian dictionary) of 1818, presented a rather balanced opinion of these outlaws:

Our people think and sing in their songs that men become *hajduks* in Serbia as the result of Turkish terror and misrule. It should be said that some went off to

---

1. In Dubrovnik, however, official records referred to these fighters as *hajduks,* or "outlaws." See Koljević, 221–22.

the *hajduks* without being forced to it, in order to wear what clothes and to carry what weapons they liked or to take revenge on someone; but the truth is that the milder the Turkish government, the fewer *hajduks* there were in the land, and the worse and more arbitrary it was, the more *hajduks* there were.[2]

The *hajduks* of Serbia were organized into bands that conducted their activities in the summer when the forests offered habitation and cover. They left behind their land and families but were given food by the *jataks,* peasants who protected them and sheltered them individually in winter when the bands dispersed. They reassembled in the spring, traditionally on St. George's Day. During the winter they dressed, and often lived, as ordinary members of the *raja.* In summer they dressed specially—in costumes forbidden to the *raja* and similar to those of the prosperous Turks. They wore soft shoes, sleeved and embroidered jackets, and breastplates decorated with silver coins. They also carried sidearms—rifles, pistols, and knives—in full view. And all of these were, of course, forbidden to the *raja.* The *hajduks* frequently dressed in blue or in green colors forbidden to all but those faithful to Islam after the eighteenth century. The wearing of green both defied Turkish decree and afforded excellent cover in the summer forest, from which they swept down on Muslim and Christian, Turk, Vlach, or Slav, honest merchant, foreign traveler, or tax gatherer with relative impunity. But among themselves they were tenaciously loyal to their oaths of brotherhood and followed scrupulously their code emphasizing honor, courage, blood vengeance, and—most particularly—a fair and open division of booty, with equal shares even for those killed in the action.

Given the disorder and corruption of the Turkish administration in its later years and the fact that most of the activities of the *hajduks* remained unreported and their identity undisclosed by the *raja* out of family loyalty or simple fear of retribution, the efforts of the Turks to suppress the brigandage were considerable and unrelenting. In nearly every subdistrict were to be found a commander and several guards, Slavs as well as Turks, whose work was to hunt *hajduks*. Occasionally they mounted a *teftis,* an attempt to intimidate villagers into identifying their *hajduks* or *jataks*. If the *hajduks* were killed in combat, the heads were mounted on spears for public display. If captured, they were impaled. Traditionally, however, they bore death bravely. Some of those who survived retired and returned to their communities, often with a guarantee arranged from the *pasha.*

2. V. S. Karadžić, *Srpski rječnik* (Belgrade: Tipographia regni Serbiae, 1898), 826–27 (Duncan Wilson's translation), quoted in Koljević, 216.

No one spoke of their former activity, but a former *hajduk* was never allowed to become a village chief.[3]

Thus, all along the Adriatic coast and throughout the loosely governed and corrupt Balkans of the seventeenth and eighteenth centuries—and presumably in Britain, Germany, Iberia, and Italy as well—brigandage certainly fed upon and perhaps was rooted in maladministration, social injustice, and economic inequality. And the *guslars*—as well as other composers of popular literature treating of outlaws throughout Europe during the time—viewed the brigands with a certain moral ambivalence that made these outlaws particularly appealing to their audiences. The singers of the *deseterci,* even the finest of them, like Tešan Podrugović, seemed at times to take a particularly gruesome delight in the depiction of violence and maiming, especially when it was inflicted on Turkish victims. And the inhumanly violent actions of certain Christian outlaw protagonists, especially in the imposition of revenge on their victims or unfaithful wives, seemed not only accepted but met with a certain approval. For the historical circumstances surrounding a particular report of an event, especially an event occurring far from their mountains, were often not understood by upland peasant singers of limited historical perspective. And thus the impulses to action of the *hajduks* of the littoral—in spite of the fact that their actions were taken at least partly within the conventions of armed societal struggle—were reported as if they were those of the *hajduks* of the Serbian hills.

But the best of the *hajduk* songs recognize the tragic ambiguity in which the protagonists find themselves. On the one hand, they are presented as heroes; their rigid allegiance to the codes of conduct and to blood vengeance, their services to the oppressed, their dash and glamour are emphasized. But their tragic situation is often understood as well. And at the same time, most outlaw-heroes—in the *hajduk* songs as well as in other works concerning outlaws—are represented as bearing some moral imperfection, a flaw that often contributes to a tragic demise.

Predrag and Nenad[4]

One of the most striking of the heroic songs, "Predrag and Nenad" seems to be on its face a *hajduk* song, concerned to express the especially poi-

3. See Koljević's discussion on 215–23.
4. *"Predrag i Nenad,"* II, 62, #16.

gnant isolation that was the *hajduk*'s fate. But "Predrag and Nenad" is strikingly unhistorical; its place names cannot be certainly located (though *Garevica,* rather than the Serbian village presently located in Croatia, seems to mean here not much more than "soot-black" mountain), and the names of the characters (*Predrag* for the older brother means "best loved" and *Nenad* for the younger "the unexpected one") seem to be more appropriate to fable, or at least to medieval tradition.[5] It is also important that the tale centers on an account of fratricide, that most seriously disordering of crimes and that crime perhaps most often recounted in the narratives of patriarchal societies. One must certainly recognize here elements that have their origins well back in the traditions of the tribal Serbs.

"Predrag and Nenad" was sent to Vuk by Jovan Berić, a Serbian writer who lived in Buda, some distance from the land of the outlaws.

Predrag and Nenad

A mother cares   for her two weakly sons
in the bad times,   in the years of hunger,
boys in one hand,   spindle in the other.
She names them well: the first, best loved, Predrag;
Nenad the next,   the unexpected one.

Predrag grows up,   works his mother's horses;
he works horses,   wields a warrior's weapons.
Then he departs,   leaves his ancient mother,
to the mountains,   there to be a *hajduk*.

She stays behind;   now she cares for Nenad.   10
As Nenad grows,   he knows not his brother.
And Nenad, too,   he works for his mother;
he works horses,   wields a warrior's weapons.
Then he departs,   leaves his ancient mother,
to the mountains,   there to be a *hajduk*.

As a *hajduk*   he is gone for three years,
a real hero,   clever and sensible,
and he's lucky,   everywhere, in fighting.

5. See Koljević, 249.

His companions   choose him as their leader,
and he leads them   for three years of struggle.   20

But he is young;   he longs for his mother.
And so he tells   his comrades, his brothers:
"You, my comrades,   you, my dearest brothers,
I long for her,   I long for my mother.
Come, my brothers,   let's divide the booty,
and each go home,   each home to his mother."
His companions   willingly obey him.

As each *hajduk*   spreads out all his booty,
he takes an oath,   swears as to his honor,
one by brother,   another by sister.   30
So when Nenad   spreads out all his booty,
he speaks to them,   to his *hajduk* brothers:
"You, my brothers,   you, my dear companions,
I've no brother,   nor have I a sister,
and yet I swear,   by our only true God;
let my right hand,   my good right hand wither,
let the mane fall   from my good horse's neck,
let my sharp sword   turn bright red with rusting,
if there is more   than this of my booty."
They've divided   by this means their booty.   40

Nenad leaves them,   rides away on his horse,
and he returns   to his dear old mother.
He is welcomed   warmly by his mother;
she gives to him   of her finest *slatko*.[6]
When they sit down   to take their evening meal,
Nenad speaks then   softly to his mother:
"O you old one,   you, my dear old mother,
if it were not   a shame before the world,
if it were not   a grief to the good God,
I would deny   that you are my mother!   50
Why did you not   bear for me a brother,
either brother   or a dear, dear sister?

---

6. Even today, upon the arrival of guests, it is customary in Serbia to serve them *slatko* (a sweet fruit preserve) and water.

When I set out   booty with my comrades,
each of those men   swore to me solemnly,
one by brother,   another by sister,
and I alone,   mother, by my weapons,
by my good horse,   on which I was mounted."

His old mother   laughs a bit at her son:
"Now, young Nenad,   do not be such a fool!
I did give birth   to a brother for you;   60
Predrag, my son,   he is your own brother.
Just yesterday   I heard news about him,
that he's around,   and he is a *hajduk*
on the mountain,   on green Garevica,
and he leads them,   his comrades in his band."

Then young Nenad   says this to his mother:
"O you old one,   you, my dear old mother,
make me a suit,   make me a fresh new one,
all done in green,   from the best of green baize
and not too long,   short like a small bush tree,   70
for I'll go there,   I will seek my brother,
to satisfy   my own lifelong desire."

Then his mother   replies to her dear son:
"Now, young Nenad,   do not be such a fool,
for play like this   will land you in your grave."
But young Nenad   will not hear his mother;
instead he does   whatever pleases him.
She makes a suit,   a new suit to fit him,
all done in green,   from the best of green baize,
and not too long,   short, like a small bush tree.   80
He mounts again   his fine horse, rides away,
and he goes forth   to search for his brother,
to satisfy   his own lifelong desire.

On his way there   he does not say a word,
nor even spit,   nor whisper to his horse.
But when he comes   to Mount Garevica,
he now calls out,   cries like a gray falcon,
"Garevica,   oh, you tall, green mountain,

is there on you   a hero of a man,
my true brother,   my own, dearest Predrag?   90
Do you harbor   on you a true hero,
who could help me   find my own blood brother?"

Predrag lounges   under a green fir tree;
Predrag rests there   and drinks the fine, red wine,
and when he hears   this unfamiliar voice,
he quickly speaks   to his comrades, brothers:
"O my dear men,   my comrades and brothers,
go down the road,   prepare an ambush there,
and await him,   await this unknown man.
Don't injure him,   neither must you rob him,   100
but bring him back,   alive, to me up here.
Where'er he's from,   he is one of our own."

Now thirty youths   take up their positions
in three places,   ten in each of the three.
When Nenad comes   to the first group of ten,
no one of them   dares to stand up to him,
to stand up there,   even to seize his horse,
but they begin   to shoot arrows at him.
Then young Nenad   calls out to all of them:
"Do not shoot me,   you, my mountain brothers;   110
be glad that you   don't yearn for your brother,
as I do now,   and as he does for me,
he who drew me   to come here to this place."
So the first ten   then let him go in peace.

Now Nenad comes   to meet the second ten.
They too prepare   to shoot arrows at him,
and young Nenad   calls out to all of them,
"Do not shoot me,   you, my mountain brothers,
be glad that you   don't yearn for your brother,
as I do now,   and as he does for me,   120
he who drew me   to come here to this place."
And the next ten   then let him go in peace.

And when he comes   to meet with the third ten,
they too prepare   to shoot arrows at him.

Now young Nenad   becomes rather angry,
so he begins   to fight with the thirty.
The first ten youths   he cuts down with his sword;
the second ten   he rides down with his horse.
But the third ten   run back up the mountain,
some to the woods,   others to cold water,   130
and they bring word   to Predrag, the hero,
"While you lounge here,   Predrag, this evil comes;
this unknown man,   it seems he comes for you,
and he has killed   the warriors of your band."

Predrag rises,   jumps nimbly to his feet,
and he gathers   his own bow and arrows,
goes down the road   to prepare an ambush.
He takes a seat   behind a green fir tree,
with an arrow   hits Nenad on his horse.
But he hits him   in a most vital place,   140
a deadly place;   the arrow strikes his heart.

Nenad cries out,   like a great, gray falcon,
crying, screaming,   writhing on his good horse:
"O you hero,   *hajduk* from the mountains,
may God strike you,   brother, and kill you dead!
May your right hand,   your good right hand, wither,
the hand from which   you released that arrow!
May your right eye   fall out of its socket,
that eye with which   you took good aim at me!
And may you yearn   for your brother ever,   150
as I do now,   both I and my brother,
he who drew me   to come here to this place,
to bad fortune,   and at the cost of life!"

When this Predrag   hears his brother's curses,
from his fir tree   he asks him a question:
"Who may you be,   and of whose family?"
Wounded Nenad   makes this answer to him:
"Why do you ask   me of my family now?
Do you, perhaps,   wish to marry to it?
I'm a warrior;   I am called young Nenad.   160
I've a mother,   who lives in her own care.

I've one brother,   only one blood brother;
he's called Predrag,   he's my only brother,
and I came here   to search out that brother,
to satisfy   my one lifelong desire
but with bad luck   and at the cost of life!"

When this Predrag   hears him speak these words,
he drops his bow,   he lets his arrows fall,
and he runs out   to the wounded warrior,
and he lifts him   from his horse to the grass: 170
"So it is you,   O my brother, Nenad!
I am Predrag,   I am your own brother,
and it may be   that you will recover.
I shall now tear   bandages from our shirts;
I'll wrap your wound   with this cloth to cure you."

Wounded Nenad   answers thus unto him:
"So it is you,   my only real brother!
Thanks be to God   that I now can see you;
I've satisfied   my one lifelong desire.
I won't survive   these wounds of my body,   180
but may you be   forgiven for my blood."

As he says this,   his soul leaves his body.
O'er him Predrag   wails out his own sore woes:
"O my Nenad!   a shining sun for me!
You rose early,   early in the morning,
but for me now   you have set much too soon.
You are for me   my green garden's basil;
you bloomed early,   early in the season,
but for me now   you've withered much too soon."
From his belt now   Predrag draws forth his knife.   190
He stabs himself   deeply in his own heart,
and he falls dead,   beside his dead brother.

Assisted by Dragana McFadden

Old Novak and Knez Bogosav[7]

It was Tešan Podrugović who, in his dry manner, recited to Vuk "Old Novak and Knez Bogosav," and the song certainly still bears Tešan's stamp.[8] For the sharp realism of the song—recited by a man who himself had been a *hajduk*—and the intense believability of the conversation it reports give "Old Novak and Knez Bogosav" a real psychological authority.[9]

Old Novak, who appears in several of the *hajduk* songs, usually in the vicinity of Mount Romanija in Bosnia—a traditional *hajduk* hideaway—and often with his son, is probably derived from Novak Debelić, a hero of Bulgarian songs of the mid-sixteenth century who, along with Marko Kraljević, was believed to have defended Bulgaria from the Ottomans; ultimately he may well have been historical. He could well have been a contemporary of Jerina Branković, "the damned Jerina."[10]

Old Novak and Knez Bogosav

They drank red wine,   Novak and Radivoj,
on the Bosna,   a cold, rushing river,
there at the home   of Bogosav, the knez.
After they've had   their fill of cold red wine,
Knez Bogosav   asked the old man, Novak:
"My sworn brother,   you old fellow, Novak!
tell me the truth,   so may great God help you,
what's the reason   you became a *hajduk*?
What misfortune   made you leave your own home,
to risk your head   and roam the green mountains   10
as a *hajduk*,   a devilish business,
at your old age—   not the time to do it?"

Then old Novak   spoke thus in his answer:
"My sworn brother,   my dear Knez Bogosav,
since you've asked me,   let me tell you the truth:
Yes, you are right,   I was in great trouble,

7. "*Starina Novak i knez Bogosav*," III, 9, #1.
8. *Knez* is a title of rank in the South Slavic languages, probably approximated in translation by "duke."
9. See Koljević, 246.
10. See Koljević, 231, 235.

since you would like   to know and remember.
When Jerina   was building Smederevo,[11]
she ordered me   to go and do free labor.
I worked most hard   three long and painful years;   20
I carried there   building stones and timber,
all with my own   cart and faithful oxen.
And in all those   three miserable years
I was not paid   a *para* or *dinar*,[12]
nor did I earn   a single pair of shoes.
Yet I'll forgive,   I'd forgive her, brother.
But when she built   Smederevo city,
and she went on   to building fortresses,
and she gilded   all gates, doors and windows,
she then levied   taxes on the people: 30
three full measures   of gold from each household—
brother, that's worth   full three hundred ducats!

"He who had it,   handed o'er the ducats,
handed over   and was then left in peace.
I was a man   of little property,
I had nothing   of wealth to give to her.
I took a pick   with which I did labor,
and with that pick   I became a *hajduk*.
But I could find   no peaceful place at all
in the country   of the damned Jerina,   40
and so I went   to the Drina River
and crossed into   this rocky Bosnia.

"When I came then   to Mount Romanija,
I once met there   a Turk's wedding party;
they were leading   a lovely maiden forth.
All wedding guests   passed and made no trouble
except for one,   the bridegroom, a young Turk.
He was riding   a beautiful bay horse.

11. Jerina Branković, "the damned Jerina," as she has come to be known (she is so identified later in this poem), was the daughter of Djordje Branković, and she succeeded him to power in Serbia in the later half of the fifteenth century. She sought alliances with Roman Catholics, and was feared by her people. In her fear of the Turks, she built many fortifications, including Smederevo, now a city in northeastern Serbia.

12. A *para* is one hundredth of a dinar.

He did not want   to let me pass in peace,
and he drew forth   a whip with three long tails,   50
a tasselled whip,   three tassels of copper,
and he hit me   on my back with the whip.

"I begged him thrice   not to hit me with it.
'I do beg you,   O you Turkish bridegroom,
for the sake of   your happiness and peace,
and in your hope   of a bright wedding feast,
pass me in peace,   go on your merry way.
Do you not see   that I am a poor man?'
But once again   the Turk gave me no peace,
and he went on   whipping me more and more.   60

"Then it began   to hurt me a little,
and I became   angry, no, furious.
I took my pick   down from off my shoulder,
and I struck him,   sitting on the bay horse.
I did hit him   so lightly and gently
that he fell off   the bay horse to the ground.
I fell on him,   with a few rapid steps,
and I struck him   again, two or three times.
And then his soul   parted from his body.

"I quickly searched   through his silken pockets,   70
and I found there   three purses with money.
and I took them,   placed them in my bosom.
I ungirded   his saber from his belt,
ungirded it,   and put it at my waist.
I left my pick   lying beside his head,
so that the Turks   can bury him with it.
And I mounted   his beautiful bay horse,
I rode straight up   Romanija Mountain.
All the guests there,   Turkish guests, witnessed it;
they had no wish   to follow in pursuit,   80
did not wish it,   nor did any dare to.

"It has been now   just about forty years.
I've gotten used   to Mount Romanija.
It is better,   brother, than my own home.

There I keep guard   over the mountain roads,
I intercept   folks from Sarajevo,
and take from them   booty, silver and gold,
lovely fabrics   and bolts of satin, too.
In these I dress   myself and my colleagues.
I am able   to sweep down and escape   90
and to withstand   the most dangerous threats.
I fear no one   except Almighty God."

 ## The Captivity of Stojan Janković[13]

The song that follows, "The Captivity of Stojan Janković," is a *deseterac* version of an account of events occurring on the Kotari plain northeast of Zadar at the time of the Turkish capture. Venice held Kotari most of the sixteenth and seventeenth centuries, with the exception of one brief period, which is the subject of concern here. "The Captivity of Stojan Janković" personalizes and sentimentalizes these events; its singer clearly lacks the understanding of them necessary to communicate more than an account of a noble family presented in the circumstances of peasant Serbs of the interior uplands. Thus the concern here is first with the vines, secondly with the discharge of debts incident to the recovery of the bride, and thirdly with maternal love, a powerful emotional commodity in the sentimentalization of the Serbian national consciousness.

Stojan Janković is one of the great heroes of the songs of the border raiders. Historically he was an "outlaw" Dalmatian *sirdar* in the employ of the Venetians during the seventeenth century, whose activities took him from the Bay of Kotor to Šibenik and Zadar.[14] During one of the skirmishes with the Turks he was captured and imprisoned in Istanbul, from whence he escaped fourteen months later and rejoined the Venetians. He was killed in a battle in 1867. His *pobratim* here, described as his nephew, is another hero of the songs of the border fighting, Ilija Smiljanić, who died in fighting the Turks in 1654. His death is depicted in another of the *deseterci* songs.

13. "*Ropstvo Jankovića Stojana,*" III, 124, #25.
14. See Koljević, 244, 250, and plate 4, facing 273. A *sirdar*—the word is Turkish—is a military chieftain.

The Captivity of Stojan Janković

When the Turks took   the region of Kotar,
they robbed the court   of the Jankovićes.
They took captive   Ilija Smiljanić;
they took captive   Stojan Janković too.
Ilija left   a pretty bride behind,
a lovely bride   of only fifteen days.
And Stojan left   an even younger bride,
a lovely bride,   only one week married.

The Turks took them   to great Stamboul city,
and they gave them   as gifts to the sultan.   10
There they remained,   captive nine lengthy years,
nine lengthy years   and seven months also.
And the sultan   changed them to Moslems there,
and built them courts   beside his fair palace.

Then to Stojan   spoke Ilija Smiljanić:
"O my Stojan,   my dear, beloved brother,
on the morrow,   Friday, the Turkish feast,
the sultan goes   for a walk with his Turks,
and tsarina   with her ladies as well.
If you will steal   keys to the treasury,   20
and I will steal   the keys to the stable,
we can capture   enough of the treasure
and take with us   two of his fine horses,
so we can ride   out to Kotari plain[15]
and see again   our lovely, faithful wives,
kiss their faces   unkissed by evil Turks."

The two brothers   listened to each other.
So on the morn   of the Turkish feast day
the sultan left   for a walk with his Turks,
and tsarina   walked with her ladies too.   30
Stojan stole keys   to the tsar's treasury,
and Ilija   the keys to the stable.

15. Kotari is a plain northeast of Zadar.

They took much wealth   from the tsar's treasury,
and took two steeds   to ride away on them,
and they rode out   to the Kotari plain.

When they were near   their home town of Kotar,
the young Stojan   was the first one to speak:
"O Ilija,   my dear, loving brother,
please go, brother,   unto our white manor
and I will go   into my own vineyard,   40
to the vineyard   I planted with my hands,
that I may see,   look upon that vineyard,
that I may see   who now binds and prunes it,
and by whose hands   it is kept in order."

To the white court   Ilija went quickly.
To his vineyard   Stojan came nervously.
In the vineyard   he found his old mother,
found his mother,   did Stojan Janković.
There old mother   cut the strands of her hair,
cut the strands and   tied the grapevine with it,   50
and with her tears   she watered the vine sprouts.
Of her lost son   she thought most of the time:
"O my Stojan,   O my golden apple,
your old mother   has almost forgot you;
I'll not forget   daughter-in-law Jela.
O my Jela,   fair as the unworn gold."

Stojan greeted   her in the name of God:
"May God help you,   you poor aging woman;
is there no one   that is younger than you,
to replace you   working in the vineyard?   60
Must you still work,   so old and weak you are?"

The old woman   bravely replied to him:
"Be well and good,   you unknown young hero.
I have no one   younger to assist me,
save for Stojan,   sole son of my desire.
The Turks took him   captive, to his bad luck,
and Ilija,   together with Stojan,
Stojan's nephew,   the son of his uncle.

Ilija left   a lovely bride behind,
a lovely bride   of fifteen days only.   70
And Stojan left   an even younger bride,
a lovely bride,   only one week married.
Daughter-in-law,   a child of good parents,
waited for him,   nine long years she waited,
and seven months   of the tenth year to come.
But now today   she marries another.
I could not watch,   for my heart is breaking,
to this vineyard,   therefore, I ran away."

So when Stojan   understood her sad words,
he went quickly   to the stately manor.   80
But there he found   wedding guests all adorned.
The suitors there   welcomed him with kindness.
From his horse they   led him to the table.
When he had drunk   his fill of the red wine,
he then began   to speak to all the guests:
"My dear brothers,   wedding guests all adorned,
is it all right   if I sing you a song?"
The wedding guests   answered him in one voice:
"It is all right,   sing, unknown young hero!
It is all right,   why should it not be, pray?"   90

Then Stojan sang   in a high and clear voice:
"Once a swallow   built her own pretty nest;
and she built it,   her nest, nine long, long years.
But this morning   she began to tear it.
There flew to her   a gray and green falcon
from a city,   a distant Turkish town;
he won't let her   tear up her pretty nest."

The wedding guests   did not understand this,
but Stojan's wife   understood the meaning.
She departed   from the groom there, quickly,   100
and she went up   to the high watchtower,
and she summoned   Stojan's younger sister:
"Sister-in-law,   you are like my sister,
your brother's here,   my lord is in the house!"
When the sister   of Stojan heard these words,

she hurried down   from the high watchtower.
She looked about   and 'round the table thrice,
until she saw   her brother's loving face.
And when she saw   the face of her brother,
both spread their arms   and kissed one another,   110
and with sweet tears   washed each other's faces,
with blissful tears   of happiness and love.

In their finery   the guests then cried loudly:
"Our dear master,   O Stojan Janković,
what shall we do   to repay the great cost?
For we did spend   a great deal of money
before we won   your wife to wed this groom."

To all of them   Stojan Janković said:
"Wait a moment,   guests in all your finery!
After I've gazed   a while at my sister,   120
we will attend   to the matter of costs.
That won't be hard   if we are all honest."
After he'd gazed   a while at his sister,
he gave fine gifts   to all the wedding guests:
kerchiefs to some,   linen shirts to others,
to the bridegroom   he promised his sister;
and the suitors   went home in happiness.

At supper time,   at the end of the day,
the mother came,   crying as she came home.
She was weeping,   as the cuckoo bird weeps,   130
for her Stojan   was ever on her mind:
"O my Stojan,   O my golden apple,
your old mother   has almost forgot you;
she'll not forget   daughter-in-law, Jela.
O my Jela,   fair as the unworn gold.
Who will await   this old luckless mother?
Who will walk out   to greet and welcome her?
Who will ask her,   the old luckless mother:
'Are you weary,   my dear, loving mother?'"

When Stojan's wife   heard the old mother's voice,   140
before the house   she walked out to meet her,

took the mother   in her two lovely arms,
and spoke gently   to the poor old mother:
"O cry no more,   my dearest old mother!
The sun has shone   on you, old one, this day,
for here is come   your only son, Stojan."
When she saw him,   the old, weakened mother,
when she saw him,   her only son, Stojan,
the mother fell   dead right there on the ground.

The son, Stojan,   buried his mother well,   150
as she deserved,   like a beloved queen.

The Wedding of Ljubović's Sister[16]

Filip Višnjić was a singer of the realistic and the contemporary, with a marvelous eye for detail, but he was also a great comic singer. In the comic songs a recurring character is Bey Ljubović, a Bosnian lord who is often ridiculous in his efforts to please the Turks.[17] Here he fails his own sister, and it is up to the girl to save herself or be married to an absurd bridegroom, Mustafa Aga.

Thus, after the opening hyperbole of praise for her beauty, this fine song resolves itself rapidly, in great comic style. And at the end, when the balance of things is restored, the Turk remains rich, and the lovers are united, the hearer joins the wedding guests in his approval.

The Wedding of Ljubović's Sister

For all of time,   since the world's beginning,
there never bloomed   a flower more beautiful
than does the one   in our own recent times
on the flat field,   Nevesinje's flat field,[18]
in the white court   of the bey, Ljubović.[19]
There Hajkuna,   a flowerlike girl, blooms,

16. *"Udaja sestre Ljubovića,"* III, 383, #82.
17. See Koljević, 310.
18. Nevesinje is a town in eastern Hercegovina.
19. Ljubovići were an old, well-known Serbian family from Hercegovina.

the dear sister   of the bey, Ljubović.
She's so lovely,   could be no lovelier.
She is slender,   tall and slim of body.
Her face is pale,   her complexion rosy,   10
as if she's come   to bloom before the noon
in the radiance,   in the spring sun's stillness.
And her eyes shine   like two bright precious stones.
Her two eyebrows   are like anemones,
her eyelashes   like the wings of swallows,
and her dark hair   like a spray of heather.
Her mouth invites   like a box of sugar,
and her white teeth   shine like two rows of pearls.
Her slender arms   are like the wings of swans,
and her white breasts   are like two pale pigeons.   20
When she speaks,   her voice is like a dove's,
and when she smiles,   it's like the glowing sun.

Of her beauty   word has spread all around
throughout Bosnia   and Hercegovina.
Many lovers   come to woo the maiden,
but among them   are two who come the most:
One of them is   the old aga, Mustaf,
from Novi Grad   of Krajina region;[20]
and the other   Zuko of Udbinje.[21]

One clear evening   they meet at the maid's home   30
while courting there   this most lovely maiden.
The old aga   bids a thousand ducats,
adding to that   a golden serving plate,
a baking plate   with a snake carved on it,
and in its head   a precious diamond stone,
in whose bright glow   one could dine festively,
whether at night   or even during day.
Zuko offers   but a dozen ducats,
for poor Zuko   has very little wealth,
just his saber   and his one fattened horse   40

20. Novi Grad, a town in Krajina, some thirty miles northeast of Zadar.
21. Udbinje is the area around Udbina, a town in Lika, east of Gospić.

with which he makes   his living in Krajina,
like a falcon   with his wings in the clouds.

Then Ljubović   speaks to his own sister:
"O Hajkuna,   my dear, beloved sister,
since your mother   has brought you to this world,
it was written   that someone should wed you.
Many suitors   have come here to woo you,
and among them   these two men are the best.
The very two   who've come to our court now.
And one of them   is old Mustaf Aga   50
from Krajina,   the town of Novi Grad.
Of his great wealth   no one can take measure;
he will feed you   with honey and sugar
and will clothe you   both in silk and satin.
The other one   is Zuko of Udbinje;
Zuko can say   that he has not so much,
just his saber   and his one fattened horse.
You must choose now,   my dear, beloved sister.
Tell your brother   which of them shall wed you."

The sister speaks   softly to her brother: 60
"Be of good cheer,   my dear, my good brother!
I will marry   whichever one you choose.
I would rather   marry the young brave lad,
even if he   has nothing to himself,
than that old one,   no matter how wealthy.
Wealth is neither   silver nor precious gold;
wealth is rather   when two love each other."
But to her words   her brother pays no heed,
and he gives her,   quite against her wishes,
he now gives her   to old Mustaf Aga.   70

When Mustaf goes   to his court in Novi,
he invites guests   now to go fetch his bride.
And he invites   Zuko of Udbinje,
to ride in front   and to bear his banner.
The wedding guests,   richly dressed, all gather,
and they set out   for the home of the bride.
When they arrive   at the home of the bride,

there they all feast   for three full merry days.
When they arise   on the fourth festive day,
they take with them   the lovely maiden bride.   80

As they all ride   across a level field,
the lovely girl   then commences to speak,
and she whispers   to the wedding's bridesman:
"Tell me, bridesman,   tell me true, my jewel,
who is fated   to be my bridegroom now?"

Then the bridesman   whispers to her softly:
"My dear sister,   beautiful Hajkuna,
look around you   both to the right and left,
and then look there   at that decrepit man
who sits stately,   just like an *effendi*,[22]   90
he who sits there   on a crimson cushion,
whose long white beard   is covering his chest.
That's no other   than old Mustaf Aga,
and he's fated   to be your bridegroom now."

Hajkuna looks   to her right and her left.
When she sees him,   she sighs deep from her chest,
and she whispers   to the bridesman again:
"And who's that lad,   the brave lad on white horse,
the one that holds   the banner in his hands,
his black moustache   twisted on both his cheeks?"   100

The bridesman tells   his sister-in-law straight:
"Sister, that is   Zuko of Udbinje,
the one who asked   your brother for your hand.
He asked for you,   but then he was refused."

When she hears that,   the maid drops to the ground.
All wedding guests   rush to raise the maiden,
Mustaf Aga   is the last to arrive.
There is no one   who can raise the maiden.
Then he comes there,   Zuko of Udbinje.
He quickly stakes   the banner in the ground,   110

---

22. Here *effendi* is not so much an honorific as a title.

and he offers   his hand to the maiden.
Then the maiden   rises up by herself,
and she then mounts   the horse behind Zuko.
Zuko swiftly   turns his white horse around,
and it gallops   across the level field,
like a bright star   across a silent sky.

When he sees that,   that old Mustaf Aga,
he then cries out   loud, in a stricken voice:
"Did you see that,   you honored wedding guests,
how that *hajduk*   has stolen my maiden?   120
Now do something;   run and bring her to me!"
The wedding guests   shout back all in one voice:
"Let the bold hawk   carry the tender quail.
Let him have her,   for she is meant for him.
You must return   to your court in Novi,
for such beauty   is not meant to be yours."

 ## The Death of Ivo of Senj [23]

This strange and brilliantly conceived dream-song foretells the fall of
Senj, a stronghold of the *uskoks* who had fled the Turks after the loss of
their fortress at Klis in 1537, and who had continued up the Dalmatian
coast to Senj, where they organized themselves as "outlaw" raiders under
Austrian protection and for seventy-five years raided Turkish and Venetian shipping, leading occasional forays onto the islands and even the
mainland. In 1618, as a result of an arrangement between Venice and Vienna, these *uskoks* were driven from Senj, "left without its people" as predicted in this song. [24]

Since "Ivo" (or *Ivan*) is perhaps the most common of Slavic given
names, "Ivo of Senj," who appears in several *uskok* songs, is difficult to
identify in history. A number of attempts have been made, none with convincing success. One possibility is Ivan Novaković Vlatković, whom Koljević identifies as "the duke of border raiders," a military commander of

---

23. "*Smrt Senjanina Iva*," III, 162, #31.
24. See Pennington and Levi, 138–39, and Koljević, 247. *Uskok* was a term suggesting border
raiders of the Dalmatian coast, as opposed to *hajduk,* which suggested the highwaymen of the
mountain inland.

the fortress, or even an ordinary soldier on military rolls in 1551.[25] Probably the character gains a certain universality through the uncertainty of his historical identity. For the song, in which the unread elements of the mother's dream seem to be transformed to the dreamlike pursuers of the son's report, enacts with remarkable expressionistic accuracy the experience of being pursued to the death, which must have been a psychological element in the experience of many outlaws, *uskok* and *hajduk* alike.

"The Death of Ivo of Senj" was sung to Vuk by an unknown singer, an unfortunate fact, for certainly it is one of the most formally conceived and most artful of the poems. Built on the repetitions that are always generative of symbol, in this poem the natural imagery of dream, borrowing its symbolic force from natural images with mythic meanings, gives way to a carefully tripartite narrative, in which repetition generates signification. But like all compelling dreams as well as successful narratives, we are never entirely convinced by the offered interpretation, even when that interpretation comes from a revered priest and seems substantiated by later events. For in this song it is a nightmarish reality, not a priest's reading, that reifies the dream out of which the song is originally generated.

The Death of Ivo of Senj

Ivo's mother   dreamt an unusual dream.
In her strange dream   darkness dropped down on Senj,
and the clear sky   was shattered, fragmented.
The shining moon   fell from the sky to earth,
on Ružica,   on the church there at Senj.[26]
The stars burnt out,   all of them were burnt out.
The morning star   rose high, all washed in blood,
and the cuckoo   called with its mournful cry
there in the town,   on the Senj church dome.

When she wakened,   the old one, from her dream,   10
she took her stick,   her walking stick in hand,
and she went forth   straight to Ružica church.
And there she spoke   to Nedeljko, the priest,
and told to him   her strange and frightful dream.

---

25. See Koljević, 247.
26. Senj is a coastal town in northern Dalmatia, known as a hotbed of *uskoks*.

When the old man   heard the old woman's words,
he then told her   what her strange dream did mean:
"You must listen   to what I have to say:
your evil dream   is of worse times to come,
for as darkness   dropped down upon Senj,
so Senj shall be   left without its people.   20
As the clear sky   shattered and broke to bits,
the shining moon   fell down on Ružica,
so your dear son,   Ivo, is doomed to die.
And as the stars   burned down to their last light,
so our women   shall all become widows.
And as that star   of morning was blood washed,
so you will call   just as the cuckoo calls.
And since it's here   that prophet bird did mourn,
so here shall Turks   come to ruin Ružica,
and they will kill   me also, an old man."   30

While the old priest   was still talking to her,
Ivo came forth,   that same Ivo of Senj.
His raven horse   was drenched and soaked in blood.
Seventeen wounds   bled from Ivo's body.
In his right hand   he bore his own left hand.
He rode his horse,   all black, into the church,
and then he spoke   these words to his mother:
"O, help me down,   mother, from my black horse;
with cold water   wash my old body clean,
and give to me   that wine that is Christ's blood."   40

Then his mother   quickly did as he wished.
She helped him down,   down from his raven horse;
with cold water   she washed his body clean;
she gave him wine,   the holy wine to drink.
Then his mother   put this question to him:
"What has happened,   my son, in Italy?"[27]

Ivo answered   these words to his mother:
"It all went well   in Italy, mother;

---

27. Not Italy itself but the territory on the Dalmatian coast controlled by Venice.

we took captives,   many souls for slavery;
and much plunder,   more gold we took than slaves,   50
and we were well,   we turned for home unharmed,
but when we came   to our first place of rest,
our pursuers   then came upon us there,
rode black horses,   were warriors all in black,
and black turbans   all wound around their heads.
And by the time   the first smoke cleared away,
not one of them   was among the living;
not one of us   was there among the dead.

"When we arrived   there at our second rest,
more pursuers   then came upon us there,   60
rode white horses;   they were angry warriors,
and white turbans   all wound around their heads.
And by the time   the smoke had cleared away,
not one of us   was there among the dead;
not one of them   was among the living.

"But when we came   to our third place of rest,
a third party,   pursuing, came on us there,
in black plaid cloaks,   bearing their long rifles;
their legs were burned,   burned right up to their knees.
And by the time   the smoke had cleared away,   70
and by the time   we had first engaged them,
not one of them   was there among the dead;
not one of us   was there among the living,
save your Ivo,   your son, the last to live,
and he's much hurt,   with many open wounds,
for look, I bear   here my own severed hand!"
With these words said,   he wrestled with his soul;
with these last words,   his light soul passed away.

So Ivo died,   may his mother mourn him.
May God provide   his place in paradise,   80
and give us health,   brothers, and better times.

Old Vujadin[28]

"Old Vujadin," sung to Vuk by an anonymous—and very possibly blind—singer, perhaps a Slavonian, is one of the most succinct, best made, and certainly one of the greatest of the songs. It treats of an outlaw of Livno, a southern Bosnian town near the frontier between Turkish and Venetian territories during the Ottoman occupation, which was used as a Turkish administrative center from which the beys of Sandžak and Klis governed much of Bosnia. But the center was moved after Venetian attacks, and Livno was reduced to a frontier garrison town, still often subject to the raids of both Venetians and outlaws, whether *uskok* or *hajduk,* as they are identified in this upland song.

"Old Vujadin" treats of familiar material; the torturing of outlaws and their courage under torture had been the subject of a much more primitive song recorded a hundred years earlier.[29] "Old Vujadin," however, is not primitive at all, but extremely sophisticated, organized carefully around images of seeing and blindness. Vujadin asks his sons to look at Livno, where they will be blinded; he describes the sharp view downward from the mountains of earlier times, at the moment of his being blinded. The song opens with the image of an observer of Vujadin and his sons, who curses her own eyes ("may you never see more") for failing to observe Vujadin under capture. For seeing seems a metaphor for knowledge; even, ironically, knowledge gained at the price of blindness.

Old Vujadin

A lovely girl   cursed her own seeing eyes:
"O my dark eyes,   may you never see more.
You have seen all;   today you failed to see,
as Livno's Turks,   from Livno town, passed by,
and led with them   those three forest *hajduks,*
Old Vujadin   and his two valiant sons.
The three were dressed   in magnificent clothes.
Old Vujadin   was dressed wonderfully;
he had on him   a coat made of pure gold,
one which pashas   would wear in their parlors.   10

28. "Stari Vujadin," III, 254, #50.
29. See Koljević, 243–46, 243.

And on Milić,   the son of Vujadin,
was a costume   more elegant than that.
And on Vulić,   the brother of Milić,[30]
there was a plume   waving on his headdress,
a pretty plume   composed of twelve feathers,
with each feather   bearing a pound of gold.[31]

When they rode forth,   toward Livno city,
and they saw there   that accursed city,
with the tower   gleaming in the middle,
Old Vujadin   began to speak to them: 20
"O my two sons,   my two valiant falcons,
can you see there   that accursed Livno,
with the tower   gleaming in the middle?
There they'll beat us,   and there they'll torture us,
break our swift legs   and our white arms as well.
There they'll gouge out   our dear, lovely dark eyes.
O my two sons,   my two valiant falcons,
do not show now   hearts of those old women,
but show the hearts   of the brave men you are.
Do not betray   any of our comrades,   30
do not betray   those who are helping us,
those in whose homes   we have spent our winters,
spent our winters   and kept our treasure safe.
Do not betray   the innkeeper's young maids,
where we spent time   drinking the cool red wine,
where we drank wine   in secret company."

So when they came   to the town of Livno,
the Turks placed them   in the worst dungeon there.
In that dungeon   they were three days only
while all the Turks   debated in council   40
how to beat them,   torture them cruelly.
After three days,   thinking and discussing,

---

30. Koljević suggests that the names "Milić" and "Vulić" may refer to "Milivoje" and "Vuko-
je," names given to outlaws in the earlier recorded song of which we have spoken. See Koljević,
243.

31. Thus Vujadin could have been in the service of the Venetians, for such devices—indeed,
gold decorated plumes—were often rewards for outlaws in the Venetian service. See Pennington
and Levi, 136–37.

the Turks led out   the old man, Vujadin,
and broke his legs,   and his white arms as well.
When they began   to gouge out his dark eyes,
the Livno Turks   then spoke to Vujadin:
"Tell us, you whore,   tell us, old Vujadin,
tell us, you whore,   names of your companions
and the helpers   with whom you went to hide,
you went to hide,   spent the winters with them,   50
spent the winters   and kept your treasure safe.
Tell us, you whore,   of the innkeeper's maids,
where you spent time   drinking the cool red wine,
drinking the wine   in secret company."

Old Vujadin   then spoke to them these words:
"Don't be foolish,   O you Turks of Livno!
If I did not   tell you for my swift legs,
which have helped me   outrun the fast horses,
if I did not   tell you for my white arms,
which were able   to break a lance in two   60
and to strike out   at the naked saber,
I won't tell you   for my deceiving eyes,
which have led me   to all kinds of evil,
looking down here   from the highest mountain,
looking down here   at highways here below,
where there are Turks,   where merchants are passing."

7 The Songs of the Serbian Insurrection

*B*Y THE BEGINNING of the eighteenth century many Serbs, especially from the cities and larger towns, had settled on Hungarian or Austrian lands. They formed communities there and began to generate a culture, to create a literature in a language of their own—Slavo-Serbian, which was a heavily Russianized reworking of the language of the Old Slavic texts—and to establish a consciousness of nationality, notably a "Serbian" nationality. But an overwhelming majority of the Balkan Slavs had remained behind on the Turkish lands south of the Danube, as peasants working the land and accommodating themselves as best they could to the increasingly oppressive taxes imposed by increasingly uncontrolled Muslim or Muslimized soldiers (the janissaries), colonial landowners (the *spahis*), and a political administration of *begs* and *pashas* (governors). The culture of these peasant Slavs was equally authentic if less self-conscious, their sense of nationality equally vital if less developed, their language more universally spoken if less often written than those of the Serbs north of the Danube.

Among the vital elements of that peasant culture remained the oral songs that Vuk was collecting. And in Vuk's time—and even later—new heroic songs continued to be composed and performed; Vuk himself had heard songs concerning the uprisings against the Turks in the eighteenth century, and he would continue to hear them during the insurrections that were to come in the early years of the nineteenth century. Those insurrections would generate in the minds of the Serbs on both sides of the Danube the dream of a new and relatively autonomous state that could somehow embody once more those often conflicting senses of Serbian nationality.

As Ottoman power declined and the outrages of the janissaries increased in the Balkan lands, Russia and Austria, the natural competitors among the great powers for hegemony in the soon-to-be-liberated Balkans, postponed their competition by means of a secret agreement between Joseph II and Catherine the Great in 1782. Rather, they joined forces in a war against the sultan, and provoked a Serbian uprising in 1787 in Šumadija, which was to be the Serbian peasantry's first test of military action. Belgrade was regained in 1789 by the Austrians, but the other great powers demanded a cessation of hostilities, and by the Treaty of Svištovo in 1791 Belgrade was returned to Turkish rule.

Now the Turks attempted to improve the lot of their Serbs. Selim III instituted many administrative reforms, designed to increase the loyalty of the *raja* to the Divine Porte and, perhaps through them, to restrain the power and the outrages of the janissaries. Mustapha Pasha, a newly appointed and enlightened governor of Belgrade, even banished the janissaries from his city. But they found military support in Vidin from Osman Pasvan Oglu, who ruled there as an independent military despot. Mustapha Pasha was murdered in 1801, and the janissaries returned to the provincial capital with their chiefs, the *dahijas,* to reinstitute their cruel rule. The situation was a desperate one for the Serbs living on the Turkish lands (greatly the majority of these people), especially for those in Šumadija. Aware that a policy of deliberate annihilation of their local chiefs—both *knezes* and *spahis*—was being planned by the *dahijas,* the Serbs again rose in revolt against them.

They were led in their new insurrection by Djordje Petrović, an illiterate former sergeant in the Austrian army of 1787, who after the peace in 1791 had returned to his native town of Topola, south of Belgrade, and had become a prosperous pig merchant. But Petrović—or *Karadjordje* ("Black George," after his dark hair)—proved a military genius and a new Serbian hero as well. The revolt against the janissaries broke out, again in Šumadija, in February of 1804. It was not initially a war for independence, not even against the *pashalik,* and certainly not against the sultan. But by 1805, when Karadjordje appeared near Ravanica with an army of five thousand and the newly arrived Turkish army under a new vizier for Belgrade dispersed, and when Karadjordje then occupied Smederevo, the fortress on the Danube that had long held such symbolic and real significance for the

Serbs, things began to appear differently. And when on the battlefield at Mišar, near Šabac, Karadjordje, with an army of less than ten thousand, defeated a Turkish army of at least twice its size, the *guslars* began to sing in the mountains of the struggle for independence. By 1807 Belgrade was in Karadjordje's hands.

The struggle would continue, but with somewhat less military zeal and considerably more Balkan intrigue, over the next several years. By 1809 the Turkish armies began to meet with more success. They recovered a major rebel stronghold and a point of access to the Serbs' strongest supporter, Russia, when they recaptured Niš. It was there that the Serbian commander, Sindjelić, fired his revolver at his own ammunition stores and thus deliberately destroyed his own army, and that the local *pasha* built a tower of a thousand Serbian skulls to commemorate the Turkish victory.

But Karadjordje was able to fight back and to recover most of Serbia. At one point, Karadjordje even undertook a campaign to drive to Montenegro to join forces with the rebels there. Many educated Serbs— among them Dositej Obradović, a traveler, journalist, writer, and later the leader of Belgrade's cultural life—returned to Belgrade to participate in the shaping of a liberal and forward-looking administration for a new Serbia. But the drive to Montenegro failed, and Karadjordje found himself in deep political waters. After 1809 and the Austrian defeat at the hands of Napoleon on the battlefield at Wagram, Austria and Russia were preoccupied with other matters. In 1812 the Russians, facing French invasion, made another peace with the Turks. Now the Turks attacked Karadjordje from all sides. Karadjordje retreated, hesitated, and ultimately fled across the Danube. Belgrade was reoccupied by the Turks, and by 1813 the situation again seemed hopeless in Serbia.

Another Serbian hero, a man quite different from Karadjordje, would appear to lead a second insurrection. Miloš Obrenović, a local leader twenty years Karadjordje's junior, had played a minor part in the first insurrection (perhaps partly because he believed that Karadjordje had murdered his half brother). Obrenović had stayed behind in Serbia after 1813 to help pacify the Serbs and to become a governor of three provinces (nearly all of Šumadija) in the new Turkish administration of Pasha Suleiman. He was the leading Serb in the new Turkish provincial government, for although Miloš was barely literate, he was an adroit diplomat. The Turks regarrisoned their fortresses in Belgrade and elsewhere, and diplomatic negotiations would continue for eighteen years.

But before then Miloš came to despair of peaceful methods, and on Palm Sunday of 1815, under the oak tree before the village church in his native Takovo, Miloš gathered the Christians after church services and announced his commitment to war. In six months Miloš had driven the Turks from the lands from Takovo to the Danube. The negotiations, with Napoleon now defeated and Russian assistance again forthcoming, would result in fiscal and political independence for the Serbs in the lands south of the Danube. But all was not well in the new state. A prince-judge, an Orthodox bishop, and Karadjordje himself (who made the mistake of returning to Serbia in 1817) were killed—Karadjordje under circumstances in which Miloš was clearly implicated. So if Serbia was free, it was not to be free of cruelty, and the feud between the Karadjordje and Obrenović clans would continue for nearly a century.

It would not be until 1833 that Serbia, over which Miloš had ruled since 1817 as *knez* (now hereditary prince), by act of the *skupština* (the parliament of Serbs meeting in Belgrade), would finally establish its autonomy as a state, and not until 1878 would the last vestiges of Turkish sovereignty disappear from Belgrade.[1]

On Easter Sunday of 1815, one week after Miloš's meeting before the church in Takovo and a moment in which Serbian national hopes were at their darkest, Vuk Karadžić was visiting his friend, Lukijan Mušicki, the learned archimandrite of the orthodox monastery at Šišatovac in the Srem. It was then that Mušicki introduced Vuk to Filip Višnjić, the blind *guslar* known, not for "The Death of Marko Kraljević," but rather for the songs he sang of the Serbian insurrection. Višnjić had witnessed the early years of that struggle against the Turks and had sung before the Serbian rebels in 1806. In 1809 he followed the Serbian army in the first insurrection, so he knew of many of its events firsthand. After the insurrection he had fled across the Sava River into the Srem, where he settled in a village. Now, in the days that followed that dark Easter, Višnjić sang to Vuk perhaps his greatest song, a song describing recent events, *"Početak bune protiv dahija"* ("The Beginning of the Revolt Against the *Dahijas*"). At Šišatovac Višnjić would then go on to sing Vuk fourteen other songs of the insurrection, of which "The Battle on Mišar" was one.[2]

1. For the above historical account we are indebted to Temperley, 195ff., and—for an eyewitness account—Prince Stephan L. E. Lazarovich-Hrebeljanovich, *The Servian People*, 2 vols. (New York: Charles Scribner's Sons, 1910), 2: 666–67. See also Michael Boro Petrovich, *Modern Serbia* 1: 1–128, and Koljević, 257–69.

2. See Subotić, *Ballads* 10, 23; Koljević, 280–95, 306–10.

These songs provide the major part of Vuk's songs of the insurrection, which he collected in his fourth volume. They are an impressive if flawed achievement. For in his attempt to fuse living with legendary history, this very experienced professional singer seemed at times too obsessed with detail, at times too rigidly formulaic—perhaps too close to his subject, as he would almost certainly have been. Yet at the same time the songs show a remarkable objectivity, if not moral balance.

Like any professional singer of the time, Višnjić undertook to offer his songs as sources of information as well as a means of historical and artistic expression. Thus they set forth the main outlines of recent events with a reportorial accuracy. They as well show a remarkable awareness of the real situation of both protagonist and antagonist. Often the songs express empathy for the full range of human suffering involved in the events.

The songs are informed in their tradition as well; they seem sometimes almost hagiographical in the frequency of miraculous and formulaic elements. It is in such awareness, as well as in the emphasis on recurrences of elements from the legendary songs, that Višnjić's real genius lay. For the true magnificence of the best of the songs of the insurrection is to be found in the fusion that they achieve between contemporary history and legendary past, and thus the unity of vision that they achieve over a dynamic and evolving reality, even a reality of historical circumstance seen in a darkening light.

 ## The Beginning of the Revolt Against the *Dahijas*[3]

Svetozar Koljević has said that "The Beginning of the Revolt Against the *Dahijas*" was sung by Višnjić

at the historical watershed dividing the heroic age from the ensuing era of national freedom, social conflicts, and party politics. It is this historical change which will soon make it impossible for any singer to produce major songs about contemporary history in the old heroic idiom.[4]

Certainly the song has been ingeniously fused to its tradition. For not only was Višnjić competent in his knowledge of the events of a decade earlier—events in which he had participated—but he was concerned in his singing to maintain accuracy in his representation of those events.

---

3. "*Početak bune protiv dahija*," IV, 100, #24.
4. Koljević, 290.

Thus, with few exceptions, facts and names are correctly reported in "The Beginning of the Revolt," and Višnjić's awareness of political and psychological circumstance is not only sensitive but realistically reported.

But there are other events described in this song, events that link it at once to its poetic traditions and to the folk beliefs of his people and yet seem at the same time to have been in some sense historical. Thus, of the cosmic anomalies described in the beginning of the poem, a partial eclipse of the moon and the appearance of a comet at least seem to have been actual historical events, for they are recorded in chronicles of the time.[5] Yet more important than such historical accidents—or narrative adroitness on the part of Višnjić—is his symbolic manipulation of his material. For Višnjić has been at pains here to present the very revolt he describes with a certain natural inevitability. If, as the wise old Turk, Fočo, says, "the time has come for our empires to change," one is also told that "the *raja* rose like grass out of the earth," and the metaphor is expanded when old Fočo warns his son that "grass will surely grow" between the hearthstones of the Turkish masters. Thus, with the steady extension of his natural metaphor throughout the song Višnjić makes his point: the tragedy of the Turkish undertaking to kill the Christian leaders is not in its cruelty but in its presumption against nature; when the young, as always disdainful of the wisdom of fathers, thus presume to disturb the natural order of things, they bring destruction down upon them and their empire.

To shape accurate historical reporting into such argument and to support it with convincing parallels is the work of real literary genius. It is thus that Koljević can conclude that "The Beginning of the Revolt Against the *Dahijas*" "seems to have fathomed the ultimate imaginative depths" of oral epic singing.[6]

The Beginning of the Revolt Against the *Dahijas*

O my dear God,   what a splendid wonder!
In Serbia   there was a great hurry,
in Serbia   a rush to change the laws;
there new judgments,   changes, had come to pass.[7]

5. See Koljević, 292, and Pennington and Levi, 153.
6. Koljević, 294. See also 290–95.
7. A reference to the reforms of Selim III after the Austro-Turkish War at the end of the eighteenth century. See Koljević, 257.

The Serb chieftains,   they did not wish to fight,
nor did the Turks,   the Turkish exploiters.
But the *raja,*   they were more than eager,
The poor *raja*   could pay the tax no more,
no longer bear   the Turkish oppression.
God's saints as well   were disposed to struggle,   10
for blood had boiled   right up out of the earth.
The time had come   for decisive struggle,
to shed one's blood   for the cross of honor,
and to avenge   all our brave ancestors.

The saints took arms   in the glorious heavens,
and they sent down   many signs in the skies,
above Serbia   in the unclouded skies.
And the first sign   they sent came in this way:
From Trifun's Day   to the Day of Saint George,[8]
night after night   the moon sent out her signs,   20
to tell the Serbs   to take up arms and rise.
The Serbs refused,   weren't bold enough to rise.

So then the saints   sent down a second sign:
From George's Day   till St. Demetrius's,[9]
all the banners   waved there and all bloody
above Serbia   in the unclouded skies,
to tell the Serbs   to take up arms and rise.
The Serbs refused,   weren't bold enough to rise.

So then the saints   sent another, third sign:
for loud thunder   clapped on Saint Sava's Day,[10]   30
in midwinter,   out of season for it.
And lightning flashed   then on the Day of Chains,[11]
and the earth shook,   trembled from the east,
to tell the Serbs   to take up arms and rise.
The Serbs refused,   weren't bold enough to rise.

---

8. St. Trifun's Day is the first of February, St. George's Day the twenty-third of April; thus the period is that of early spring. (All dates are according to the Orthodox calendar, or "Old Calendar"—the calendar used to determine the events in this song.)

9. According to the Orthodox calendar, from April 23, St. George's Day, until October 26, St. Demetrius's Day, the traditional day of *hajduks'* parting—thus, summer and early fall.

10. The fourteenth of January.

11. The sixteenth of January.

So then the saints   sent another, fourth sign:
above Serbia   in the unclouded skies
the sun turned black   in the season of spring,
in the spring time,   just on Saint Trifun's Day.
It did turn black   thrice in a single day,   40
and then three times   the sun danced in the east.

All this was seen   by the Turks in Belgrade,
and from the towns   of all seven *dahijas,*
Aganlija   and Kučuk-Alija,
and two brothers,   the two young Fočićes,
Mehmed Aga   along with Mus Aga,
Mula Jusuf,   a great *dahija* leader,
Dervish Aga,   supplier of the city,
old man Fočo,   a hundred-year-old man,
all of them met,   all seven *dahijas,*   50
there in Belgrade   just at the Stamboul gate,[12]
each with red cloak   draped across his shoulder.
They were crying   while watching all the signs:
"What great trouble!   What strange signs and signals!
This, my good friends,   does not bode well for us."

In their distress,   all seven *dahijas,*
in their concern,   had a dish of glass made,
with which they scooped   water from the Danube
and they took it   to the Nebojša Tower.[13]
On the tower   they placed the dish of glass   60
because they wished   to trap stars in the dish
and thus observe   all the signs from heaven,
what the future   had in store for them all.
So they all sat   around the dish of glass.
In the dish they   saw their own images.
When they saw there,   images reflected,
the *dahijas*   saw them with their own eyes,
there was no head   on any image there.

12. For military purposes Serbia was divided into seven *pashaliks:* Belgrade, Zvornik, Sjenica, Novi Pazar, Leskovac, Niš, and Vidin.

13. The Nebojša Tower was the great tower of the fortress of Kalemegdan overlooking the confluence of the Sava and the Danube and the city of Belgrade. Legend has it that it was built by the Jakšić family in the fifteenth century.

When they saw it,   all seven *dahijas,*
they then seized there   a steel pointed pickaxe   70
and they shattered   the glass dish to pieces,
threw the pieces   off from the white tower,
from the tower   down into the Danube,
so there would be   no trace of that glass dish.

In their distress,   all seven *dahijas,*
sad and worried,   set out on a short walk,
down Nebojša,   the tower of Jakšićes,
and then went on   to a large coffee house.
There they sat down   in the large coffee house.
They sat down there   one beside another,   80
old man Fočo   at the head of table,
with his white beard   all the way to his waist.
Then they shouted,   all seven *dahijas:*
"Come here quickly,   you *hodjas* and *hadjis!*
And bring with you   the holy books of yours,
to read in them   what these signs are saying,
what the future   has in store for us all."

They hurried here,   the *hodjas* and *hadjis;*
they brought with them   all of their holy books.
They read in them,   tears rolled down their faces,   90
and then they spoke   to seven *dahijas:*
"Our Turk brothers,   you seven *dahijas!*
Our holy books   now tell us this wisdom:
there were such signs   like the signs that you saw
above Serbia   in the unclouded skies,
there were such signs   five hundred years ago;
the Serb's empire   did perish at that time.
We did conquer   the empire of that time,
for we brought down   two great Vlach emperors:
First, Constantine,   in Tsarigrad city,   100
by the Šarac,   by the rushing river;[14]
second, Lazar,   on Kosovo's flat field.

14. An apparent reference to the waters of the Bosporus.

"Miloš killed there   Tsar Murad for Lazar,
but he did not   finish him properly,
so that Murad   was still alive with us
until we won   all the Serbian empire.[15]
Then Tsar Murad   summoned all his viziers:
'My Turk brothers,   companions and viziers!
I am dying,   but I won the empire.
Listen to me,   give heed to my advice,   110
so that your reign   will last for a long time.
Do not be harsh   and cruel to the *raja*,
rather be kind,   gentle to the *raja;*
let the taxes   be but fifteen dinars,
and in no way   more than thirty dinars.
Do not levy   other fines or taxes.
and do not make   the *raja* destitute.

"'Do not lay hands   on the Christian churches.
Do not meddle   in their laws or conduct.
Don't avenge me   on the wretched *raja;*   120
though my belly   has been slit by Miloš,
that was strictly   a soldier's rotten luck.
For one cannot   conquer any empire
on a soft bed,   smoking one's tobacco.
Do not force them,   the *raja*, to hide out
in the forests,   to be afraid of you.
Treat the *raja*   as if they were your sons,
and then your rule   will last for a long time.
If you refuse,   do not wish to heed me,
but are violent,   cruel to the *raja*,   130
you will surely   lose the empire I've won.'

"The tsar died there   and we were left behind;
we did not heed   our mighty tsar's advice.
We've committed   many awful crimes here,
and we've trampled   on their laws and customs.
We have brought them   pain and destitution,

---

15. The fall of Serbia is usually associated with the fall of the fortress of Smederevo, which occurred in 1459.

imposed great fines,   stiff fines on the *raja*,
and thus transgressed   against the laws of God.

"And now the signs   have appeared in the skies,
and now someone   will again lose empire.   140
Don't be afraid   of a high, mighty king;
no king will dare   rise against any tsar,
and no kingdom   can defeat a tsardom,
for that is how   God has arranged his world.
But be aware   of the needy *raja*.
When they take arms,   that flotsam and jetsam,
in Medija[16]   Turks will greatly suffer,
and the women   of Sham[17] will loudly cry,
for the *raja*   will cause them much heartache.

"O Turk brothers,   you seven *dahijas*,   150
it is just this   that our holy books say:
Your stately homes   will be burned to the ground.
You *dahijas*   will surely lose your heads.
'Mong your hearthstones   the grass will surely grow.
Our minarets   covered o'er by cobweb,
no one to call   the faithful to prayer.
Along our ways,   along our cobbled roads,
where once the Turks   came and went in business,
where their horses   wore down the paving stones,
there will be grass   growing in the hoof-prints.   160
The roads will wish   to see the Turks again;
there'll be no Turks   for the roads to see them.
And this is what   our holy books tell us."

When they heard that,   the seven *dahijas*,
all *dahijas*   fell into deep silence
and pensively   looked downward to the earth.
None can argue   with those same holy books;
none can deny   or can gainsay the books.
Old man Fočo   twisted his long white beard,
bit with his teeth   into that long white beard.   170

16. *Medija* is Medina, in South Arabia, the destination of the hegira.
17. Sham is an area located today in western Iraq.

He too knew not   what to say to the books,
for he himself   was amazed by all this.

Mehmed Aga,   a Fočić, bowed not down,
bowed not his head   but raised his voice instead:
"Raise your heads high,   you *hodjas* and viziers,
pray to our God   and keep the calls to prayer
day after day,   five times in every day,
and have no fear   for us, the *dahijas*.
For just so long   as there's health and reason,
and just so long   as we have our fortress,   180
we will control,   have charge of this city
and the *raja*   all around the city.
So if the kings   are fearful to attack,
how will they dare,   the *raja*, to cause trouble?
Each one of us,   we seven *dahijas*,
has much treasure,   has whole stores of treasure.
And what treasure?   All soft golden ducats.
All that treasure   is lying there unused.
With us, brothers,   we four *dahijas* here,
Aganlija   and Kučuk Alija,   190
and I myself   and Mula Jusuf too,
each one of us   has large unknown treasures,
all uncounted,   each in two treasure troves.
The four of us,   when we wish to rise up,
when we rise up   onto our nimble feet,
and open up   our stores full of treasure,
we shall scatter   ducats on cobblestones.
With gold ducats   we can form an army,
the four of us,   greatest of the *dahijas*.
We shall divide   our great army in four,   200
divide in four,   we four loving brothers.[18]
We shall set out   from our Belgrade city,
we shall go through   seventeen provinces,
and we shall kill   all the Serbian *knezes*,
all the *knezes*,   all the Serbian chieftains.

18. The four *dahijas*, commanders of the renegade janissary, had a relatively free hand in Serbia after the death—the murder—of the enlightened Mustapha Pasha in 1801.

We'll also kill   their most able leaders,
the Serbian priests,   the Serbian schoolmasters.
And there'll remain   only infirm children,
infirm children   less than seven years old,
and they will be   the proper *raja* then.   210
They will serve us,   Turks, well and faithfully.

"Till I kill him,   the knez, Palalija,
from a village,   pretty Begaljica;[19]
he is pasha,   but I am sub-pasha.[20]
Until I kill   that *knez*, Jovan, also
from a little   village of Landovo;[21]
he is pasha,   but I am sub-pasha.
And Stanoje,   the chieftain of Zeok;[22]
he is pasha,   but I am sub-pasha.
Until I kill   Stevo Jakovljev, too,   220
from Lijevče,   the hajduks' hiding nest;[23]
he is pasha,   but I am sub-pasha.
And Jovan, chief   of Krsnica village.[24]
Until I kill   the two Čarapićes
from Avala,   mountain by a white stream,
who are able   to come out to Vračar
and in Belgrade   incarcerate the Turks;
they are pashas,   but I am sub-pasha.[25]

"Until I kill   the valiant Black George
from Topola,   proud and haughty village,[26]   230
for he does trade   with Vienna's emperor;
he is able   to buy ammunition

---

19. Knez Palalija was a local leader from the village of Begaljica, southeast of Belgrade, halfway between Belgrade and Smederevo.

20. The local Christian authority (often a *knez*) was under the authority of the pasha by Turkish law, but often had more control of events than his superior. It is this reality of authority that is under discussion here. The repetition of the statement, "he is pasha but I am sub-pasha," reveals the resentment of the Turks at the realities of local power.

21. A village in Šumadija.

22. A village Zeoke near Čačak in south-central Serbia.

23. A village in the mountains in central Serbia.

24. A small town near Smederevo, in northeastern Serbia.

25. Vasa and Marko Čarapić were Serbian *knezes* who died in the fighting. Marko was executed in the manner later described, but Vasa died in battle sometime later. See Koljević, 291.

26. Topola, a town in central Serbia, was the birthplace of Karadjordje.

from Varadin,[27]   the lovely white city,
and all weapons   that they need for fighting.
He is able   to wage war against us;
he is pasha,   but I am sub-pasha.
Until I kill   the archpriest, Nikola,
from Ritopek,   a beautiful village;[28]
he is pasha,   but I am sub-pasha.
Until I kill   Djordjije Guzonja   240
and his brother,   Arsenije, as well,
from Železnik,   a beautiful village,[29]
who are able   to besiege Topčider.[30]
Until I kill   the arch-priest Marko, too,
from a village,   lovely Ostružnica;[31]
they are pashas,   I am but sub-pasha.
Until I kill   those two abbots also,
Hadji Djera   and Hadji Ruvim too,
who both know how   to liquify pure gold
and then to write   many letters with it,   250
slandering us,   *dahijas,* to the tsar,
and to advise   the poor *raja* as well;
they are pashas,   but I am sub-pasha.[32]

"Wait till I kill   Ilija Birčanin,[33]
that *ober-knez*   from below Medjednik.
For it has been   full three years now, brothers,
since he's become   such an arrogant lord;

27. A town in Vojvodina, now a part of Novi Sad.
28. The archpriest Nikola is from Ritopek, a small village about twenty miles southeast of Belgrade.
29. Two local Serbian leaders from Železnik, a small town about fifteen miles southwest of Belgrade.
30. Topčider is today a suburb of Belgrade.
31. Ostružnica is a village by the Sava, in Posavina district, where the first people's assembly was held in 1804.
32. Hadži Ruvim was in fact the archimandrite of the monastery at Bogovadja near Valjevo. He was killed in the center of Belgrade, as set forth later. Not set forth here are the circumstances of his death. Since he had refused to betray his rebel colleagues, the Turks tore the flesh from his body with pincers. See Koljević, 291.
33. Ilija Birčanin was a Serbian chief who, as Višnjić tells us here, was captured by the Turks and executed on the bridge across the Kolubara River in Valjevo. Vuk saw Marko Kraljević, of whom Višnjić had also sung with great imagination, as a prototype for Ilija Birčanin. See Koljević, 87, 87 n, 291.

where'er he goes   he rides an Arab horse
and another   he leads, too, by the rein,
and he carries   a mace by the saddle.   260
He even folds   his moustache in his cap.
He won't allow   Turks into his province;
when he catches   a Turk in his province,
then with his mace   he breaks his bones and ribs,
and when that Turk   is about to expire,
Ilija shouts   to his *hajduk* servants:
'Hey, my servants,   throw that bastard dog there
where the ravens   even can't find his bones.'
And when he brings   his taxes to us Turks,
he bears weapons;   when he would speak to us,   270
he puts his hand   over his *jatagan*,[34]
with his left hand   he hands us his taxes:[35]
'Mehmed Aga,   here are your damned taxes!
The poor people   have sent you their greetings;
they can no more   pay you such high taxes.'
When I begin   there to count his taxes,
he casts a fierce,   furious glance at me:
'Mehmed Aga,   will you really count it,
though already   I've myself counted it?'
Then I don't dare   to count it any more,   280
but throw the tax   beside me on the pile.
I cannot wait   to be rid of trouble,
and I don't dare   even to look at him.
He's, too, pasha,   but I am sub-pasha.

"Wait till I kill   that chief Grbović, too,
from Mratišić,   a beautiful village;[36]
he is pasha,   and I'm but sub-pasha.
Wait till I kill   chief Aleksa also
from a village   pretty Brankovina,
and Jakov too,   brother of Aleksa.[37]   290

34. A *jatagan* is the pistol worn in the belt which is traditional to *hajduks*.

35. The offering of the left hand, the hand reserved for earthy acts, is deemed insulting by Muslims.

36. Milovan Grbović, a Serbian leader from Mratišić, a village near Valjevo, in western Serbia.

37. Jakov Nenadović, the brother of one of the early martyrs of the first insurrection, and

When the sultan   and the emperor quarreled,
they were captains   in the royal army.
They wore tall hats   adorned with gold pieces,
and they plundered   many small Turkish towns;
they plundered them,   then set them all afire.
When the sultan   and emperor made peace,
they surrendered,   the two, to the sultan,
and they became   chieftains of the sultan.
They then slandered   many Turks to the tsar.
Seven pashas   they have slandered wrongly,   300
slandered wrongly,   and brought death upon them.
They are pashas,   but we are sub-pashas.[38]

"Until I kill   the knez of Tavnava,
Chieftain Stanko   from Ljutić village there;[39]
until I kill   the chief of green Mačva
Martinović   Laza, from Bogatić;[40]
they are pashas,   but I am sub-pasha.
Until I kill   the *knez* of Pocerje,[41]
from Metković,   Mihajlo Ružičić;[42]
he is pasha   but I am sub-pasha.   310

"Wait till I burn   Rača by the Drina,
until I kill   Hadji Melentije,
who has traveled   across the wide blue sea
and visited   the Mecca of the Vlachs.[43]
On his journey   he stopped by in Stamboul,

himself an early rival of Karadjordje, was an important Serbian rebel leader. See Ranke, 125, 142, and—in the definitive English-language history of Serbia for the period—Petrovich, *A History of Modern Serbia*, 1: 46.

38. Aleksa and Jakov Nenadović belonged to a leading Serbian family from Brankovina near Valjevo. Aleksa was, as Višnjić tells us here, captured by the Turks and executed on the bridge across the Kolubara River in Valjevo. See Koljević, 291.

39. A village in Tamnava, a district in western Serbia north of Valjevo.

40. Laza Martinović, a Serbian leader from Bogatić, a town fifteen miles west of Šabac Mačva is a region in northwest Serbia, at the intersection of the Drina and the Sava rivers. Much of the fighting in the early years of the first Serbian insurrection took place in this region.

41. Pocerje (*pocerje*, "from around Cer") is the region near Cer Mountain, south of Šabac.

42. Knez Mihajlo Ružičić was from the village of Metković in the area south of Šabac.

43. Hadji-Melentije was the abbot of the monastery Rača by the Drina River near Bajina Bašta. He visited Jerusalem, hence the added "Hadji" to his name. Vlach is a pejorative expression for Orthodox Serbs.

from the sultan   he received a permit
for a hundred   golden yellow ducats,
to build a church   for all the Vlachs back home,
to build a church   over seven long years,
but he built it   all in one single year.   320
It has now been   six years of those seven;
he is building   a tower next to the church;
in the tower   he stores ammunition
and in darkness   he is bringing canons.
You see clearly   he's awaiting something.
So then we'll go   out to all provinces
and cut down there   all the Serbian headmen.
As for *raja,*   how can it trouble us?"

All *dahijas*   jumped up to their feet there
and bowed deeply   down to Mehmed Aga: 330
"Thank you, thank you,   Mehmed Aga Fočić!
you're so clever,   enough for a pasha.
We shall make you   a pasha of our own;
we shall always   follow your wise advice."

Then Old Fočo   began to speak these words:
"What a wise lad!   What a clever discourse!
Clever discourse   worthy of a pasha!
Take, my dear son,   Mehmed Aga Fočić,
take a handful   of straw in your white hand,
and wave the straw   over a burning fire.   340
You will either   quench the fire with it,
or you will make   an even stronger fire.
You'll be able,   God gives you the power
to assemble   such a mighty army.
And you can go   to all Serb provinces.
You can capture   one Serb *knez* by deceit
and you'll lure him   with false word of honor.
You'll lose honor,   trust of all the others.
You'll capture one;   two others will escape.
You'll capture two;   four others will escape.   350
And they will set   your houses on fire,
you, *dahijas,*   will perish by their hand.

"So don't do it   the way you are planning,
but you listen   closely to an old man.
I have read and   studied our holy books.
Our rule, pashas,   will not last much longer.
The time has come   for our empires to change.
But you, my sons,   be good to the *raja;*
make the taxes   lower for the *raja;*
let the tax be   as Murad advised us;   360
forget the fines   and the other taxes.
Become brothers   with Serbian chieftains.
Give them presents,   give them noble horses,
and lesser gifts   to the village leaders,
and with their priests   be honorable friends,
so that we all   can long survive in peace,
for our empire   cannot last much longer.
What good is it   all your priceless treasure?
You can mill it;   there's no way to eat it."

Then in answer   young Aga Fočić spoke: 370
"O my father,   I won't heed your advice."
He said those words   and jumped up to his feet,
and after him   rose all the *dahijas.*
They placed canons   round the city walls.
For gold ducats   they gathered an army.
The four of them,   the greatest *dahijas:*
Aganlija   and Kučuk Alija,
Mula Jusuf,   Mehmed Aga Fočić,
all divided   their armies in four parts,
all in four parts,   like four loving brothers.   380
Then they opened   the gates of white Belgrade,
and they rode out   with their troops for census,
and to visit   all seventeen provinces.

They tricked the chief,   the Serb chieftain there;
lured, then captured   the *knez*, Palalija,
and they killed him   in the town of Grocka.[44]
And Stanoje,   the chief of Zeok town,

44. Grocka is a town southeast of Belgrade.

they lured, captured,   and then they murdered him
in his own home,   a stately white manor.
They took also   brave Marko Čarapić,   390
they lured, captured,   and then they murdered him.
Janko Gagić,   the commander, also,
he from Boleč,   a rather small village.[45]
They killed as well   the good *knez*, Teofan,
from Orašje,   Smederevo province.[46]
They killed also   Resava's *knez* Petar.[47]
They tricked and trapped   Mato the commander
from Lipovac   close by Kragujevac,
killed him as well,   so young and full of zest.
At Moravci[48]   they went into the church   400
and there they killed   Hadji Djera as well.
Hadji Ruvim   they took to Belgrade fort
and they killed him   right there in the fortress.

Mehmed Aga   arrived at Valjevo,
but Grbović   was somewhat more clever,
so Grbović   escaped the deadly snare.
But Aleksa,   *ober-knez,* surrendered,
as did also   Ilija Birčanin.
Mehmed Aga   imprisoned both of them,
tied them firmly   by their manly white hands,   410
then he took them   to Kolubara's bridge.[49]
When Aleksa,   *ober-knez,* realized
that the Turks meant   to murder both of them,
he then addressed   Mehmed Aga Fočić:
"O my master,   Mehmed Aga Fočić,
spare me my life,   and let me fight for it.
I will give you   sixty sacks of treasure."
Mehmed Aga   then spoke to Aleksa:
"O Aleksa,   I cannot release you
if you gave me   a hundred treasure sacks."   420

45. Boleč is a village near Belgrade, somewhat to its southeast.
46. A village south of Smederevo.
47. A district near the Resava River in central Serbia.
48. Moravci is a small village in central Šumadija, near Ljig, with a monastery close by.
49. The Kolubara River flows by Valjevo and empties into the Sava.

To the aga   spoke Ilija Birčanin:
"O my master,   Mehmed Aga Fočić,
spare me my life,   and let me fight for it,
I will give you   a hundred treasure sacks."
Mehmed Aga   then spoke to Ilija:
"Don't be a fool,   Ilija Birčanin.
Who would set free   a cunning mountain wolf?"
Mehmed Aga   then called forth his hangman.
The hangman drew   a saber from his skirt
and he cut off   the head of Ilija.   430

Then Aleksa   sat down on the same bridge
and he began   to speak to the people:
"May God strike dead   any Christian brother
who believes in   the word of Turk again!
O you, Jakov,   brother of the same blood,
do not keep faith   ever with any Turk.
Where you meet Turks,   always fight them bravely."
And Aleksa   would have gone on talking,
But the hangman   then interrupted him,
drew his saber   and cut off his head there.   440
The two *knezes*   were thus cruelly killed
there on the bridge   over Kolubara,
Knez Aleksa,   Ilija Birčanin;
Hadji Ruvim   in the heart of Belgrade,
all in one day,   almost at the same hour,
the radiant sun   above them grew quite dark.

Mehmed Aga   hurried to his lodging;
he hoped to catch   other Serbs unawares;
he hoped to find   another Serb to kill.
But when the Serbs   discovered the danger,   450
they ran away   from the town's central part,
so no one else   came to Mehmed Aga.
When he saw that,   Mehmed Aga Fočić,
it came to him   that he was in error.
And right away   he regretted his acts.
But it was now   much too late for regrets.

He called to him   twelve of his brave soldiers,
Uzun also,   who made coffee for him:
"Listen to me,   falcons, my dear soldiers,
saddle quickly   and mount your swift horses   460
and then gallop   to Topola village,
and see if there   you can kill that Black George.
If that Black George   escapes us at this time,
you understand,   no good will come of it."

When they heard that,   the twelve falcon soldiers,
they right away   mounted their swift horses,
and with Uzun,   the coffee man, in front,
they all galloped   toward Topola village
on Saturday,   the day before Sunday.
On Sunday morn   they came to Topola   470
before the dawn   and before the bright day.
They surrounded   George's large white manor,
and they threatened   to attack right away.
From the two sides   they began to cry out:
"Come out quickly,   you Djordje Petrović!"

Who will deceive   a fierce mountain dragon?
Who will catch him   in his sleep unawares?
So that brave George,   he has made a habit
to rise early,   and always before dawn,
to wash himself,   and to say his prayers,   480
and to drink down   a glass of his *raki.*[50]
So on this day   Black George rose quite early
and he went down   to the lower cellars.
But when he saw   the Turks around the house,
he did not want   to answer their summons.
It was his wife,   his young wife that answered:
"God be with you,   Turks, this night before dawn!
What at this time   could you wish from us here?
Black George was here   a few moments ago;
he was here then,   but he just departed,   490
and I don't know   just where he could have gone."
And that Black George   watched them, and he listened.

---

50. Today the morning *raki* is still a habit among the Balkan peasantry.

After Black George   finished counting the Turks,
he drank his glass,   and he readied his gun.
He took enough   powder and enough lead,
and then he went   out into his pigsty,
where he joined   twelve good, faithful herdsmen.
When he came there,   he woke up the herdsmen.
He spoke to them   in the following way:
"O my brothers,   my good, faithful herdsmen,   500
you must get up,   and open the pigsty.
From the pigsty   then drive all the swine out;
let them wander   wherever they wish to.
But you, brothers,   listen to my advice:
make ready now   your multicolored guns.
If God grants it   that things do so happen
as I have planned   for them to be today,
I will make you   all honorable men;
I'll cover you   with pure gold and silver,
and I'll dress you   in pure silk and velvet."   510

The good herdsmen   could hardly wait to go.
They drove the swine   out of the large pigsty,
they made ready   their multicolored guns,
and they followed   Black George, their dear master.

So Black George then   went straight to his own house.
When that Black George   and his men saw the Turks,
then Black George spoke   to his men with these words:
"Listen to me,   my twelve faithful hersdmen,
each one of you   aim closely at one Turk,
but do not fire   your multicolored guns   520
until you hear   my own gun firing first.
I will target   the Turk, Uzun Mehmed,
and you will see   what will become of him."

When he said that,   Karadjordje Petrović,
he fell to earth   and he fired his rifle.
He fired his gun,   and it was not in vain;
what he aimed at,   the shot reached its target.
Uzun Mehmed   fell dead from his bay horse.
When they saw that,   the twelve faithful herdsmen,

twelve shots were heard,   and all at one instant.   530
Six of the Turks   fell dead from their horses.
The other six   ran away on horseback.

Black George then spoke   throughout Topola town,
and he gathered   an even larger group.
They all followed   the tracks left by the Turks,
and all the way   to Sibnica village.[51]
There all the Turks   took refuge in the inn;
they were praying   to their mothers for life.
There that Black George,   with men, surrounded them.
Then he spoke out   through all of Sibnica   540
and all the men   of Sibnica joined him;
all together   there were a full hundred.
Then right away   they set the inn on fire.
Three of the Turks   lost their lives in the fire;
the other three   ran out before the Serbs.
The Serbs killed them   all right there on the spot.

George then sent forth   messages everywhere,
to the country's   seventeen provinces,
to all leaders   and village commanders:
"Each one of you,   kill your own sub-pasha!   550
Send your women   and children to hiding."
When they heard that,   the Serbian chieftains,
they all heeded   George's urgent message.
They all got up   on their own nimble feet,
they all girded   their battle ready arms,
and they all killed   each his own sub-pasha,
sent their women   and children to hiding.

So when Black George   roused his Serbian people
and thus started   a struggle with the Turks,
he then set out   for all the provinces.   560
He set on fire   all Turkish watchtowers,
and he tore down   Turkish summer houses,
and he attacked   the Turkish settlements.
He set on fire   all Turkish settlements,

---

51. A village northwest of Topola.

he placed women   and men under saber,
and brought bad blood   between the Serbs and Turks.
The Turks still thought   the *raja* not a threat,
but the *raja*   is the life of the towns.
The *raja* rose   like grass out of the earth;
they chased the Turks   into the great cities.   570

Black George hurried   from one town to another,
and he spoke out   to all the town folk there:
"Listen to me,   you Turkish citizens!
Open the gates   of your pretty cities,
and hand over   the villains among you,
if you would wish   to live your lives in peace,
for we've no wish   to destroy your cities.
If you don't want   to hand over to us
all the villains   that are still among you,
then those cities   which the *raja* built here—   580
for nine long years   they've built up those cities—
the *raja* shall   destroy them in one day,
and start a war   with the sultan himself.
And when we start   a war with the sultan,
even if all   seven kings rise and try
to bring peace here,   they will not be able.
We shall fight on   to the very last man."

Then citizens   began to shed their tears,
and to Black George   they spoke these very words:
"O bey, Black George,   chieftain of Serbia,   590
we shall give you   what the *raja* asks for.
Do not destroy   the sultan's fair cities;
do not begin   a war with the sultan.
We'll hand over   the villains among us."

And the people   of the Turkish-held towns
opened the gates   of their pretty cities,
handed over   the villains among them.
And those villains,   the Turkish exploiters,
they were given   to Serbian rebels.
O my great God,   O Mother of God,   600
when the same Serbs   took the Turkish villains,

the exploiters,   into their eager hands,
then they began   to march them one by one
across the field   without any clothing,
without sheepskins,   and without long-sleeved robes,
without turbans,   and without the small caps,
without their boots,   and without the slippers;
then they beat them,   naked, barefoot, with maces:
"Hey, sub-pasha,   now where are our taxes?"

There in midfield   Black George drew his saber,   610
and he cut off   the heads of the villains.
When he finished   decapitating Turks,
cutting the heads   off the Turkish villains,
then George went on   and entered the cities.
What Turks he found   inside the white cities,
who deserved it   also were beheaded.
He released there   all of those who wished it,
those who wanted   to become new Christians.

When he began   to rule over Serbia,
he made Serbia   again a Christian land,   620
and he kept it   safe there beneath his wing,
from Vidin town   to the Drina River,
from Kosovo   to that Belgrade city.
Black George then spoke   to the Drina River:
"Drina River,   O you noble border
between Bosnia   and our own Serbia,
it won't be long,   a little time indeed,
before I cross   your turbulent waters
and I visit   honorable Bosnia."

 ## The Battle on Mišar[52]

There are two versions of "The Battle on Mišar," the one Višnjić sang to Vuk (which is translated here) and a shortened and politically truncated version. Višnjić's song, while it cannot be called objective since it realistically presents its events only through the eyes of differently committed

---

52. *"Boj na Mišaru,"* IV, 148, #30.

observers, nevertheless neatly opposes two points of view—that of the raven, apparently pro-Serb, who reports the events of the battle to the Turkish wife, then that of a Turkish soldier's wife. Thus it provides an account of the battle balanced between emotional significance and fact as well as between Turkish and Serbian experience, and at the same time it suggests something of the range of experience attendant upon the Turkish defeat. The shortened, and clearly inferior, version presents only the first half, the pro-Serbian half, and ends with the song's most famous, and most stirring, line (which occurs midway through the longer version): "For this Serbia will not be pacified!"

It seems clear that Višnjić's intention here is hardly simple nationalism. Yet, his "Battle on Mišar" is quite clearly and deliberately an ironic parody—perhaps of the chauvinism stirred by the Kosovo songs, but certainly in order to underline the comparison between the long-remembered defeat of the Serbs with their long-awaited victory being here described. For example, in his "Mišar," which opens with a raven recounting a battle to the wife of the losing commander, "Tsar Lazar and Tsaritsa Milica" of the Kosovo cycle is ironically echoed. Here the report is made to the wife of the Turkish commander, and the reader is made aware, not of Serbian defeat but of Serbian victory. Yet, simultaneously, both the cruelty of the Turks and the suffering of their leader's wife are sympathetically presented. And yet again, this wife is not always generously treated; at one point she hisses like a snake and at the conclusion she dies like an animal—Višnjić uses the verb *crče*, which is reserved for the death of animals, to describe her death.

The military engagement that Višnjić's song so accurately recounts occurred on August 13, 1806, on the plain of Mišar, a few miles west of Šabac, one of the westernmost of the Turkish forts along the south bank of the Sava. It was the Serbian rebels' first major engagement in pitched battle against the full might of a Turkish army, an army of at least twenty thousand men under the command of the cruel but valorous young Kulin Kapetan. On the field that day the Turks were confused and defeated by Karadjordje and his army of ten thousand Serbs, and Kulin Kapetan was killed. So Mišar was indeed a famous victory; it was there that the Serbs first showed themselves to be a match for the Turkish army and that Karadjordje demonstrated his brilliance as a tactician and field commander.[53]

53. Ranke, 163, 167–69; W. A. Morison, *The Revolt of the Serbs Against the Turks (1804–1813)* (Cambridge: Cambridge University Press, 1942), xx.

"The Battle on Mišar" was sung out of a consciousness of a cultural and poetic tradition available to its singer, a tradition of which his own song is a living part; it was also sung out of the consciousness of a man telling of events immediate to his own experience and significant to his sense of history. Perhaps such doubled awareness—at once both passionate and distanced, intensely immediate and topical and at the same time literary, or at least culturally historical—such a balance, or such a duality of awareness, is achieved only rarely and is not long to be sustained.

In any event, the heroic song in Serbia was soon to enter upon a period of decline. After Višnjić's death in 1834 in his village of Grk and his burial beneath the oak cross with a *gusle* carved upon it, there would be no more great poems recounting contemporary deeds of heroism sung, although *deseterci* songs are still composed and sung, even today.

The Battle on Mišar

Two black ravens　fly out across the sky
over Mišar,　over that wide, wide field,
over Šabac,　over that white city,
beaks all bloodied,　right up to their eyeballs,
feet all bloodied,　up to their very knees.[54]
They've flown over　the fertile Mačva plain;
they've soared across　churning Drina's waters;
they've passed over　the honest Bosnian land;[55]
now they descend　on bitter border land
into Vakup,　that cursed provincial town,[56]　　　10
on the tower　of Kulin Kapetan.[57]
When they alight,　they both begin to caw.

54. Like the "wide" (*široko;* here *širokoga*) field and the "white" (*bijeli;* here *bijeloga*) city, the description of the beaks and wings recalls not only "Tsar Lazar and Tsaritsa Milica" but other earlier songs; one example already seen is "The Death of the Mother of the Jugovićes," lines 57–60.

55. The Drina, a river flowing north into the Sava, separates Serbia from Bosnia. Why Bosnia (or Bosna), whose Islamized nobles were loyal to the Turks in 1806, is "honest" (*čestita*) here is unclear; Koljević conjectures that since the adjective is inappropriate to the context one must read it as simply formulaic. See Koljević, 282.

56. Vakup, today Kulen Vakuf, is in western Bosnia, some fifty miles northeast of Zadar, then located on the "bitter border lands" between the Venetian territories and the Turkish lands, a region of much outlawry.

57. The title *Kapetan* was, in its original meaning, a noble rather than a military rank, a Turkish designation of landlord; it is so used throughout this poem.

Now there comes out   Kulin Kapetan's wife;
as she comes out,   she softly speaks to them:
"My two ravens,   my two brothers in God,
have you lately   crossed the lower border,
over Mišar,   over that wide field there,
over Šabac,   over that white city?
Did you see there   many Turkish soldiers
around Šabac,   around that white city?   20
With those soldiers   many Turkish nobles?
Did you see there,   my most treasured husband,
the exalted   Lord Kulin Kapetan,
he who leads there   a hundred thousand men?[58]
For he promised   to the great tsar himself,
that he'd surely   pacify all Serbia,
that he'd gather   taxes from the *raja,*
that he'd capture   the Serb Karadjordje,
and bring him back   alive to the great tsar,
that he would kill   for him the Serbian chiefs,   30
those who started   first the Serbs' uprising.
Did he capture   Karadjordje for the tsar?
Did he impale   Jakov on a sharp pole?
And did he flay   skin from living Luka?[59]
Did he make fires   to roast the Cincar's flesh?[60]
Did he run through   Čupić with his saber?[61]
Tore he apart   Miloš with four horses?[62]
And thus has he   pacified all Serbia?

---

58. Višnjić's head counts are a bit exaggerated. According to Vladimir Stojančević's "*Srpska nacionalna revolucija i obnova države od kraja XVIII do 1839,*" in a book that he edited, *Istorija srpskog naroda od Prvog ustanka do Berlinskog kongresa, 1804–1878,* vol. 5 of Sima Ćirković, ed., *Istorija srpskog naroda* (Belgrade: Srpska književna zadruga, 1981), 1:40, there were at Mišar some twenty thousand Turks opposing ten thousand Serbs.

59. Luka Lazarević, the brother of Knez Ranko, another of the early Serbian martyrs, was a priest, a Serbian rebel leader, and one of Višnjić's principal heroes. See Ranke, 112, 125, 168–69. Also see Koljević, 283.

60. Janko Popović, a Wallachian or "*Cincar,*" was one of the Serbian chiefs. See Stojančević, 40.

61. Stojan Čupić, a Serbian military leader of great skill and rapport with his troops and one of Višnjić's principal heroes, defended the Mačva. See Ranke, 162.

62. Miloš Stojčević, from Cer Mountain, south of Šabac, was a small but bold *hajduk* leader under Karadjordje. See Ranke, 166.

"Does he come here,   my Kulin Kapetan?
Does he still lead   the proud Bosnian army?[63]   40
Is he coming?   Will he be with me soon?
Does he not bring   Mačva's cattle with him?
Does he not bring   Serbian slave girls with him,
who can serve me   with true obedience?
O tell me, when   comes Kulin Kapetan?
When will he come,   when should I expect him?"

The two ravens   give this answer to her:
"O my lady,   Kulin Kapetan's wife,
we would answer,   if we could, with good news,
but we cannot,   for we must tell the truth.   50
We did lately   cross the lower border;
we passed over   Šabac, that white city,
over Mišar,   the wide field of Mišar,
and we saw there   many Turkish soldiers
close by Šabac,   that white city close by.
In that army   were many Turk leaders,
and we saw there   your most treasured husband,
the exalted,   brave Kulin Kapetan.
And then we saw   also Karadjordje,
there on Mišar,   that wide field of Mišar.   60

"Djordje had men,   fifteen thousand Serbians.
With your husband,   brave Kulin Kapetan,
there were many,   one hundred thousand Turks.
And we saw there,   we saw with our own eyes,
these two armies   fiercely fight each other,
there on Mišar,   the wide field of Mišar.
One was Serbian,   and the other Turkish;
before the Turks   was Kulin Kapetan;
before the Serbs   was Djordje Petrović.
The Serb army   overcame the Turkish.   70
In that struggle   Kulin Kapetan died;
this Petrović   was the man who killed him.
With him died there   full thirty thousand Turks.[64]

63. The "Bosnian" army is, of course, the Muslim or Turkish army.
64. Like his head counts, Višnjić's body counts are a bit overblown, although there is no
doubt that Turkish losses were heavy.

The Turks' leaders,   many of them, died there;
each one of them   better than the others,
all those who came   from proud, rocky Bosna.
So it's certain   that he won't be coming;
he's not started,   nor will he ever come.
Don't hope for him;   no need to wait for him.
Bring up your son,   send him to the army,   80
for this Serbia   will not be pacified!"

Now when the wife   of Kulin has heard this,
like a serpent   she then hissed angrily.
To the ravens   the lady said these words:
"O you ravens,   this is most awful news!
But tell me this,   my two brothers in God,
when you were there,   when you saw the battle,
whom else saw you   that you knew by his name
from Bosnia,   honest, rocky Bosna,
who has died there   on Mišar, the wide plain?"   90

So the ravens   answered to the lady:
"We know them all,   O lady, Kulin's wife;
we know them all,   and we shall tell of all,
each chief by name,   and how each has perished,
just who it was   that died there, my lady.
One who died there   was Mehmed Kapetan,
Zvornik's Mehmed,   he of the white-walled fort;
Miloš killed him,   Miloš of Pocerje.[65]
Another died,   Pasha Sinan Pasha,
from Goražde,   in Hercegovina.[66]   100
Luka killed him,   Luka Lazarević.
Another died,   Mullah Sarajlija,
Čupić killed him,   Čupić, at Drenovac.[67]
Another died,   Asan Beširević;

---

65. Mehmed Kapetan was a town father of Zvornik, an important Turkish trade center on the west bank of the Drina; he died in the battle with two of his sons. See Ranke, 143, 168.

66. Another important Turkish military commander who died at Mišar, Sinan Pasha was from Goražde, a town near the west bank of the Drina and some forty miles east of Sarajevo.

67. "Mullah" (Islamic scholar) is used here as a given name, and except that he is *"Sarajlija"* (from Sarajevo), he is not otherwise identified. Drenovac is a large village on the west bank of the Sava, above Šabac. And Čupić is Stojan Čupić; see note 61.

he met his fate   there in Kitog's green grove.[68]
He was done in   by Smiljanić the priest.[69]
Another died,   Derventski Kapetan;
Jakov killed him,   Jakov of Valjevo,[70]
cut off his head   there on the Dobrava.[71]

"But a few Turks   reached the Sava River,   110
swam across it   on their good war horses,
fled to safety   over to Austria.[72]
Had they been saved   their mothers would be glad.
But word got out;   Janko the Cincar heard.
Lazar Mutap,   he received word also.[73]
These two strapped on   all their shining weapons,
crossed the water   onto the Austrian land.
Close they followed,   pursued the fleeing Turks,
and they caught them   at their first stopping place,
there at the mouth   of the Bosut River.[74]   120

"Just as the Turks   climbed down from their horses
before the inn,   Bosut's white-walled inn there,[75]
from the one side   Janko the Cincar cried,
'Hold it, you Turks;   you have not escaped us!'
From th'other side   Lazar Mutap cried out.
When he heard it,   Ostroč Kapetan heard,
then that young lad   became quite terrified,

68. Asan Beširević, presumably the son of Bešir Pasha, vizier of Bosnia, is here reported to have been caught in the debacle of Kitog Forest after the battle, in which a Turkish force attempting to escape across the Drina was trapped in the dense forest on the west bank of the Sava, attacked on all sides, and destroyed by the Serbs. See Ranke, 169.

69. Prota Nikola Smiljanić, an Orthodox church prelate, also led the Serbs in battle at Mišar. See Stojančević, 44.

70. "Derventski Kapetan" was one of the senior Turkish commanders at Mišar. Jakov Nenadović is "of Valjevo" because he was of the leading family of that district and because it was he who freed that city of Turks. See Ranke, 168.

71. The Dobrava is a tributary of the Sava that flows north to join it just below Šabac and very near Mišar field.

72. The Austrian lands at the time were separated from the Turkish territories by the Sava. The text reads *Njemačka* (German).

73. Lazar Mutap was a Serbian duke (voivode), who would later distinguish himself in the service of Karadjordje. See Stojančević, 5.

74. The Bosut, a northern tributary of the Sava River, flows south to join it a few miles northeast of the mouth of the Drina and some thirty miles northwest of Šabac.

75. Here the village of Bosut, at the mouth of the river.

and Haj Mosto   fell to earth in a faint.[76]
Then the Cincar   and Mutap fell upon them;
Mutap cut off   the head of Haj Mosto,   130
and Janko cut   the head from Ostroč's neck.
Dedo escaped,   Dedo from Gradačac,[77]
but he would not   have gotten away thus,
had he not friends   who knew him over there,
for Austrians   were the ones who hid him.

"When the Serbs killed   that Ostroč Kapetan,
then they ran wild   just like ferocious wolves;
they seized treasures,   vast treasures of the Turks;
and then they took   the Turks' splendid horses;
they hurled corpses,   Turks, into the Sava.   140
To that river   they spoke these very words:
'Sava's waters,   full of waves, icy cold,
swallow, Sava,   these Turks, our enemies.'
So they killed him,   killed Ostroč Kapetan,
in Austria,   before the white-walled inn,
for they fear not   emperor nor sultan."

When Kulin's wife   heard these woeful tidings,
she cried aloud   —even God can hear her—
and her laments   were like the gray cuckoo's;
she twisted and turned   like a wounded swallow.   150
But now she spoke,   utters bitter curses:
"White-walled Šabac,   may your walls be blackened,
and may you burn   to ash in a fierce fire,
for near to you   were all the Turks vanquished!
O Karadjordje,   I pray God will kill you,
for from the first,   when you quarreled with us,
many mothers   you have left lamenting,
and many wives   you've sent to their parents,
many sisters   you have dressed in mourning.

---

76. Ostroč Kapetan was a Turkish commander at Mišar. See Stojančević, 40. Haji Mosto (here *haj*) apparently either was not historical or was simply a youth from a local Turkish family.

77. Gradačac is a Bosnian town some one hundred miles west of Šabac. *Dedo* (literally, old man) is probably Husein Beg Gradašević, "The Dragon of Bosnia," a Bosnian loyal to the Turks who was an important and feared military leader.

Now you've broken   my own heart with sorrow,   160
for you've cut down   my good lord and master,
killed my husband,   brave Kulin Kapetan.
Father Luka,   may you still bear grave wounds!
Why did you kill   Pasha Sinan Pasha,
he who was wise,   and could lead all Bosna?
O you Miloš,   may musket fire kill you!
Why did you kill   our Mehmet Kapetan,
he, our right arm,   the lord and protector
of Bosnia   and of its provinces?
And you, Jakov,   may God rightly kill you,   170
and may your house   be emptied, deserted!
Why did you kill   our Dervent Kapetan?
And you, Čupić,   may you have your black grief!
Why did you kill   Mullah Sarajlija,
he, wise enough   even to judge the tsar?
Grove of Kitog,   may your green be withered!
You, Smiljanić,   may you drown in sorrow!
Why did you kill   Asan Beširević,
he, fairest man   in all of Bosnia?
He left behind   a golden girl betrothed.   180
Cincar Janko,   may the good Lord kill you!
It's not enough,   crimes you did in Turkey,
so you now go   and ravage Austria!
Why did you kill   our Ostroč Kapetan,
a fiery lad,   his mother's only son?"

These words she speaks,   Kulin Kapetan's wife.
She speaks out thus,   and wrestles with her soul,
gives up the ghost,   drops dead, no more to live,
her heart broken   from so much bitter grief.

Assisted by Dragana McFadden

Selected Bibliography

I. ANTHOLOGIES OF SERBIAN EPIC POETRY

English

Bartok, Bela, and Albert B. Lord, eds. *Serbo-Croatian Folk Songs: Texts and Transcriptions of Seventy-Five Folk Songs from the Milman Parry Collection, and a Morphology of Serbo-Croatian Folk Melodies.* New York: Columbia University Press, 1951.

————. *Yugoslav Folk Music.* Vol. 1: *Serbo-Croatian Folk Songs and Instrumental Pieces from the Milman Parry Collection.* Albany: State University of New York Press, 1978.

Bowring, Sir John, trans. *Narodne srpske pjesme: Servian Popular Poetry.* London: Baldwin, Cradock and Joy, 1827.

Butler, Thomas, ed. and trans. *Monumenta Serbocroatica: A Bilingual Anthology of Serbian and Croatian Texts from the 12th to the 19th Century.* Ann Arbor: Michigan Slavic Publications, 1980.

Chatterton, Julia. *Jugo-Slav Folk Songs.* London: J. Curwen and Sons, 1930.

Ćurčija-Prodanović, Nada, ed. and trans. *Heroes of Serbia.* London: Oxford University Press, 1963; New York: Henry Z. Walck, 1964.

Furnas, Philip W. *The Serbo-Croatian Narrative Folk Songs Translated into English with Introduction and Notes.* Cambridge: Harvard University Press, 1938.

Goy, E. D., ed. and trans. *Zelen bor/A Green Pine: An Anthology of Love Poems from the Oral Poetry of Serbia, Bosnia and Hercegovina.* Belgrade: Prosveta and Vukova Zadužbina, 1990.

Lockhart, John Gibson. *Translations from the Servian Minstrelsy to Which Are Added Some Specimens of Anglo-Norman Romances.* London, 1826.

Low, D. H., trans. *The Ballads of Marko Kraljević.* Cambridge: Cambridge University Press, 1922. Reprint, New York: Greenwood, 1968.

Manning, Clarence A., and O. Muriel Fuller. *Marko, the King's Son, Hero of the Serbs.* New York: McBride, 1932.

Matthias, John, and Vladeta Vučković, trans. *The Battle of Kosovo*. Athens: Ohio University Press and Swallow Press, 1987.

Meredith, Owen, trans. *Serbski Pesme; or, National Songs of Servia*. London: Chapman and Hall, 1861.

Mijatovitch, Chedo. *Servia and the Servians*. London: Pitman, 1908; Boston: L. C. Page, 1908; *Servia of the Servians*. London: Pitman, 1911, 1915; New York: Charles Scribner's Sons, 1913, 1914.

Mijatovitch, Elodie Lawton, trans. *Kossovo: An Attempt to Bring Serbian National Songs About the Fall of the Serbian Empire at the Battle of Kossovo into One Poem*. Abridged. London: Wm. Isbister, 1881.

Miletich, John S., ed. and trans. *The Bugarštica: A Bilingual Anthology of the Earliest Extant South Slav Folk Narrative Song*. Urbana and Chicago: University of Illinois Press, 1990.

Morison, Walter Angus, ed. and trans. *The Revolt of the Serbs Against the Turks (1804–1813)*. Cambridge: Cambridge University Press, 1942.

Mrkich, Dan, trans. *Kosovo: The Song of the Serbs*. Ottawa: Commoners' Publishing Society, 1989.

Muegge, Maximilian A., ed. and trans. *Serbian Folk Songs, Fairy Tales and Proverbs*. London: Drane, 1916.

Noyes, George Rapall, and Leonard Bacon, eds. and trans. *Heroic Ballads of Servia*. Boston: Sherman, French, 1913.

Parry, Milman, Albert Lord, and David E. Bynum, eds. *Serbo-Croatian Heroic Songs*. Cambridge: Harvard University Press, 1953; Belgrade: Serbian Academy of Sciences, 1953, vols. 1–4, 6, 16, and forthcoming.

Pennington, Anne, and Peter Levi, eds. and trans. *Marko the Prince: Serbo-Croat Heroic Songs*. New York: St. Martin's Press, 1984. London: Gerald Duckworth, 1984.

Petrovitch, Woislav M. *Hero Tales and Legends of the Serbian*. London: Harrap, 1914; New York: Farrar and Rinehart, 1934.

Rootham, Helen, trans. *Kossovo: Heroic Songs of the Serbs*. Oxford: B. H. Blackwell, 1920.

Stanoyevich, Beatrice Stevenson, ed. *An Anthology of Jugoslav Poetry*. Boston: Richard G. Badger, 1920.

Wiles, James W., trans. *Serbian Songs and Poems: Chords of the Yugoslav Harp*. London: Allen and Unwin, 1917.

Zimmerman, Zora Devrnja, ed. and trans. *Serbian Folk Poetry: Ancient Legends, Romantic Songs*. Columbus, Ohio: Kosovo, 1986.

Serbo-Croatian

Djurić, Vojislav, ed. *Antologija narodnih junačkih pesama*. Belgrade: Srpska književna zadruga, 1965.

Karadžić, Vuk Stefanović. *Srpske narodne pjesme*. Ed. Ljubomir Stojanović. 9 vols. Belgrade: Državno izdanje, 1891–1901.

————. *Srpske narodne pjesme*. Ed. Vojislav Djurić, Svetozar Matić, Nikola Banašević, Vido Latković. 4 vols. Belgrade: Prosveta, 1953–1954.

————. *Srpske narodne pjesme.* Ed. Vladan Nedić. Belgrade: Prosveta, 1969.

————. *Srpske narodne pjesme iz neobjavljenih rukopisa Vuka Stef. Karadžića.* Ed. Živomir Mladenović and Vladan Nedić. 5 vols. Belgrade: Srpska akademija nauka i umetnosti, 1973–1974.

————. *Srpski rječnik.* Belgrade: Tipographia regni Serbiae, 1898.

Milošević-Djordjević, Nada, ed. *Narodne epske pesme.* Belgrade: Nolit and Prosveta, 1980.

Pavlović, Miodrag, ed. *Antologija lirske narodne poezije.* Belgrade: Vuk Karadžić, 1982.

Radojčić, Djordje Sp., ed. *Antologija stare srpske književnosti.* Belgrade: Nolit, 1960.

II. CRITICAL SOURCES

English

Barac, Antun. *A History of Yugoslav Literature.* Belgrade: Committee for Foreign Cultural Relations, 1955, and Ann Arbor: Michigan Slavic Publications, 1973.

Bloomfield, Maurice. *The Religion of the Veda.* New York and London: G. P. Putnam's Sons, 1908.

Brkić, Jovan. *Moral Concepts in Traditional Serbian Epic Poetry.* The Hague: Mouton, 1961.

Clissold, Stephen, ed. *A Short History of Yugoslavia from Early Times to 1966.* Cambridge: Cambridge University Press, 1966.

Dvornik, Francis. *The Slavs in European History and Civilization.* New Brunswick: Rutgers University Press, 1962.

Edwards, Lovett F. *Yugoslavia.* New York: Hastings House, 1971.

Gimbutas, Marija. *The Goddesses and Gods of Old Europe 6500–3500 B.C.* Berkeley and Los Angeles: University of California Press, 1982.

————. *The Slavs.* New York and Washington: Praeger, 1971.

Higgins, David H. Introduction, commentary, notes, and bibliography. *The Divine Comedy,* trans. C. H. Sisson. Chicago: Regnery Gateway, 1981.

Jelavich, Barbara. *History of the Balkans,* 2 vols. Cambridge: Cambridge University Press, 1983.

Koljević, Svetozar. *The Epic in the Making.* Oxford: Clarendon, 1980.

————. Introduction, *Marko the Prince: Serbo-Croat Heroic Songs,* ed. and trans. Anne Pennington and Peter Levi. New York: St. Martin's Press, 1984; London: Duckworth, 1984.

Kostelski, Z. *The Yugoslavs: The History of the Yugoslavs and Their States to the Creation of Yugoslavia.* New York: Philosophical Library, 1952.

Kotur, Krstivoj. *The Serbian Folk Epic: Its Theology and Anthropology.* New York: Philosophical Library, 1977.

Prince Stephan L. E. Lazarovich-Hrebeljanovich. *The Servian People.* 2 vols. New York: Charles Scribner's Sons, 1910.

Lockwood, Yvonne R. *Yugoslav Folklore: An Annotated Bibliography of Contributions in English.* San Francisco: R. & E. Research Associates, 1976.

Lord, Albert Bates. *The Singer of Tales.* Cambridge: Harvard University Press, 1960.

Low, D. H. "The First Link Between English and Serbo-Croat Literature." *Slavonic Review* 3 (1924): 362–69.

Mihailovich, Vasa D., and Mateja Matejic. *A Comprehensive Bibliography of Yugoslav Literature in English 1593–1980.* Columbus, Ohio: Slavica, 1984; *First Supplement 1981–1985* (1988); *Second Supplement 1986–1990* (1992).

Petrovich, Michael Boro. *A History of Modern Serbia 1804–1918.* 2 vols. New York: Harcourt Brace Jovanovich, 1976.

Ranke, Leopold von. *A History of Servia and the Servian Revolution.* Trans. Mrs. Alexander Kerr. 2d ed. London, 1848. Reprint, New York: Da Capo, 1973.

Subotić, Dragutin. "Serbian Popular Poetry in English Literature." *Slavonic Review* 5 (March 1927): 628–46.

———. *Yugoslav Popular Ballads: Their Origin and Development.* Cambridge: Cambridge University Press, 1932.

Temperley, Harold W. V. *History of Serbia.* London, 1917. Reprint, New York: Howard Fertig, 1969.

Waring, L. F. *Serbia.* London: Williams and Norgate, 1917; New York: Holt, 1917.

West, Rebecca. *Black Lamb and Grey Falcon.* New York: Viking, 1968.

Wilson, Duncan. *The Life and Times of Vuk Stefanović Karadžić, 1787–1864: Literacy, Literature and National Independence in Serbia.* Oxford: Clarendon Press, 1970; Ann Arbor: Michigan Slavic Materials, 1986.

Serbo-Croatian

Ćirković, Sima, ed. *Istorija srpskog naroda.* 6 vols. Belgrade: Srpska književna zadruga, 1981– .

Jireček, Josef Konstantin. *Istorija Srba.* Belgrade: Slovo ljubve, 1978.

Koljević, Svetozar. *Naš junački ep.* Belgrade: Nolit, 1974.

Latković, Vido. *Narodna književnost.* Belgrade: Naučna knjiga, 1975.

Matić, Svetozar. *Naš narodni ep i naš stih: Ogledi i studije.* Novi Sad: Matica srpska, 1964.

Murko, Matija. *Tragom srpsko-hrvatske narodne epike.* 2 vols. Zagreb, 1951.

Nedić, Vladan, ed. *Narodna književnost.* Belgrade: Nolit, 1966.

Stojanović, Ljubomir. *Život i rad Vuka Stef. Karadžića.* Belgrade and Zemun: Makarije, 1924.